PRAISE FOR

Take Your Lead

"As an educator, leader, and project manager, I felt deeply honored to review this work before its release. Richard's insights are both timely and timeless—his words inspired me on multiple levels. The diagrams, illustrative examples and personal narratives are not only engaging but also deeply practical. This book is a powerful tool for anyone seeking to build resilient, empathetic leadership and team culture. I'm grateful for Richard's voice and Dr. D's reflections in this space—it has strengthened my own connection to purpose and the work I've been called to do."

—Dr. Elwanda M. Bennett,
MEDP, PMP

"Richard Dillard truly has the heart of a servant leader—always giving himself away for the benefit of others. In *Take Your Lead* Richard takes us on a personal journey of how he constructed his *Personal Leadership Platform* and then gives the reader some practical tools to apply in constructing our own. No matter where you are in your maturity as a leader, the Leadership Enrichment LIFE-cycle (LEL-c) is a continual improvement process that can help you construct (or improve) your personal platform, as well as that of your organization. You will find yourself returning to this book as your personal and organizational platforms mature."

—Evan Breedlove,
LT COL, USAF (RETIRED)

"If you are stone-cold serious about becoming the best leader YOU can possibly be and raising the lid on leadership in your organization, I highly recommend *Take Your Lead*. But do not approach it the same way you would any other book about leadership; READ it for content first, then go back and STUDY it critically. This is not a typical 'feel good' or 'happy talk' generic leadership 'how-to' guide—this book requires work on your part. This book compels you to look at AND evaluate the person that you see in the mirror every morning. You will have to look deep within yourself and your organization—even in places that may make you a little uncomfortable. But if you can find the strength to open your mind for honest evaluation, this book will without a doubt help you and your organization reach maximum potential!"

—Frank Ciszek,
MSGT, USAF (RETIRED)

"Grow, change, or wither." Leadership and organizational behavior are dynamic, ever-evolving fields that demand constant reflection and adaptation. For those willing to challenge their perspectives and elevate their leadership approach, *Take Your Lead* by Richard S. Dillard and Dr. Brian G. Dillard offers a transformative journey. Rooted in the authors' own experiences, the book offers practical tools and profound insights that seamlessly integrate leadership with organizational culture and performance. The book explores innovative methods for leadership development while clearly defining the personal growth necessary to enhance both individual and organizational performance.

"Richard and Brian share a deeply personal and authentic narrative which emphasizes the importance of introspection, emotional intelligence, and moral authority as the foundations of effective leadership. Their concept of the "Leadership Platform" introduces a refreshing framework that evolves through real-life experiences, guiding leaders to align their values, beliefs, and behaviors in a meaningful way. Unlike conventional leadership guides, *Take Your Lead* challenges readers to embrace "non-neutral learning," a transformative approach that pushes beyond comfort zones and demands sustained personal growth. *Take Your Lead* is a true call to action for those ready to commit to authentic, purpose-driven leadership. Highly recommended for individuals willing to undertake the hard work of building something meaningful and lasting."

— Cynthia J Martin,

ORGANIZATIONAL TRANSFORMATION
AND PERFORMANCE

"I've had the privilege of working with Dr D and it is clear that the concepts contained and explained in these pages are not just an intellectual exercise… he practices what he preaches. In the following chapters, you'll find many ideas to challenge your conceptions of leadership. The authors also provide many thought exercises to "make real" the concepts they explore. If you find yourself stuck, or questioning the next step on your leadership journey, this book is for you. As the Dillard brothers suggest…just start!"

—Kevin Kennedy,
LT GEN, USAF (RETIRED)

"This book is not for the faint of heart! If you're looking for a light read that won't challenge your illusions of yourself, then look elsewhere. If, on the other hand, you want something that can help you become the leader you really want to be, then dive in! This book will present you with timeless truths and hard-won expertise that are sure to challenge any self-deception or illusions you have as a leader and enable you to perceive the reality. It will also give you tools and a method to move forward to where you truly want to be as a leader and a human being. If you do nothing more than read it and think about the ideas presented, it will be valuable, but for those who put into practice the ideas presented, the benefits can be beyond counting."

—Dr. Dan O'Connor,
RESEARCH DIRECTOR IN DEFENSE & SPACE;
PHD IN VALUES-DRIVEN LEADERSHIP,
BENEDICTINE UNIVERSITY

"An Exceptional Book on Leadership. Blends leadership and management into a coherent discipline that, if followed, should lead to success in any organization. Wish I would have had been able to read it when I was transitioning from the Army to Industry!"

—William L. Bond,
MAJOR GENERAL, U S ARMY (RETIRED)

TAKE
YOUR
LEAD

*The Motivational Leadership Book
for Motivated Leaders*

Richard S. Dillard &
Dr. Brian G. Dillard

Take Your Lead: The Motivational Leadership Book for Motivated Leaders
Richard S. Dillard & Dr. Brian G. Dillard

© 2025 by Richard S. Dillard & Dr. Brian G. Dillard
Published by Tyleum Group LLC

Tyleum Group LLC
2810 N Church St PMB 954281
Wilmington, Delaware 19802-4447 US
WWW.TYLEUMGROUP.COM

Ordering Information:
Quantity sales. Special discounts are available on quantity purchases by corporations, associations, and others. For details, contact the publisher at the address above.
Orders by U.S. trade bookstores and wholesalers. Please contact Publisher: Tel: (618) 920-6164; or visit the following to send Direct Message to Authors:
WWW.LINKEDIN.COM/IN/RSDILLARD/
WWW.LINKEDIN.COM/IN/DR-BRIAN-DILLARD-60861165/

Printed in the United States of America
Publisher's Cataloging-in-Publication data
    Richard S. Dillard, Author
    Dr. Brian G. Dillard, co-Author
    Take Your Lead : The Motivational Leadership Book for Motivated Leaders /Richard S. Dillard & Dr. Brian G. Dillard
    p. cm.

ISBN (Hardcover) 979-8-9989890-0-1
ISBN (Paperback) 979-8-9989890-1-8
ISBN (eBook) 979-8-9989890-2-5
ISBN (Audiobook) 979-8-9989890-3-2

First Edition

TABLE OF
CONTENTS

PREFACE

L EADERSHIP AND ORGANIZATIONAL behavior are
phenomena. They are dynamic and captivating. Rich in
complexity and depth, they rank among the most extensively
studied topics in management. Fueling it all is a seemingly endless
stream of information, which researchers use to continually
examine how various leadership styles influence everything from
employee motivation and productivity to organizational culture
and effectiveness. At the same time, a vast array of individuals—
from business moguls to budding entrepreneurs, tenured profes-
sors to undergraduate students, senior pastors to lay leaders and
government officials to public servants—strive to stay current
with the latest research findings, books and empirical studies.

What if, despite (or perhaps because of) that abundance, we're
still largely unable to realize its full potential—for ourselves and
the organizations we serve—due to the persistent paradigms that
keep us trapped in rigid hierarchies, unadaptive environments,
and transactional relationships? Now, imagine a world where
leadership isn't confined to boardrooms or hierarchical structures and where leaders aren't constrained by their job titles or

positions when it comes to changing the organizations they serve. Instead, it's a highly personal and constructive proposition that has the power to unleash dynamic organizational forces that transcend boundaries, ignite innovation and foster genuine human connection. This book challenges the traditional paradigms of leadership and invites you to explore a new realm where your leadership is perpetually renewed. Join us on a journey to rethink and reframe what it means to lead in the 21st century—where the true power of leadership lies not in authority but in authenticity... not in a position but in a platform... not in any old platform but in your *Leadership Platform*.

More on that shortly, but before we begin our journey together, we would like to express our sincere gratitude. We're honored you would choose to spend some of your time exploring the phenomenon of leadership with us. We also want to applaud you for your motivation, and we want you to know that the powerful ideas presented here are for you, regardless of where you are in your career progression or in life! And to help you get the most out of this book, we're sharing the following hallmarks of our approach:

1. **Vision:** It is written by two authors with a combined 82+ years of professional experience, yet we don't want you to take our words as final. What we're offering is a fresh perspective and the opportunity to propel untapped depths of potential toward unrealized heights of performance, personal and organizational.

2. **Strategy:** This offering uses a format where key sections are written by the author, Richard Dillard

('Mr. D'), based on observations and experiences from the past 41 years. These sections are frequently punctuated by some **Reflections** and **Opportunities** from a co-author, Brian Dillard ('Dr. D'), adding perspective from his 41 year career to date and even a little humor to lighten things up.

3. **Structure:** It is carefully designed to elicit a response and produce what we'll present later as "non-neutral learning opportunities" for the reader; initially through active, participative engagement with the book (i.e., structured learning) and later in what you do with it through daily activities (i.e., unstructured learning) related to work, family, or community reinvestment.

4. **Function:** Our singular goal was to transcend the constraints of traditional writing, compelling you to embrace a new way of thinking that leads to deeper knowing, ignites a passion for doing, and culminates in higher levels of performing.

5. **Form:** This is what follows function. It's the new shape of things as decision becomes destiny, commitment becomes catalyst, action becomes accustomed and effort becomes excellence. We have no way of predicting what that will look like for you. This remains, as it has always been, your domain.

6. **Feelings:** Today, more emphasis is placed on this facet of our human experience than perhaps at any other time in history. And we know first-hand there will be times when you will not feel like

doing it, nor will you feel that it is even useful or necessary...whatever 'it' becomes for you as a result of engaging with this book. While feelings are tied to emotions and both play significant roles in your decisions, commitments, actions and efforts, they are often misplaced—both in order and relation.

a. Order: Feelings that follow form are less deceptive than those that attempt to produce a forced form prematurely.

b. Relation: Emotions that rise to support these feelings are more powerful and sustainable than those typically accompanying impulsive or reflexive responses.

So here's a foresighted suggestion from your fellow sojourners: Don't rely on feelings to shape form. **Decide, commit and act even when you don't feel like it.**

Is it simple? **Yes.**
Is it easy? **No.**
Does it work? **Absolutely.**

Now, back to the real substance of the subject matter at hand. Although this book explores the topic of leadership, our approach differs significantly from that of many other authors who have examined this complex phenomenon. The entire Preface actually serves as an illustrative example. It's intentional and, for us, unavoidable. We are convinced that something equal to leadership must be examined first...a primer for what awaits.

So, what's so important that it warrants this kind of attention before we start to unpack the leadership phenomenon? In the simplest terms, the relationship between management and leadership and the cause-effect dynamics of leadership, organizational culture and performance as it relates to long-term competitive advantage.

SETTING THE SCENE

Business management and improvement methods, models and theories are widely taught, extremely prevalent and in use everywhere in the public and private sectors. They all have a common aim: to help managers effectively and efficiently achieve better organizational outcomes, regardless of vision, mission, or values. Yet there are two aspects of modern management that stand out from the rest: leadership and organizational culture.

Before diving in to address leadership head-on, we're taking a few pages to examine the principal idea that, no matter how valid or robust management concepts may be, individually or collectively, they cannot compensate for a defensive and non-adaptive organizational culture. Further back and higher up in the cause and effect value chain, it is clear from decades of research that organizational culture ultimately determines the efficacy of management and, as a result, organizational performance and long-term competitive advantage. But when truly examined, it is leadership that emerges as the means by which a more constructive and adaptive organizational culture can be established.

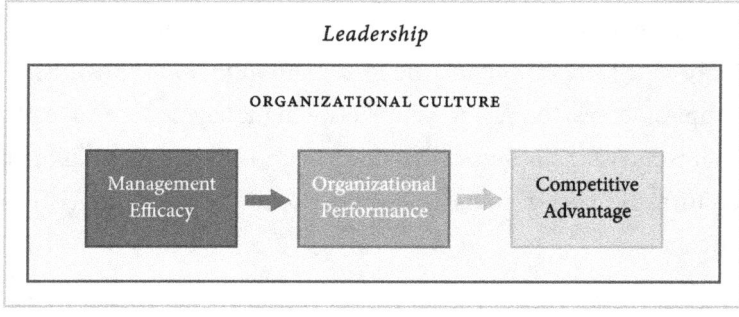

For this book, *management efficacy* is defined as how efficiently a manager guides their team to achieve better results from the goals they establish…better organizational performance outcomes that secure and preserve competitive advantage. It is measurable and encompasses leadership, communication, decision-making and adaptability, ultimately leading to higher employee engagement, productivity and overall team performance. To 'set' goals is incredibly important for an organization and one of the core activities of management. But what it takes to 'get' those goals is in the domain of leadership. Herein lies **an incredible opportunity**, and it comes in the form of our ability and willingness as leaders to promote a culture that produces those results over time. This is because the real measures of merit in goal-getting through short-, mid- and long-term objectives are efficiency-oriented (progress made toward goal completion, or what it takes to reach an objective and reduce time to value) and effectiveness-oriented (outcomes produced by goal completion, or what happens as you achieve an objective and begin to realize that value over time).

In the pages that follow, our goal is to clearly establish that a constructive and adaptive culture is not just preferred but required to reach and achieve goals through incremental objectives over time. We'll also establish that leadership is the first-cause of organizational culture, and that it is essential to unleashing a wealth of previously untapped personal and organizational potential. And when this happens, a newfound capacity for managing to achieve higher levels of organizational performance and long-term competitive advantage can be realized.

WHERE DOES IT ALL START?

Well… right from the beginning. We've already alluded to the idea that management is the process of effectively and efficiently working with people and resources to accomplish organizational goals (Bateman & Snell, 2011, p. 14). This sounds like a lofty endeavor. And it is if you do not have the right set of tools or the skills to use them.

In order to gain competitive advantage through the accomplishment of organizational goals, Bateman & Snell (2011) further suggest that managers abide by fundamental principles to fulfill the core management functions of planning, organizing, leading and controlling. And as every new manager quickly discovers, there are myriad management strategies and tactics that can be applied in the fulfillment of these core functions.

According to 12manage.com (2012), there are as many as 400 business management approaches with an additional 2000 business concepts to be explored through their management dictionary. Yet there is one thing they have in common: all are designed and/or applied to help managers effectively and efficiently achieve organizational goals. This is what classifies them as "management" approaches.

With so many options from which to choose, is it any wonder the late Dr. J. Clayton Lafferty once quipped over 38 years ago: "Management is a uniquely thinking activity" (Human Synergistics, Inc, 1987)? Any manager today with more than a little experience knows he was right. Managers must accurately assess and understand the environment—external and internal—to be successful, and not simply pick from the management cafeteria any approach or concept they 'hope' will work. They must be careful to select the best management methods and models, and they must apply the most useful theories. Well that would take experience…yes? Maybe not.

The late Dr. W. Edwards Deming, world-renown American statistician, professor, author, lecturer and consultant would often say in interviews and throughout his popular four day management seminars: "There is no substitute for knowledge" (Deming, 1994). He would go on to say something to the effect that, if you didn't have a method for managing you were 'goofing off' and to do your best without knowledge actually has the effect of making things worse. In other words…take the time to educate yourself, on the situation, the people involved, the Whisky 5 Hotel (what, when, where, who, why, how). Education will not guarantee you make the right decision or choose the best method or get the best results, but it can help you with comparing what's available and with recognizing the less effective ones faster as you apply them. This is because the more knowledge you have, the more options you have.

This also means that managers must approach every decision based on what Lafferty (1987) termed 'thinking activity' and Deming (1994) ultimately labeled 'profound knowledge.' They both knew that as managers strive to gain **competitive advantage** for their organizations by achieving goals through planning, organizing, et al., they would need to remain adaptive (e.g., the ability to adjust or modify). Adaptability is an essential ***organizational performance*** enabler for rapid and successful change implementation in response to shifting environmental conditions, and one of the most

important factors that influence an organization's responsiveness is ***culture*** (Bateman & Snell, 2011, p. 72). And this may come as a surprise, particularly to those who consider themselves great managers; the first cause of organizational culture is ***leadership***... not management.

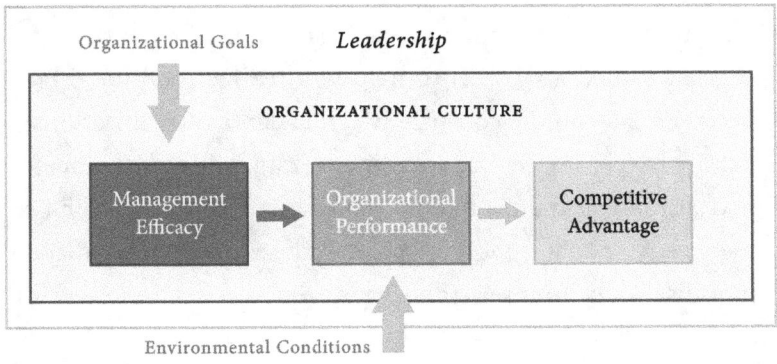

The effort to achieve organizational goals amid changing conditions in the external environment (largely uncontrollable legislative, economic and market shifts) requires rapid adaptation, which is a function of culture. If culture remains unadaptive, the efficacy of management is impacted negatively and, ultimately, organizational performance and long-term competitive advantage are compromised.

While management is focused on planning, organizing and controlling organizational capabilities—process, technology, and data—for maximum effect (i.e., outcomes), leadership is focused on creating the most constructive and adaptive culture wherein people can exploit and continually renew those capabilities for better organizational performance and increased competitive advantage.

The phenomenon of leadership deserves special and focused attention, so we wrote a book on it...this one. But we felt that it was necessary to hardwire the *leadership-culture-performance* connection and call specific attention to the impact of culture on the efficacy of management and the extent to which managers are able to successfully apply a variety of strategies and methods to increase organizational performance and maintain a competitive advantage.

The aim of this Preface—like the rest of the book—is today's professional manager, and its goal is threefold: (1) to help you recognize the impact culture is having on your efforts to achieve organizational goals, (2) to help you realize the incredible potential that a more constructive and adaptive organizational culture has for improving performance and long-term competitive advantage and (3) to help you resolve that culture can be managed and that it must be managed by the best method and most useful theories related to leadership.

PERCEPTION OF THE NEED

Making the case for a connection between culture and management efficacy, Bateman & Snell (2011) assert: "Most companies today know that adopting a customer orientation, improving quality and making other moves necessary to remain competitive

are so essential that they require deep-rooted cultural change."
Reinforcing this connection is mounting evidence from research
on the impact of culture for more than half a century underlining
(e.g., non-financial ROI) and bottom lining (e.g., financial ROI)
real value for companies willing to engage in the effort. Ask
almost anyone in business today and they'll tell you: "organizational culture can and should be managed."

Yet in spite of assertions by the experts, mounting evidence
and widespread agreement, culture change remains elusive for
many organizations and largely unhampered by meaningful
activity since the term first appeared in scholarly journals in the
early 1980s or became popular management jargon in the early
1990s. Why is that? Perhaps it's reflective of a general distrust
of the experts or an inability to fully understand or appreciate
the evidence. Or perhaps organizational culture simply gets
overlooked or eclipsed by faster, easier and more popular management strategies.

As you know from reading to this point, the challenge begins
with leadership. Both *culture* and *change* (or culture change)
require leadership. Leadership is the supreme cultural antecedent.
Dr. Deming (1986) taught that companies must "Adopt and
institute leadership" (p. 54). He also taught that in order "To
manage, one must lead. To lead, one must understand the work
that he and his people are responsible for" (p. 76). And we agree
with Dr. Deming that this includes knowing his people, not just
the work. This idea will get explored deeply in the remainder
of this book, but for now it's important to emphasize that this
"knowledge of people" includes more than just their name, job
title and surface-level interests, but their hobbies, how many kids
they have, their favorite team, etc. Perhaps most importantly,

what turns them up versus shuts them down. We're not saying that you need to become close personal friends, only that building these constructive relationships can become a conduit for the exchange of better information, and that information can develop into new ways of working that routinely exceed expectations.

There is no other responsibility of management where this is more appropriate than when it's applied to organizational culture. While oft-criticized for being a "management basher", Dr. Deming knew in the middle of last century that a large part of the work we are responsible for is related to people and the culture of the organization. He also knew we were (a) in a crisis and didn't know it and (b) largely still unaware of the real power of leadership when it comes to transformation. To give us the opportunity of getting *Out of the Crisis* (Deming, 1986), he introduced 14 Points for Management (Ch. 2) to apply and Seven Deadly Diseases (Ch. 3) to avoid. Then, in *The New Economics* (Deming, 1994), he proposed a System of Profound Knowledge to aid management in their responsibility of transforming the prevailing managerial style with what we're going to refer to as *Real Leadership*—a term you will see repeated throughout this book because it's the only way you can truly **Take Your Lead**.

That same need to transform management (and organizations) with *Real Leadership* still exists today. It is a cycle that starts with each new generation entering the workforce. Tragically, most of the effort is still expended on managing common resources equally available to all organizations such as property, procedures, and so on. Little, if any, effort is expended on leading human resources or building a constructive culture; aspects unique to each organization and key differentiators that offer substantial competitive advantage. A key finding of Right Management from one of their global studies of nearly 29,000 employees from ten major industry sectors in 15 countries across the Americas, Europe and Asia-Pacific was that "Fewer than half of all employees work in an organization that is perceived as having capable leaders and people systems that drive the right behaviors. Leaders play a key role in creating a culture of engagement by directly or indirectly impacting all factors of engagement" (2010). This positions culture change as a key differentiator between merely managing and actually moving to the next level, and changing it requires *Real Leadership*.

Building on this concept, Human Synergistics® International (2012)—herein referred to as Human Synergistics International or simply Human Synergistics—asserts that leaders shape the way people think and behave… they set the agenda. Leaders influence the organization's culture and in turn the long-term effectiveness of the organization. Leaders and managers set the context within which organizational members strive for excellence and work together to achieve organizational goals (The Impact of Leaders on Culture, paras 2 and 3). Taking it a step farther, Allan Stewart, president of Human Synergistics Canada, writes in *How Leaders Impact Culture* that, in reality, "…everything is driven by the organization's leaders (past and present)" and, therefore, "…leadership skills and qualities are essential to building a constructive culture" (2021). In *Leadership/Impact® (L/I)*, an assessment that measures the impact leaders have on performance, Robert A. Cooke, Ph.D., Human Synergistics International CEO and distinguished academic, concludes that managers cannot be considered to 'lead' (i.e., guide or direct) unless they, in some way, "…transform, shape, and influence the environment within which people operate and the ways in which they approach their work and interact with each other" (2012).

Getting directly at the core issue holding organizations back in their effort to transform managership with *Real Leadership*, Shaun McCarthy, Chairman of Human Synergistics in Australia and New Zealand suggests "…those in leadership positions know what needs to be done. They know how to lead. They **know** what an effective culture looks like…they just don't **do** it" (2005). Leaders either translate "knowing" into action, or "doing", or there is a *knowing–doing* gap that the organization falls into, thus ignoring their role in managing organizational culture altogether or merely paying it lip-service.

McCarthy concludes "Few leaders intentionally set out to create a defensive culture [or one that is unadaptive and averse to change]. They simply do not understand the impact of what they do and how they do it" (2005). Lack of understanding this impact helps explain why many leaders personally fail and why many organizational cultures suffer from lackluster leadership—a topic we address exhaustively in the rest of this book.

From all of these observations and conclusions, it stands to reason that leadership shapes culture; culture determines the efficacy of management; managerial effectiveness drives performance; and organizational performance sustains competitive advantage. Unfortunately, the perception of the need to renew and improve organizational culture is not widely held in management circles and, if it is, it doesn't run very deep. If you have not heard or already acted accordingly, people don't leave bad companies on their own…they leave bad managers. No matter what they put as their reason for leaving, you can probably tie it back to a single manager that did not do their job effectively; did not lead.

CASE IN POINT

Consider one example from the commercial mid-market. INXS Global (the company name is fictional; the illustration is factual) formed in the late 1990's through the merger of three separate organizations, each operating to some extent on a global scale. In the years that followed, INXS Global struggled to become a viable competitor in their market, in spite of throwing a host of new management approaches at the problem. This is not uncommon or unusual. Many companies struggle during post-merger integration...particularly with the clash of cultures.

After some initial strategy sessions, the largest revenue producing business unit (BU), one of three in the new INXS Global, emerged with a plan to add new service lines (innovation), improve current products (quality), provide exceptional customer value (service), decrease time to market (speed) and implement waste reduction programs (cost). To meet these objectives and fulfill the fundamental success drivers for competitive advantage (Bateman & Snell, 2011, pp. 9-13), cross-functional teams from across the BU were busily engaged in: (a) expanding services lines, adding a leading-edge service offering to the portfolio; (b) initiating an 18-month, $1.5 million software development project, converting a clunky legacy system over to a new service oriented architecture (SOA) platform; (c) adding online self-service capability to the customer portal and streamlining off-site call center operations, decreasing call center volume and improving first contact resolution; (d) adapting product development through the creation of a hybrid methodology using Agile and traditional Waterfall to define smaller, more iterative release packages that reduced development time for more rapid product deployment; and (e) implementing Lean Six Sigma (LSS) as a means of eliminating waste, with the goal of decreasing overall process cycle time and saving the business unit hundreds of thousands of dollars year over year.

Sounds impressive, right? It was! They certainly had a team of high-performance managers that accomplished a lot together. And their focus appeared to be on all the right things; inclusive of all 5 management objectives for delivering competitive advantage. No doubt about it. And for a short period of time, it worked as advertised in all the management journals. Between 1999 and 2002, everything appeared to be heading in the right direction.

By 2003, however, it was a different story. As a result of external market pressures and an inability to respond with necessary agility, the company was forced to dismantle the product development group in that particular business unit altogether, and to defund all major new product/service initiatives enterprise-wide. Essentially, they could no longer afford to pursue the goals originally established to grow the organization. In fact, INXS Global launched multiple rounds of lay-offs—"right-sizing" as the latest management buzz-word of the era would prefer it be called— and some of the members that remained were forced to accept demotions in lieu of a lay-off as the organization "restructured" while others had their salaries red-circled to avoid additional cost. Ultimately, both voluntary and forced attrition would continue through 2009, leaving INXS Global a skeleton of what it was after the merger. What explains this?

History and a host of other related examples from "business-as-usual" will show that lay-offs and overall decline were inevitable. The positive results they achieved, primarily between 1999 and 2002, were not sustainable because the culture of INXS Global was defensive and non-adaptive—a direct result of not making culture change a strategic priority for post-merger integration. As a result, this lack of readiness for change undermined the efficacy of every other management approach they implemented in the effort to improve performance and remain competitive.

THE NATURE OF ORGANIZATIONS

The reality is every organization struggles with the impact of culture on the efficacy of management, including high-growth organizations like ENRON, high-reliability organizations like NASA, and high-precision organizations like those currently providing services in our Nation's independent health care systems. For most in today's global economy, across the competitive landscape pressures to succeed are exceedingly great and margins for error infinitesimally small. If there is a silver lining in all of this, it is the fact that we do not have to go back very far in history or look very hard in literature to ascertain the precursor of what is taught today in business school as the "ENRON Scandal"[1] in the Energy industry (2001) or to find the cause of Space Shuttle Columbia's disaster[2] (2003) or to determine what precipitated the need for the 100,000 (now 5,000,000) lives campaign[3] in Health Care (2005).

It is now well documented, in each case, that lack of strong leadership played a significant role and that failure to change organizational culture was a principal cause. Moreover, thanks to the work of companies like Human Synergistics International, Kilmann Diagnostics, Denison Consulting, et al., we do not have to search endlessly for a viable way to correctly diagnose leadership and organizational culture, or to improve their impact on managerial and organizational effectiveness.

On the upside, the data shows that more companies in the United States and United Kingdom are starting to pay more than just lip service to workplace culture. A recent research project conducted by Censuswide on behalf of Redgrave (2025) revealed that "…91% of survey recipients say the leadership team prioritizes workplace culture, with half saying it's a top priority." On the downside, many—safe to say, most—can't sustain it. This same study showed: "Almost 9 in 10 respondents have experienced cultural deterioration in a workplace." But, in their words…

> *"…perhaps the most telling factor is **ineffective leadership**. A quarter of those who have seen culture deterioration in an organization before say a primary cause was a lack of clear leadership and direction. Almost a quarter (24%) say this was due to inconsistent communication from management, while 24% say that a change in leadership or organizational restructuring was the primary cause."*

This explains, in a nutshell, why this Preface is so necessary in terms of establishing the aforementioned *leadership-culture-performance* connection.

We believe part of the challenge lies in a misunderstanding of how organizational culture is defined and a misattribution of how it is created.

Organizational Culture Defined

Organizational culture has been described in different ways by many authors. For example, Verbeke, Volgering, and Hessels (1998) identified 54 different definitions in the literature between 1960 and 1993" (p.567).

After their own exhaustive research, Cooke and Rousseau (1988) attested: "While specific definitions differ, they all tend to emphasize certain things: (1) Culture is something *shared* by members of an organization; (2) *values* (what is important), and *beliefs* (how things work), are central components of culture; and (3) culture encompasses *norms and expectations* that influence the way members of organizations think and behave."

Having worked extensively with Human Synergistics International's *Organizational Culture Inventory*® (OCI®) and for more organizations than either of us care to count over the years, we've adopted what some consider to be a "middle-ground" definition that balances ideational (i.e., unobservable assumptions, values, beliefs and ideas shared by members of an organization) views of culture with opposing adaptationist (i.e., observable customs, rites, ceremonies, stories, heroes and other patterns within the organization) views (Szumal, 1998, p.2).

Dr. D's Reflections

In one of my classes on Innovations in Technology, students investigated a new technology from a list of ten and argued for or against its adoption. Although the adopting company was fictional, one assignment required assessing the social aspects of implementing the technology. This highlighted the importance of organizational culture, which can influence products and services, impacting the company's reputation and diluting its hard-earned differentiators.

As measured by the OCI®, organizational culture refers to the behavioral norms and expectations that: (a) guide the way people interact with one another and approach their work and (b) reflect shared values, beliefs, and/or other organizational factors. This definition forms the basis for the rest of this book.

How Culture is Created

Culture begins with the founders of an organization and continues to develop through successive leaders as the organization matures and grows. In the *How Culture Works* Model, Human Synergistics International suggests that founders begin to establish organizational culture (i.e., the internal environment) as they consider the complexity and volatility of the external environment. This culture is rooted in the assumptions they make about people, the world and the way things work, as well as the values they espouse. If the sets of assumptions and values are coherent, they provide a broad base for viewing, feeling and approaching the world—a philosophy for subsequent generations of organizational leaders. To the extent they are shared widely and strongly, they provide a basis for a consistent pattern of expected behaviors. Over time, this pattern becomes discernible in the ways that people relate to each other and that seem to work, and eventually the pattern becomes a comprehensive framework (i.e., culture) that guides an organization's "way of doing things". This way of doing things ultimately determines individual, group and organizational outcomes through the impact it has on the efficacy of every management method, model or theory-in-use. A principal caution here is that these assumptions occur very early in this process and they are seldom, if ever, questioned thereafter.

As it turns out, this is problematic. If your like us, you remember what your Dad told you: "When you assume, you make an…". Well, you can finish that. The point is, it's good to revisit these assumptions if you want to create a constructive and adaptive culture. So, does that mean the less the ambiguity, the better the culture? Maybe! It all depends on whether leadership has the courage to call into question their own assumptions about people, the world, and the way things work.

General Types of Culture

Organizational cultures can be weak or strong depending on the level of influence they exert over how people think and behave (Bateman & Snell, 2011, p. 72). They can also exist at three different levels in the same organization, at the same time: dominant culture, subcultures, and counter-cultures (Cooke & Rousseau, 1988). While the overall culture will reflect dominant norms, subcultures reflect where differences are (i.e., occupational groups, departments, tenure, functions, etc.) and counter-cultures reflect where there is a conflict with other subcultures or with the dominant culture (i.e., shared values, behavioral norms, etc.). It's helpful to remember that no two people are completely alike. We were all raised differently, by different people, in different homes, etc. The variables in play are exponential.

Your awareness of different types of organizational cultures as you lead is as important as awareness of different national cultures as you travel abroad. The difference is, you can measure and improve the former to achieve the types of outcomes all of us are after in business; you are generally stuck with the latter and have to make the best of it until you get back home.

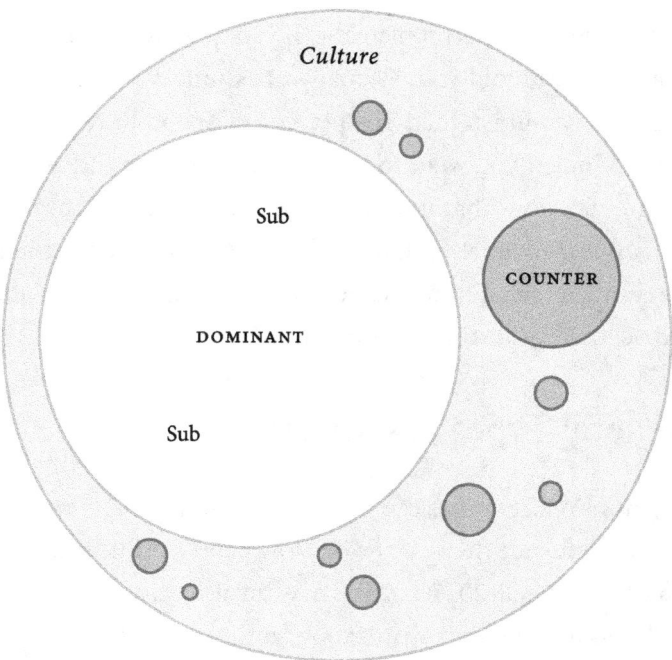

Culture

Sub

COUNTER

DOMINANT

Sub

Differentiating dominant culture from subcultures and counter cultures can offer significant advantage to leaders who want to focus change efforts on what is needed,where it is needed most.

Perhaps you read, as we did, in one of your management courses that an organization can be broken down along the lines that:

- roughly 50% of your workforce will produce 50% or less of an organizations overall output,

- around 40% of your workforce will produce between 50% to 100% output, and

- less than 10% of your workforce will be willing to work at a level above 100%.

The tendency of an inexperienced manager would be to rely on the 10% to carry the team and not address the 50%. Even though it's easy, don't fall for that. You will burn out that top 10% and it is not sustainable. Let the top 10% do their job and work to remove barriers around their successful work. Concentrate on empowering the other two groups, applying leadership, and ensuring the culture is one where everyone is able to contribute in ways that elevate individual, group, and organizational performance. **That is the challenge…**

To help address that challenge directly, according to the *Organizational Culture Inventory®*, organizational cultures can exhibit various behavioral norms and be categorized into one of three dominant clusters: (a) *Constructive* (i.e., interact with others and approach tasks in ways that meet higher order satisfaction needs), (b) *Passive/Defensive* (i.e., interact with others in ways that will not threaten personal security) or (c) *Aggressive/Defensive* (i.e., approach tasks in forceful ways to protect status and security) (Szumal, 1998, p. 3).

As Mr. D has previously discussed in Miracle Cure: The Amazing New Elixir of Corporate Culture (Dillard, 2009), the two ends of the organizational culture continuum are Defensive/Non-adaptive (e.g., Unhealthy) and Constructive/Adaptive (e.g., Healthy).

Culture Continuum

Unhealthy Healthy

DEFENSIVE/NON-ADAPTIVE

· There is competition between the parts
· Marked by placing blame on someone/something else
· Fear and preservation of the status quo pervades

CONSTRUCTIVE/ADAPTIVE

· There is collaboration and cooperation among the parts
· Marked by personal responsibility and accountability
· Individual initiative and engagement pervades

Generally, unhealthy organizational cultures are inactive or reactive and characterized by: (a) competition between the parts, (b) a focus on fixing the blame, not the system and (c) fear and preservation of the status quo.

In contrast, healthy organizational cultures are proactive and characterized by: (a) high levels of collaboration and cooperation, (b) high levels of personal responsibility and accountability and (c) high levels of individual initiative and engagement.

These characteristics make all the difference in the effectiveness of any approach to management through the leadership-culture-performance connection introduced earlier. And to advance the concept that organizational culture has an impact on the efficacy of management, we need to first hardwire the connection.

THE CONNECTION EXPLAINED

The broad application of *Leadership/Impact®* by Human Synergistics International in several countries has revealed that most top executives want to influence people to behave constructively but are unconsciously leading people in ways that cause them to behave defensively, either through their own defensive behavior or the organizational practices they deploy that encourage people to behave that way (McCarthy, 2005). The data that were reviewed in arriving at this conclusion included responses from over 2,000 senior executives and over 14,000 direct reports.

Not surprisingly, people look to what goes on around them on a day-to-day basis to determine how they should approach their work and interact with one another, and what they see causes them to conclude the type of behavior that is required to "fit in":

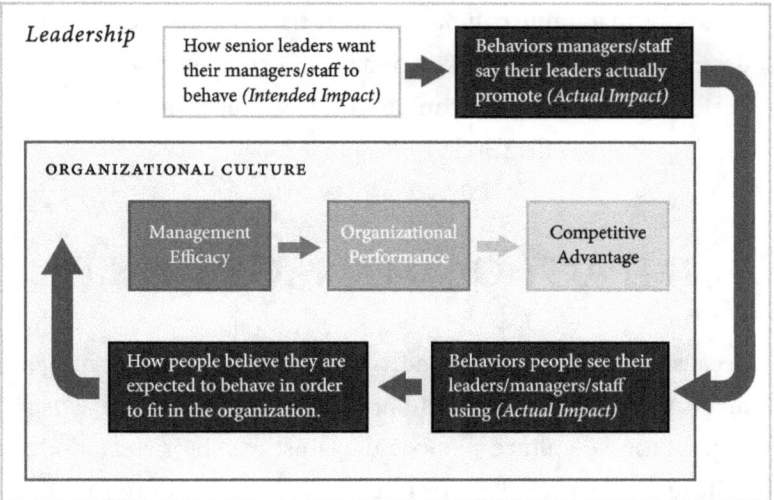

Senior leaders and managers operate within cultures that encourage the very behaviorthey are described by others as using themselves. Conversely, cultures are reflectingthe behaviors of those in leadership and management positions.

Because of the impact senior leaders have, how they really intended for their managers/leaders to behave gets thwarted by the behaviors they actually promote. And because of the leadership-culture connection, the very behaviors employees see from their managers/leaders gets interpreted as what is expected in order to fit in and get on within the organization. If these expectations lead to behaviors that are defensive, it can produce "…lower levels of individual satisfaction and motivation, lower levels of teamwork and co-operation, and lower levels of customer service and quality….That's the leadership-culture-performance connection" (McCarthy, 2005).

Regardless of how valid or robust a management method, model, theory or approach may be, imagine trying to achieve organizational goals with the outcomes listed above. There is no doubt that culture impacts managerial effectiveness, which determines the extent to which management's effort to improve performance and deliver competitive advantage will be successful. It's a "cause-effect" relationship.

IMPACT ON MANAGEMENT

Because there are literally hundreds of different business management approaches and 2000 additional business concepts, of which organizational culture is one and against which organizational culture can be evaluated for impact, this Preface examines the impact of organizational culture on the efficacy of management and hence competitive advantage in the context of the five fundamental success drivers that Bateman & Snell (2011) call specific attention to: Innovation, Quality, Service, Speed and Cost (pp. 9-13). This will clearly establish the connection between organizational culture and performance through the impact it has on the efficacy of management, as well as underscore the reasons companies like INXS Global failed to sustain competitive advantage.

The table below provides a good summary of the impact of organizational culture on the five fundamental success drivers of management, and it is followed by a detailed explanation.

Culture

	PASSIVE/DEFENSIVE	AGGRESSIVE/DEFENSIVE	CONSTRUCTIVE
INNOVATION	Suppresses	Neutral Impact	Encourages and Sustains
QUALITY/ SERVICE	Negative Correlation	Significant and Negative Correlation	Significant and Positive Correlation
SPEED	Impedes Action	Builds Barriers	Promotes Teamwork and Breaks Down Barriers
COST	Increases Turnover and Reduces NPAT	Increases Turnover and Earnings/Sales Volatility	Lowers turnover and increases Earnings/ Sales Ratios and NPAT

Driver (row label at left)

Unless otherwise cited, all results and conclusions are drawn directly from the research and development work of Robert A. Cooke, Ph.D. and J. Clayton Lafferty, Ph.D. at Human Synergistics International, as well as from analysis performed by Sanders & Cooke (2005)[5] on results from a comprehensive application of the *Organizational Culture Inventory*® (OCI®). Though there are many culture assessments on the market today, the OCI® was selected because (a) it is a survey-based quantitative assessment that is more useful for relating culture to performance than a qualitative assessment, (b) the norming base is large and statistical validity high compared to every other assessment and (c) it is the most familiar of all the assessments, textually and experientially, to this author.

Innovation. OCI® results reveal that organizations with *Constructive* cultures, where members capitalize on individual differences to enhance performance, encourage creativity and sustain innovation. In stark contrast, *Aggressive/Defensive* cultures are shown to have a neutral impact on innovation while *Passive/Defensive* cultures, which tend to be traditional, conservative, and run on the basis of rules and regulations (i.e., Conventional), actually encourage members to conform, follow rules and procedures and maintain the status quo. An unnecessarily Conventional culture can suppress innovation and make it difficult for the organization to adapt to changes in its environment.

According to the Harvard Business Review Blog Network post: Six Secrets to Creating a Culture of Innovation (Schwartz, 2010), an IBM poll of 1500 chief executive officers (CEOs) across 60 countries revealed creativity as the "…most important leadership competency." It also revealed that eighty percent of CEOs believe the "…business environment is growing so complex that it literally demands new ways of thinking." Tragically, less than fifty percent believed their organizations were equipped to deal with it effectively.

Creativity is the predecessor of innovation and vital as a leadership competency. Given the leadership-culture-performance connection, it becomes clear how organizational culture impacts the effectiveness of management when it comes to delivering performance and competitive advantage through innovation.

Quality and Service. While Batemen & Snell (2011) address quality and service separately, they are inextricably linked by the following: (a) "Quality is further provided when companies provide goods and services to the wishes of the individual consumer" (p. 10) and (b) "service means giving customers what they want or need, when they want it" (p. 11). As a result, they are addressed together in this book.

Based on the *How Culture Works* (2025) model, both group (i.e., unit-level) and organizational quality are outcomes of culture, as is quality of service. In 2001, the OCI® was used to assess culture at 90 newspapers as part of *The Impact Study*, a multi-faceted research project of the Readership Institute at Northwestern University. The results revealed that *Constructive* cultures have a significant positive relationship with product and service quality (Sanders & Cooke, 2005). This means that the relationship between *Constructive* cultures and higher quality is statistically significant (i.e., the correlation is clearly on the positive side of zero, with +1 or -1 being the perfect positive or negative correlation and zero representing no correlation, and there is only a 0.1 percent chance that the relationship observed is the result of chance). In contrast, this same study revealed that *Passive/Defensive* and *Aggressive/Defensive* cultures have a significant negative relationship with product and service quality. While this does not establish causation, a strong correlation like this is enough to conclude with confidence that organizational culture does have an impact on management's effort to deliver performance and competitive advantage through quality and service.

Speed. Whether the focus is making faster and better decisions, reducing time to market, or decreasing overall process cycle-time, the need for speed in today's rapidly changing and competitive global marketplace is growing. Due to the interdependency of functions and interoperability of processes in our complex business systems, it is not enough to maintain isolated pockets of speed. Organizations must now work to improve teamwork and inter-unit coordination, two outcomes of culture at the group level. *Constructive* cultures are dominated by Affiliative norms that directly promote teamwork and cooperation. Members communicate openly, are thoughtful and approachable, and show genuine concern for each other, all of which breaks down barriers to teamwork and inter-unit coordination so the organization can move faster. In contrast, *Aggressive/Defensive* cultures tend to be Perfectionistic and Oppositional, which slows things down and builds up barriers to cooperation, while *Passive/Defensive* cultures tend to be Dependent and Avoidance oriented, slowing responsiveness and impeding action. In either case, defensive cultures, passive or aggressive, wreak havoc on management's effort to deliver speed for performance and competitive advantage.

Cost. There are numerous cost-drivers in business. This book examines turnover, earnings/sales ratios and net profit after taxes (NPAT) to uncover the impact of culture on cost.

Estimates on the cost of turnover range from 30% of an employees' annual salary to over 150%. OCI® research related to the Readership Institute study of 90 newspapers revealed *Constructive* cultures have a significant negative relationship with turnover, while the defensive styles both exhibited positive correlations with *Aggressive/Defensive* exhibiting the highest.

Based on OCI® and financial data from 69 companies, Sanders & Cooke (2005) were able to identify a strong positive relationship between *Constructive* cultures and higher earnings/sales ratios. No relationship was found between either type of defensive culture or the earnings/sales ratios; however, the *Aggressive/ Defensive* styles were found to have a significant relationship with volatility.

A nine year longitudinal study between 1996 and 2004 with the OCI® at Lion Nathan, the largest brewer in New Zealand and second-largest in Australia, revealed annual rate of change increases in NPAT for seven consecutive years. Over this same time frame, the culture of Lion Nathan moved from a defensive culture (i.e., primary styles were *Aggressive/Defensive*; back-up styles were *Passive/Defensive*) to a predominant *Constructive* culture. The shift started to take place between 1996 and 1997, such that a significant increase in the *Constructive* styles could be observed as early as 1998; the same year Lion Nathan posted their first rate of change increase to NPAT.

From each example, it is clear that organizational culture has an impact on management's ability to deliver performance and competitive advantage by controlling cost.

SUMMARY AND TRANSITION

Organizational culture seems to make no distinction between the "proposed" usefulness of management methods, models or theories being applied toward accomplishing goals, improving performance or gaining and retaining competitive advantage. It impacts all of them indiscriminately. But while evidence that organizational culture impacts the efficacy of management appears conclusive, culture change remains largely elusive for most organizations. In fact, it is rarely given serious consideration as a strategic priority and, even when it is, very little ever gets changed.

And it isn't that managing culture has been tried and found wanting. It is found to be too difficult and left untried. But this begs the question: "Where did all the evidence in support of culture change come from?" It came from organizations with leaders who dared to change themselves and, as a result, their cultures. So we know it can be done.

With that established, a second question should be asked: "Was it worth the effort?" This Preface explored five fundamental success drivers that connect culture with the efficacy of management, and as previously discussed (Dillard, 2009), in every case culture change was successful it was well worth the effort:

- A study of 200 blue-chip enterprises in 22 industries over an 11 year period by Kotter and Heskett of Harvard Business School found that organizations with the strongest adaptive cultures had significantly higher performance than firms with rigid or weak cultures.[6]

- Values guru Richard Barrett found that the return on assets and return on equity in companies with the 'best' (defined here as *Constructive*/Adaptive) cultures was higher than the S&P 500 from 1991 through 1997.[7]

- Examining 950 businesses across sectors, Denison Consulting also found a correlation between culture and the bottom line. Such cultural traits as involvement, consistency, adaptability and mission were positively linked to operational performance measures, including return on investment, product development, sales growth, market share, quality and employee satisfaction.[8]

- Hospital Corporation of America (HCA) found that its 12 highest performing hospitals in terms of financials were also its 12 highest culturally performing hospitals, enjoying an employee engagement ratio of 5.68, as compared to an average of 2.44 for the entire system (173 hospitals) and 1.83 for its lowest performing hospitals. HCA also found a steadily decreasing employee turnover rate of 16.6 percent for the highest performers versus a steadily increasing turnover rate of 23.3 percent for the lowest performers.[9]

And what about INXS Global? A few years back, I had an opportunity to catch up with a senior leader from the business unit introduced earlier. The reason for his call was to ask if I would be interested in helping them with culture, leadership and teams/teamwork so that they would be ready to respond in a way that would help them take advantage of the market upswing they were anticipating. My sincere hope was that they would take up the challenge. They didn't... at least not with me. How about you?

Though history is fixed and we'll never know for certain, we're convinced they would have been in a better competitive position had they made organizational culture a post-merger strategic priority. And we don't say that hypothetically. In an article that first appeared in CMA Management over a two decades ago, Gitelson, Bing and Laroche (2001) start off by sharing the following insights: "According to a KPMG study, '83% of all mergers and acquisitions (M&As) failed to produce any benefit for the shareholders and over half actually destroyed value'. Interviews of over 100 senior executives involved in these 700 deals over a two-year period revealed that the overwhelming cause for failure 'is the people and the cultural differences'. Further, difficulties encountered in M&As are amplified in cross-cultural situations when the companies involved are from two or more different countries."

Based on the totality of evidence available, a number of conclusions can be drawn when it comes to managing culture: (1) leaders shape organizational culture through their leadership strategies and actions and (2) operating culture has an impact on the efficacy of their management strategies and actions, as well as performance. Because this leadership-culture-performance connection determines the extent to which managers will be able to accomplish organizational goals, adapt to the external environment and gain/retain competitive advantage, it is in every manager's best interest to both discover more and then do something about improving culture. Leadership is all that is required. But not just any leadership; a *Real Leadership* that you can read more about in the rest of this book as you endeavor to…

FOREWORD

IN THE EARLY part of the 20th century Thomas Kuhn wrote what has become one of the most influential books of our times: The Structure of Scientific Revolutions. In this landmark work, Kuhn brilliantly described how every historical breakthrough is a really a break WITH. In other words, they reflect a "break with" old ways of thinking, of doing and of being—just as they speak to the importance of engaging in an intentional process of developing new skills, new habits and new tools if we are to achieve excellence and ensure relevance in an ever-changing world.

The book you are holding in your hand is a genuine BREAK WITH.

The rate of change in today's society is unprecedented. The globalization of markets, the rapid proliferation of technology and information and the increasing appetite for top-shelf talent is placing tremendous demands on people and organizations alike. And it will not get easier anytime soon. So how can we position ourselves to flourish and thrive in our individual spheres of influence? I'd offer the solution is clear, and it is what Richard & Dr. Brian Dillard call: *Real Leadership!*

The common denominator among organizations that set the standard for achieving sustained excellence is the quality of their leaders. Not just any leadership and not just at the top of the organization. No matter how you look at the data, it's clear that leaders who succeed in creating a great workplace are those who can develop shared trust, take pride in what they do, and enjoy the people they work with. In other words, they are self-motivated life-long learners who are committed to leading at a higher level.

To lead at a higher level is to accept that the development of people—customers, workmates, partners—is as important as organizational performance. In the words of leadership expert Ken Blanchard, leading at a higher level is "a process." Specifically, a process by which we constantly push the bounds of our own potential while committing to act with respect and care.

In the most successful organizations, be they for-profit businesses, non-profit charities, schools, hospitals, military units or any entity for that matter, leadership is considered a shared responsibility. In other words, it is more about exercising moral authority than it is about wielding formal authority. All choice and no chance, *Take Your Lead* begins with acknowledging that leading well is hard work. But it's worth the effort if you are serious about becoming the leader you want to be and others deserve to see.

One of the great tragedies I've witnessed time and time again occurs when people spend their days just going through the motions without associating what they are doing with a sense of greater purpose. Instead of looking for ways to constantly give their best in support of a cause, campaign or mission bigger than themselves, they choose to lead small lives. And the saddest part about it is that they don't have any idea what they are missing.

If you are looking for something more than just another book on leadership; specifically, a book that challenges you to rethink and reframe how you view your potential to promote positive change, this book is for you. The most powerful incentive known to humankind is our own assessment of our behavior, our accomplishments, and most importantly, our potential. When we believe we are able to meet our personal goals and objectives, we feel validated and fulfilled. We also feel as if we are living up to the image of who we want to be, which ultimately fuels the intrinsic motivation we need to consistently raise the bar on our performance en-route to becoming the best possible version of ourselves.

Remember, when it comes to doing our part to promote positive change in our surroundings, we not only need the courage and the scholarship, but the practical skills to do so. As the experts at the Great Workplace Institute have confirmed in their decades of assessing, measuring and recognizing the best organizations around the globe, what separates the good from the great, the ordinary from the extraordinary, the average from the outstanding comes down to a single line: It's not what you do. It's *how and why you do it* that matters most.

So no matter where you are in your current leadership journey or what kind of organization you are in, *Take Your Lead* will equip you with new skills, new habits and new tools to develop your own insight on how to lead well. It will give you everything you need to transform your new insights into practical action—again and again, as our ever-changing world demands. All that's left to do is take up the challenge.

Enjoy the journey.

John E. Michel, Brigadier General
United States Air Force, Retired
President Food is Love Foundation and Co-Founder,
Soulcial Kitchen & Skyworks Aeronautics.
Board Member, Social Entrepreneur & Community Strategist.
O'Fallon IL, June 2025

ACKNOWLEDGEMENTS

T HERE ARE MORE people to thank and acknowledge for this book than the entire length of it would afford. Regardless, we would be remiss to avoid an attempt.

First, we are profoundly grateful to our Heavenly Father for His steadfast love and manifold wisdom; to the greatest, most *real leader* who ever walked planet Earth: **our Lord and Savior, Jesus Christ;** and to the Holy Spirit for illuminating the path through the inspired Word (Logos). May this book be used as Bach intended his music: Soli Deo Gloria (for your Glory alone) and for the benefit of others. May it also be for our own good in changing, growing and leading, as we continue to learn what it means to love ourselves the way you love us and to love others as we love ourselves.

Next, to our family. Thanks for all your love and support. Perhaps more than all else, for giving us the room to take risks and make mistakes, for modeling forgiveness through our long and inelegant learning journey and for never wavering in your allegiance to what we believed to be our mission and purpose. There is no way to fully express how we feel about you in mere words, but we pray to have provided enough evidence by our actions for you to already know.

Next, to Andrea L. Wagner for her power of editing over the first two books back in 2012, now being combined and updated herein. And to Caerus Kourt, our book designer, responsible for this present masterwork.

Finally, to all who truly understood what it meant to *Take Your Lead* and demonstrated it by your commitment in time, talent and treasure to coach and mentor us over the years. To all those who signed up to read the draft manuscript and write the Foreword or a word of commendation or praise. We hope you find in these pages some of the return on your investment in us. And to all who have been a part of our professional journey over the last 40+ years, including all the Imaginary Leaders who taught us so much about what to avoid...

Thank you!

DEDICATION

THIS BOOK IS dedicated to anyone who is curious about their leadership. Not just the phenomenon, but about how they are leading and how to become better at who they are and what they do as a leader. If this describes you, this book is written to meet you precisely where you are at as a leader today, regardless of whether you consider yourself a beginner, novice or expert.

Though it didn't start out that way, for us, as Brothers and Irish Twins—sandwiched in the middle of 5 additional siblings—writing this book turned out to be a tribute to our Dad: **Tommy Eugene Dillard**.

Here's why...

In the 1930s, poet and historian Carl Sandburg was finishing his six-volume work entitled *Abraham Lincoln: The Prairie Years and The War Years*. Sandburg called his 75th and final chapter "A Tree is Best Measured When It's Down," a line he borrowed from an old woodsman's proverb. Sandburg chose that line because he was writing of the events immediately following Lincoln's assassination, and because he felt that until a life is "down" we are unable to accurately measure the length of its significance, the breadth of its impact, and the depth of its character.

Like the proverb states, while alive, no man or woman can be fully measured. Only with the passing of time can anyone's life be properly evaluated. The gushing praise of flatterers and the derisive contempt of adversaries alike are best gauged and reappraised against the lasting results of a person's words and deeds.

Never is this truer than when applied to Leaders. Among the few from which we've had the privilege of being trained, our Dad stands out to us most. Born about the time Sandburg was wrapping up his biographical masterpiece on Lincoln, he tragically passed away in 1974 at the age of 40 from lung cancer. But the length of his significance, the breadth of his impact, and the depth of his character have only elevated in consequence for us over the last 50 years.

He was raised dirt-floor poor in rural Arkansas (Crittendon County) wearing burlap sacks for clothing and dropping out of school before finishing the 3rd grade. He did this in order to pick cotton instead. Yep! We come from a family of sharecroppers, and life was very simple for them. They lived by the proverb: "If you don't work you don't eat!" (2 Thessalonians 3:10). A phrase often repeated in our home as we were growing up.

Eventually, these humble beginnings (and our Mom) would lead Dad to a faith in Christ and to the manifestation of his confession in baptism. There are photos that serve to memorialize this event, as well as a few others from his brief time with us, but they could never truly capture the length of significance, the breadth of impact and the depth of meaning it has had, and continues to hold, on our lives. We surmise that only an eternity of sharing with him the presence of Almighty God is big enough to do that. But what is truly measurable and meaningful this side of eternity is this; that *in the soil of his personal transformation was planted the seeds for our own*. One such seed was humility and the 'wisdom' that grows from it through lifelong learning. Growing up in South Detroit in the 1960s and '70s, we were blessed to learn about the grace of God from many other members of our family, but it was Dad who instilled in us the fear of God. Solomon stated that this is the beginning of wisdom, which Jesus Christ confirmed is shown right by the lives of those who follow it.

These humble, simple beginnings have subsequently taken us on the learning journey of a lifetime, but we'll never forget where we came from or how it all started. In fact, as we reflected back on over 4 decades in our own careers, we were continually reminded of "the wisdom of Dad" while writing this book. We haven't always gotten it right. We've made a ton of mistakes, taken unnecessary risks and botched things up good at times. But it is equally true that, we learned a lot from our missteps, endeavored never to repeat them and sometimes—just sometimes—got it right the first time. And for leaders, wisdom is indispensable. It rules the day when our decisions and actions are guided by thoughtful consideration, moral integrity, and a deep understanding of others, such that we consistently act justly, love mercy, and walk humbly.

To the extent this is true of us and of the ideas contained in the pages of this book, we give the credit to Dad. Of course our Mom, Carol Ann Dillard (née Petrosky), played a huge role in the years after his passing. In fact, we are exceedingly grateful for the opportunity we were afforded until early 2022 to repeatedly express our gratitude to her for picking up where Dad left off in the wisdom category.

So, as you read, remember that we endeavored to look back and reflect on the man who touched our lives… to keep Dad's legacy intact. We hope to both honor and remember him. Surely, his life of character and consequence will continue to have the impact of positive influence in our family for generations to come. With that in mind, may this book enrich your personal leadership, enhance the positive impact you have on those who choose to follow your lead and enable you to elevate the level of performance in your organization.

Another Leadership Book?

Y ES AND NO! We'll explain.

It is a book and it is about leadership, but it is not just about the abstract management concept that elicits the typical nod followed by a big yawn. **It is really all about 'You, the Leader!'** This is a distinction with a difference that will become clear as engage the rest of this book. It's important because, as Leaders go, so goes the Team, the Group, the Organization, the Nation, et al. Yet in spite of this multi-millennial axiom, and the haunting notion that we could very well be the best leadership-educated society in the history of business, our encounters with genuine leaders remain extremely rare. *Take Your Lead* examines this perplexing phenomenon and qualifies the principle cause as an unwillingness and/or inability to *take new leadership information and use it to improve our performance*. It also provides the solution: a Leadership Enrichment LIFE-cycle (LEL-c) to help individuals and organizations build and sustain durable *Leadership Platforms* by pursuing the performance waypoints of learning, changing, growing and leading through successful navigation of their emotional connectors: awareness, acceptance, action and achievement. If you are ready to enrich your personal leadership and raise the level of leadership in your organization, this book is for you.

And if you are still reading this, it is likely that you have more than just a surface-level interest in leadership. Perhaps you've already finished numerous books on the topic of leadership and have chosen this one to expand your point of view. Perhaps this is your first book on leadership and you're just hoping to elevate your awareness, or you're doing research for a term paper and need another reference for citation. Or it could be that you want to dig deeper into leadership as it relates to organizational culture and performance.

But we caution you ahead of time—this book and its measures of merit are a little different than the typical leadership development offering. It won't offer instant solutions or allow for a casual engagement by the passive reader. No! It offers much more than that. It offers an active reader the opportunity to develop leadership in a way never before encountered. And all you'll have to do in order to capitalize on it is ***reject the notion that reading equals leading***. No one becomes a better leader just by reading books about leadership; it doesn't work that way. Reading about leadership won't make you a leader any more than reading a car manual makes you a mechanic, but it is often a good place to start and a better practice to continue.

The principal measure of merit for ***Take Your Lead*** is the extent to which it can steal you away from the impersonal and perfunctory activity of building leadership sandcastles (subject to the evening tide) so that you can ***move toward the personal*** *and thoughtful actions of building Leadership Platforms* with firm Footings, solid Foundations and strength-tested Framings. With your commitment and this book as a guide, a personal and organizational *Leadership Platform* can emerge to actually withstand the world's difficult tests of time and torrent.

In Part 1, your thinking will be transformed by ideas and concepts not normally associated with leadership, but nevertheless vital to our success as leaders. In Part 2, you'll be offered the opportunity of adopting the Leadership Enrichment LIFE-cycle; a process for developing and sustaining *Real Leadership*. Our sincere hope is that you'll take it personally and apply it as the basis for *reflecting on yourself as a leader and improving the impact you have on those who choose to follow.* Then we hope you'll use the strength of your personal *Leadership Platform* to elevate the level of your organization's Leadership and, ultimately, transform the world as you…

TAKE *Your* LEAD!

Real Leadership Undiscovered

HERE IS ABSOLUTELY no doubt in my mind; each of us has crossed paths with someone who could be described as a 'leader' at some point in our personal, professional or social lives. Simply put…someone you are willing to follow. Whether that is into battle or into the board room. This is the person that if asked, you would take a bullet for because you believe the world is a better place with then in it. It matters not where or when we're born, what our background is, or how much education we've had. We all tend to know when we've been in the company of a leader. Not so much because of what they said or what they did, but because of how they made us feel (about them and about ourselves) and because of the positive impact they had on us and those around us. The impression is so remarkable that, when personally asked about it sometime later, we can recall the encounter in vivid detail. More than this…we actually talk about it without being asked. And, if more than one of us experienced the encounter, it inevitably gets recalled organizationally, during water-cooler conversations, lunch breaks and team meetings. This happens with such rapacity that the story could border on legend as time progresses. And it would seem that, no matter how long the encounter, we emerge a little better off and somewhat lost in amazement and wonder. We also emerge with a willingness to follow this individual…to appoint him/her as our leader, if given the opportunity.

This response to an encounter with *Real Leadership* is not unexpected. The history of leadership suggests that its roots are submerged in the idea of movement or advancement by appointment. In Theory and Practice of Leadership, Roger Gill does a masterful job of explaining how the term "leader" was historically used:

> *The word 'Lead' comes from the Old English 'laedan', corresponding to the Old Saxon 'ledian' and Old High German 'leiten', meaning 'take with one', to 'show the way' (Hoad, 1988). Ledere was the term for a person who shows other people the path to take and guides them safely along the journey (Kets de Vries and Florent-Treacy, 1999: 5). The Old Icelandic derivative 'leidha' meant 'the person in front', referring to the person who guided ships through the pack-ice in spring. The word 'leader' appeared in the English language in the thirteenth century, but 'leadership' appeared only in the early nineteenth century.* (Gill)

According to the Online Etymology Dictionary, the suffix "-ship" comes from the Old English '-sciepe', and the Anglian '-scip', which means "state, condition of being", which is from the base '*skap-', which means "to create, ordain, appoint." So a basic understanding of the term **"leadership"** includes achieving the state or condition of being capable as a leader, and then, by the appointment of others, showing them the path to take and guiding them safely along the journey. This *movement by appointment* requires that we: a) first become someone capable of leading and b) get "appointed" by others to lead.

Seems straight-forward enough, doesn't it? Well, if you've been at this as long as we have, you've likely made a number of observations about leaders along the way. And, if you're like us, some of those observations have really made you scratch your head trying to make sense of it all. We don't say that hypothetically. We say that because of more than 82 combined years of professional experiences and numerous conversations we've had along the way about this idea of leadership. Whether conversing with family, friends, co-workers, clients, fellow volunteers or those considered civic and business leaders, we continue to find a number of consistent observations.

Perhaps the most consistent observation is how truly rare our encounters with *real leaders* are. Yes! Just as we know when we've encountered a leader, we know when we haven't. And when we haven't, we also know, and can easily recall, the negative impact they had on us personally, and those around us organizationally. Our own experience validates this. Over the past 41+ years, we can count on one hand

Mr. D's Introspections

This may not seem significant until you consider that I have held over 50 professional and social roles, including 36 unique positions with 22 organizations spanning 12 career fields and 7 industries in the commercial sector and 11 positions with 8 organizations in the government and non-profit sectors. And if you are tempted to question just how much I care about this phenomenon called leadership, I named my 4th daughter in a way that her initials spell the word LEAD!

the number of *real leaders* we've had the privilege of encountering in a direct-reporting relationship. In all those encounters there have been more times than not we are left with the question of "who put that person in charge?". Who in their right mind thought that individual could lead others to achieve anything. How many times have you asked yourself that question? Now, compare it to the number of times you encountered someone you were willing to follow. Take note of both as they will be relevant as we journey through this book.

Another observation is regarding the classes of leaders we encounter. By my estimation, there are two distinct classes:

1. **LEADERS-IN-POSITION (entitled)** who imagine they are being followed, and

2. **LEADERS-IN-PERSON (earned)** who actually look around every once in a while to find out who has chosen to follow them.

Compounding this observation is the fact that one of these leaders is an imposter (a fake) and, unfortunately, it's the class of leader found most often: *leaders-in-position*. Interestingly enough, this class of leader may actually hold a high rank or title in the organization, but it begs a question: "What should they be called if no one is actually following them?" If they are leading at all it would have to be through what we'll call an Imaginary Leadership, which stands in polar opposition to what this book is about: *Real Leadership*! Do not kid yourself into thinking there is no risk in promoting the wrong people into a position of leadership. Imaginary Leaders can and, in fact, do cause a lot of harm to organizational cultures and if not identified and corrected, it ends with little to sustainable performance. In fact, they often regress an organization to the point of extremely negative outcomes.

A third observation is related to the sheer amount of information available on the subject of leadership. It seems that new ideas are released every day. We have literally been peppered with countless leadership books, seminars, blended learning curriculums, assessments, et al., coming at us from every life venue (i.e., business, church, school, politics, etc.). Here's some perspective: a Google search for the word "leadership" in 2012—when the first edition of *Real Leadership! Are You Ready?* was published—returned approximately 495,000,000 results. Yes... that's 495 million. That same search on Amazon would have returned 119,798 results, ranging from books, eBooks, CDs, DVDs, Posters, et al. From the business venue alone, during my visit to 12manage.com in 2012, they advertised as many as 400 different business management approaches with an additional 2000 business concepts to be explored through their management dictionary. Over 90 of these were classified under the heading: "Leadership. Methods, Models, and Theories (A-Z)." **Today (2025), a Google search will return 1,770,000,000—over 1.7 billon—results on the word 'leadership', a more than 260% increase in just the last 13 years.**

These three observations alone were enough to put us in a real quandary. For all this new information on the subject, we would have expected the frequency of our encounters with *real leaders* to be far higher. But it isn't. We would also reasonably expect to find more *leaders-in-person* over the course and scope of daily living, whether the context is personal, professional or social. But we don't. We still find more *leaders-in-position*. Why is that? Well, it may seem overly simplistic, but you must want to be a leader, and many don't. For various reasons throughout history people have decided not to lead or develop into someone worth following. Sometimes accepting the responsibility is to great a burden, or maybe the fear of failure is too much that they would rather not. Whatever their reasoning, it says a lot about their character to admit they have limitations and stay out of positions that require leading others. Would that more take pains to do this. But the reality is that the allure of titles and more money draws professionals unwittingly into positions of leadership. But just starting your own company or being appointed or selected by someone above you in the organizational hierarchy for a vertical promotion doesn't mean that those who fall below you in that paradigm-past structure want to, or will, automatically accept it and start following your lead.

Could it be that, for all this information and all our education on leadership, we still lack the scholarship to learn from it? Or is it that we lack the courage to actually apply what we've learned? Or is it as Malcolm Muggeridge once predicted about Western Man…we've educated ourselves into imbecility? Either way, an affirmative answer to any one of these questions begs another: Is that okay? As we began to dig deeper to find the answer, we stumbled upon some startling things.

First, there remains a lot of confusion. The term 'leadership' still carries with it about as many definitions and meanings as there are people who consider themselves leaders. Ironically, the term carries equal weight with those who are impacted by these "leaders" on a daily basis, but the meaning for them tends to be substantially different. This isn't all that surprising. With the rarity of *real leaders*, the preponderance of imaginary *leaders-in-position* and the sheer amount of new information mentioned earlier, most now tune out at a mere mention of the word Leadership.

They've already heard it all and have "had it up to here" with all the talk about leadership, so little effort is ever applied to defining it personally and little consensus is ever reached on how it should be defined organizationally. At the end of the day, if you are in the oft-times unenviable position of leading others, you and you alone define what leadership means and the results you will have the potential to achieve, whether you know it or not. But more than likely, without investing in defining and developing your leadership, you will not rise to the occasion of creating a constructive and adaptive culture that produces sustainable performance and better outcomes, but you will default to the level of your training or, even more base still, what you believe needs to get done to make the problem quickly go away or to get the next promotion and pay raise.

Opportunity: *Different situations may require different styles or approaches from your leadership (e.g., Situational Leadership). Agree or disagree, and why? Put that in your notes. Oh yes, part of the challenge in reading this book is writing…your writing. It'll become more apparent as you progress through the pages. Start now.*

Either way, there remains a lot of confusion about management and leadership. The terms (and skills/qualities) have largely become a distinction without a difference even though the best information we have available tells us that, while related, they are profoundly different. Going back to the classes of leaders just presented, *leaders-in-person* don't need to hold a position of leadership to be effective. They don't need to have a budget, control any assets, or own any processes to lead. They simply care enough about their impact on others to actually check whether anyone is following. They may or may not like what they find, but at least they can stop imagining like the *leaders-in-position* and start working with others to find out what is holding them back. The fact is, there isn't a role on earth that is so directly tied to, and ultimately dependent upon, others (i.e., followers) than that of leader. In contrast, the role of manager, while as useful and necessary for personal and organizational success, fails this basic people-test because its principle focus is on something different: assets, task accomplishment, process, etc. It is not predominately focused on people and, when it is, it views employees as "assets of" the company, rather than "assets to" the company. Worse yet, when management begins to shift its focus away from tasks to people, it ends up taking the shape and form of its own sinister imposters: micro-management, command and control, carrots and sticks motivation and management by objectives. All are equally devastating to leadership and achieving the outcomes they are responsible for producing for and with others.

As mentioned, both leadership and managership are essential components of outstanding personal and organizational success, but they are, as my good friend Dave Guerra says, "…best appreciated as polar complements….two sides of one coin." This means we need to understand the difference between leadership and managership, develop both skills/qualities to be successful and know when and how to skillfully apply each to increase personal and organizational performance. We encourage you to find out more about Dave's thought-leadership by reviewing *Superperformance: New Profound Knowledge for Corporate Leaders*. It is available on Amazon in paperback and through Kindle as an eBook.

Safely and securely leaving the task of increasing clarity on the distinction between leadership and managership to Dave Guerra (and a host of others), we want to address the confusion on, and lack of progress toward, defining and then taking Leadership to a meaningful level. We'd like to spend time on understanding this confusion and limited progress, and why there is such a lack of congruity between how leaders imagine they are leading and how they are actually impacting their down-line (a.k.a., direct reports).

How is it that, when you start to assess and analyze leadership, there appear to be many *leaders-in-position*, entitled by promotion, without the benefit of followers? They by right have direct reports and positional power to impact outcomes, but they are not leading. In contrast, why do we still find scarcely few *leaders-in-person*, earned by appointment, with followers en masse? Through their personal power they positively impact others and outcomes with or without positional authority.

We believe the primary reasons for this persistent confusion are that leadership remains largely impersonal and is considered mostly unnecessary. Sure, based on things routinely measured, on all outward evidence, things look fine and career progression—typically restricted to upward mobility—is on-track.

All "required" training gets checked-off on leadership topics like ethics, collaboration, empowerment, teaming, etc., the performance appraisal ticket gets punched in the development category year after year and we methodically advance through the prescribed leadership curriculum and up the corporate ladder. Unfortunately, the things less measured—the inward evidence—points to the fact that very little of the new leadership information we're exposed to gets personalized and seldom, if ever, gets leveraged for improving our impact as leaders or raising the level of leadership in our organizations.

Opportunity: *How do you measure leadership? Is it quantitative or qualitative? Is the measure fair? How do you know? Put this in your notes.*

Conditioned by the culture (e.g., defensive/non-adaptive) within which we work and the structures (i.e., hierarchy, decision-making, etc.) and systems (e.g., training, appraisal, etc.) that work on us each day, leadership ends up being viewed by many as just another professional requirement...a superfluous exercise of "going through the personal development and empowerment motions" at work. It is anything but personal and only useful and necessary to the extent it checks the right professional boxes. But in all fairness, can we blame them? No! Who wouldn't be tempted to conclude after a few successive promotions in this type of culture—with these types of structures and systems in place—that positional power is what counts and personal power is unnecessary? Now we're not suggesting that positional power isn't important. The fact is, it can be a great force for good leveraged by leaders holding higher positions of authority in common hierarchical organizational structures. But as many of us already know by experience, any strength abused rapidly becomes weakness; and over-reliance on positional power at the expense of developing real personal power is an all-to-common mistake for leaders.

One of the biggest and most immediate negative consequences of this mistake is that it naturally increases what some refer to as "Power Distance", which is one way to describe professional relationships. A primary reliance on positional power increases that distance and results in clearly distinguishable lines of authority; more formal, less relaxed communication; and authoritative/directive approaches to decisions and actions in a "superior-subordinate" relationship. In contrast, a primary or balanced reliance on personal power decreases power distance and produces less formal, more relaxed communication and participative/consultative approaches to decisions and actions in a "leader-follower" relationship while still maintaining lines of authority. In the final analysis, positional power is simply not enough to be effective as a leader…it will help you to *Take Your Lead*. We must have personal power. The challenge that all of us face here is that the former comes with "title territory" and doesn't need to be developed while the latter requires a lot of hard work.

We promise that we'll get to deeper explanations for all of this in Part 1, as well as what can be done about it in Part 2. But before going there, now that we understand more about what causes the confusion, let's try to add more clarity to what is meant by *Real Leadership* as it will help you to...

Real Leadership IS/IS NOT

A s mentioned, there has been so much written and taught about leadership over the years that most people automatically tune out at hearing the word, particularly those who believe they are already leading. The reality is, there are many who are leading poorly without even realizing the negative impact they are having on others. Also, there are those with leadership potential that is largely unrealized because they never thought of themselves or their leadership in the ways we're about to describe. Either way, the result is the same: *Real Leadership* remains undiscovered. To break away from this negative impact from limited thinking, we've included below five ideas about leadership. They are not popular but they are vital to a basic understanding of *Real Leadership*, so we hope you will give them careful consideration.

1. **There is effective and ineffective Leadership.**
   There is ample evidence (re: *Leadership/Impact®*
   from Human Synergistics International) to suggest
   that leaders who employ more Prescriptive than
   Restrictive strategies across a few key areas or
   domains will promote higher levels of individual,
   group and organizational effectiveness. These areas
   include personal strategies related to aspirations
   and conduct, interpersonal strategies related to
   one-on-one interactions with others and organizational strategies related to using systems, structures
   and resources to influence the thinking, behavior
   and performance of others (Cooke, Leadership/
   Impact Feedback Report). *Real Leadership* is
   effective leadership!

2. **There is right and wrong leadership.** In a
   post-modern era that has made it politically
   incorrect to talk about right and wrong while
   simultaneously over-relying on massive code
   of ethics policies to encourage right behavior
   (remember ENRON had an industry leading code
   of ethics policy), it is important to note that "effective" leadership does not equal "right" leadership.
   There is a difference. Consider the simple idea that
   leadership is renewable energy and, as such, can
   be exchanged between producer and consumer.
   It can be produced/consumed for good/benefit
   or for harm/detriment. Countless examples of
   applied leadership throughout history clearly fall
   into both camps. Leadership, like any great might,
   does not make right. If there is one lesson to learn,

it is that MOTIVE (e.g., intention) determines the MEANS (e.g., methods) by which we reach ENDS (e.g., goals/objectives). In this sense, Leadership, as attained and applied through the Leadership Enrichment LIFE-cycle, is intended to be governed by righteousness or "the moral law", otherwise motive, means and ends get perverted and bad things naturally begin to follow. *Real Leadership* is right leadership!

3. **Leadership may not be private, but it sure is personal.** No question. Leadership is as much about self as it is about others, but not in the way you may be thinking. To be both effective and right as a leader, we must attend to self-leadership; the governance of one's own person. Without self-governance, there is little of real value to give away and/or little that others will perceive as being worthy of following. Ever wonder why senior leaders resign after compromises of integrity (i.e., extra-marital affairs, embezzling, etc.)? Stephen Covey picked up the flavor of this critical ingredient in our leadership enrichment recipe when he clarified in habit #5 of *The 7 Habits of Highly Effective People* the first component of Greek (Aristotelian) philosophy on Rhetoric: credibility or ethical appeal (ETHOS). In order to be influential as a leader, we first need to maintain high standards of personal moral excellence (a private matter, as Dwight L. Moody quipped: "Character is what you are in the dark")... otherwise no one will allow us to get close enough to really understand

their concerns (PATHOS) or consider us credible enough to receive—let alone dare ever act on—our words (LOGOS), nor will they, as a result, ever choose to follow our lead. And if you question this idea or are tempted to wonder whether it matters, consider the results of a Baylor University study, recently conducted by Mitch Neubert and Dawn Carlson. According to the online article: *As the Leader Goes, So Goes the Company* (Carlson), their findings suggest that ethical leadership does indeed lead to better performance in the workplace and that Servant Leadership leads to more creative behavior on the part of employees. *Real Leadership* must first become personal, but it cannot stay private.

4. **Leadership bears no relation to your title, rank or position.** Leadership finds its roots in those who choose to follow. Put another way, there are no leaders without followers. If no one is following, you are not leading, regardless of your title, rank or position. Never forget that. It will come in handy as a humbling agent when you start believing too much in your own "stuff." Lead long enough with any success and you will be tempted to "over-believe" in your own capabilities... some of us sooner than others, but all of us at

Mr. D's Introspections

Because of the certainty of being tempted to over-believe in my own capabilities, I've hardwired my Leadership Platform with a practical warning to guard against it and include the following admonition as reminder: "Keep those who follow FIRST!"

some point. Conversely, anyone can lead from any station in their personal, professional and social lives if they are committed to becoming someone worth following. This will require that you break out of the mold that suggests your level of influence is tied to your position in the family, the organization or the community. If you haven't already, begin to reject this lie firmly and see yourself, others and the world differently. *Real Leadership* is a leadership made by the appointment of those who choose to follow your lead.

5. **Leadership is perishable.** As renewable energy, *Real Leadership* finds its source of renewal in: (a) your commitment to get better at who you are and what you do in the organizations where you work and (b) those inside the organization that actually make the choice to follow you each and every day. At any time, these followers can opt out. Remembering this will help you, over time, to consistently give them the best reasons to stay "in". More importantly, the longer they are "in", the more you will be able to develop them as leaders and they, in turn, will be able to attract other followers. *Real Leadership* is continually renewed and improved, and so is the organizational culture these types of leaders create!

The ideas just presented form a basis for the rest of this book and with it, your best opportunity to *Take Your Lead*. And taking advantage of this opportunity will require your commitment to thinking differently about leadership in Part 1 and then creating your own *Leadership Platform* for continual renewal and improvement in Part 2. As a result, you will gain the ability to positively and publicly impact others by the authority of your example rather than the authority of your title/rank, and you will prevent your leadership (and culture) from ever deteriorating. There is more, however, to this idea of leadership being personal that must be addressed. After all, it really begins with your personal commitment, not someone else's. So let's talk about you and me as *real leaders* you as a real leader endeavoring to...

Real Leaders

OUR FOCUS UNTIL now has been on our encounters with other leaders and the impact they've had on us. Yet for all of this there remains a central question: "How do **others** feel when they leave their encounters with **us**?" More directly, "How is it for **you** as a leader?" Ever wonder what is said about **your leadership** in water-cooler conversations or what your impact as a leader really is?

Opportunity: *Do you know? Do you care? Does it matter? Be prepared for the answer, as it may surprise you. Write in your notes what you think your impact is, or could be, as a leader. This keeps you in the leadership mindset.*

It wasn't long into our professional and social careers before these thoughts began to haunt us. With all the new information about leadership available to us, we began to wonder whether we were learning, changing and growing to the point of impacting others in a positive rather than a negative way. Were we leaders and, if so, what kind of leaders? What kind of impact were we having? Were the groups we led and organizations we worked for better off than they were before their encounter with us? Suffice it to say, the process of finding out yielded the book in your hands. We were taught, like many others have been, to leave something in better condition than what you found it. This is your impact. You can only judge your intent. Others will judge your impact.

We've been reading about leadership for years. And you're doing that here, perhaps for the umpteenth time. But it doesn't automatically follow that we will become better leaders. To become better leaders, we have to move beyond just reading about and understanding the concept of leadership. To improve outcomes for our organizations, we have to do more than just pay lip service to leadership and the operating culture it creates. We have to do something purposeful and deliberate…something more than just building leadership sandcastles. We need the strength and stability of personal and organizational *Leadership Platforms* that won't get washed away by the rising tide. If you have a desire to lead, proactively seek out opportunities to do that. For those of us that served in the military—Mr. D in the Marines and Air Force and Dr. D in the Air Force, both retired—this is part and parcel of any successful career.

The effort to truly comprehend the difference between getting by with a leadership sandcastle and building a durable *Leadership Platform* literally forced us to walk through more than four decades each of personal, professional and social history…a history marked by both success and failure. As mentioned, we started our journey in the Military, being taught that the first principle of leadership was to "know yourself and seek self-improvement."

Mr. D Vignette: For me, the leadership goal was singular and simple at the time: become the best Marine in the Corps. As a result of setting very specific goals, I was meritoriously promoted 3 times in my first 2 years on active duty. Success! My focus rapidly shifted, however, to overcoming the challenges and trappings that accompany perfectionism; a tendency I picked up from our Mom's side of the family, all of whom loved me but were certainly not infallible. This particular enrichment was hard/painful, as it was precipitated by a divorce (the loss of my first family at an extremely young age). Failure!

After more career success in the Marines, my leadership enrichment focus shifted again through yet another painful transition as I made the decision to leave the Corps after almost 10 years. I've often described taking that uniform off as one of the hardest things I've ever had to do. There are a few colloquialisms of our day that underscore the difficulty of this transition. The most well-known is: "Once a Marine, Always a Marine." The lesser known is: "You can take a Marine out of the Corps but you can't take the Corps out of a Marine."

In the years that followed this painful transition, I experienced more career advancement (rapid promotions over a decade-long run up the corporate ladder) and set-backs (a demotion followed by three job losses in a five year period between 2004 and 2009). And since publishing my first book on Leadership back in 2012, I've suffered 3 additional job losses because of tyrannical managers within terribly defensive operating cultures…a total of 7 in an 18 year period. In more than a few instances, I voluntarily initiated my departure in order to get away from the people punishers to whom I found myself reporting. In other instances, I was voluntold to leave for reasons of "irreconcilable differences".

As it turns out, all of this pain motivated me to pursue a better understanding of what really was happening, and why…what the leadership phenomenon was really all about. Eventually, it led me to new discoveries about my *Personal Leadership Platform* through numerous psychometric assessments. I found that they revealed extremely difficult improvement opportunities for me in key areas of leadership mindset, expressions and conduct. It also led to my discovery and application of numerous group and organizational assessments that were designed to raise the level of leadership, release new potential for teamwork and create more constructive/adaptive organizational sub-cultures.

We realize that sounds like a lot of disappointment and hard work, and it was. But we don't believe that this experience is all that uncommon for those learning to lead. Perhaps you have found your own leadership largely undiscovered and, as a result, your effectiveness as a manager has plateaued. Or worse yet, perhaps it's now moving in a downward direction. Or maybe you've already been confronted with aspects of your own leadership sandcastle that ought to be, but haven't been, improved. If so, we're confident that you've experienced no less disappointment and, if you want to improve your performance as a leader or the performance of your organization through leadership, it will require the same hard work.

Opportunity: *Add your frustrations and failures in the notes section. Keep in mind a positive approach to this is not having any regrets, just lessons learned. A lesson is not truly learned, however, until you have made a change to elicit a different outcome.*

And this idea leads to the uniqueness of this book and how it is set up. It is steeped in unique concepts that will first elevate your thinking about leadership and then enrich your ability to lead through a proven lifecycle of continual renewal and improvement as you...

Leadership Book

CREATING A MEANS to take new leadership information and use it to continually improve personal and organizational performance is what this book is about.

Part 1 is designed to provide you with some new information by introducing the idea of a *Leadership Platform*…what it is and why it is important. It is not designed to teach you everything you can know about leadership. There are many other books designed to do that. By the end of Part 1, however, you'll be thinking a little differently about leadership and perhaps be a bit curious about the actual impact you are having on others, as well as the impact of leadership on your organization. This is already a giant step up from simple reading. And by now you may be asking: "What's with all the 'Opportunity' segments?

These are meant to allow for micro changes in thinking such that new behaviors can emerge. These micro changes will afford you the opportunity to flex when necessary, depending on the circumstances, as you read and digest the information presented.

Opportunity: *There is an inherent challenge for anyone who is reading this book. One is that anywhere you run into new information that doesn't square with the old, you'll begin to think there may be a "problem." The challenge is choosing to see it as "opportunity." This puts any new knowledge you gain from this book into a positive context and moves you closer to a desired outcome, whatever that may be for you, your group, your organization, based on where you are today and where you'd like to be tomorrow.*

Part 2 is designed to provide you with the means to take this new information (in addition to any information you have) about leadership and use it to improve your impact as a leader and to elevate the level of leadership in your organization. By the end of Part 2, you should be building your own *Leadership Platform* and aiding in the effort to improve the *Leadership Platform* of your group or organization as the practitioner of your leadership.

Again, in Part 1, we're thinking about leadership in a whole new way. In Part 2, we're engaged in the effort of doing something to ensure the impact of leadership, both personal and organizational, is more constructive. This is the best outcome we can, and should, expect from all our encounters as leaders, and it should be expected given all the information we have available to us. Keep in mind that the adage "practice makes perfect" is a fallacy as human perfection does not exist…neither does perfect practice. If you strive for perfection, you will never achieve it and you will be disappointed; something we will explore at length together later in this book.

> **Opportunity:** *Practice does make better because it allows you to make mistakes, and you will make mistakes. What have you learned from mistakes? Include some of the mistakes you have made in your notes. Again, awareness is key here to not repeating them.*
>
> _____
>
> _____
>
> _____
>
> _____
>
> _____

And in case you're tempted to question whether this truly matters, it does. Improving the positive impact of leadership has been shown time and again to produce increased levels of personal and organizational effectiveness, financial performance and long-term success. This we feel extremely comfortable

Dr. D's Reflections

Being a practitioner of leadership isn't just about education... it is about application.

promising to you, the reader, thinker and doer. Positivity also releases endorphins, which as we understand it will make you feel better physically as well as mentally.

What we can't promise is that the next few pages will be easy. We wish that were so, but it isn't. This read will prove difficult, at times, but if you are willing to become a *real leader*, this is the way. Our hope is that you'll strive alongside us long enough to finish the book and, if you do, we promise it won't be viewed as the end of your learning about leadership. Rather, you'll view this as a "certificate of beginning" if you're just starting out, or a "certificate of becoming" if you've been a student of leadership for a while. Either way, there is opportunity here for you to learn, change, grow and lead through awareness, acceptance, action and achievement. The upside potential for your organization and those you lead is near limitless as you start to...

PART I

Backdrop for a
Leadership Platform

[Written by Mr. D with reflections by Dr. D.]

> *This section is designed to help you rethink leadership, so you can reframe it in Part 2. It describes the genesis of creating my first Leadership Platform. Throughout, you will find that Dr. D has made some incredible contributions through his personal reflections. Your journey up to this point will have been different but understanding a bit here in Part 1 about where this whole concept started and how it continues to evolve will prove helpful in Part 2. So, here goes...*

T HE YEAR WAS A.D. 2000. It was the beginning of a new millennium and, as I was about to discover, the beginning of a whole new chapter when it came to my life's purpose and my personal potential for leading.

It was after spending 16+ years of playing "sometimes the instructor; always the student" of leadership that I found myself in another professional mentoring relationship with a co-worker. Mentoring has always proven to be extremely rewarding for me, and I routinely find ways to develop as a leader and develop other leaders in my personal, professional and social engagements through both formal and informal relationships with mentors and protégés. In fact, early in my career, I learned that mentoring and coaching were "best-practices" in leadership development, so I adopted them as a part of my personal development plan. Unfortunately, like many best-practices, I also learned that they are often overlooked in personal and organizational development efforts.

This time, my mentoring relationship was with a Recruiting Manager named Lisa Sokolowski. Over time, meaningful conversations about leadership, teams/teamwork and organizational effectiveness were routine, and both Lisa and I were reaping the benefits of our time together. Then something unusual happened. What I fully expected would be just another mentoring meeting turned into an event that would literally grab me by the nape of the neck and shake me awake to something that I had never thought about when it came to my leadership.

Here's how it happened. For months, Lisa was an active participant in our mentoring relationship, sharing vulnerabilities; patiently listening and responding to my recommendations regarding leadership development opportunities, which she would regularly act on. She took copious notes and kept a logbook of our time together. She really took it seriously while, at the same time, taking herself lightly. I learned so much from her about this. But that wasn't what truly changed my thinking about leadership. In a fleeting moment, Lisa asked me whether I had ever attempted to document everything I believed and endeavored to pass on about leadership.

Since I had never given it serious thought, my immediate negative response was flippant and I was content to let the rock sink there. Not satisfied with my reply, Lisa immediately challenged me to coalesce my thoughts on leadership into a single coherent form... to codify my leadership and the impact I intended to have as a leader into a single platform. That's what she called it...a *Leadership Platform*. She further challenged me to document how I developed as a leader, why it was important, what activities and tools enabled the effort, which pitfalls and traps should be avoided, etc. In essence, to capture the process I moved through so that she and others could follow it. Her justification for the request was rational. If I was having an impact through one-on-one coaching and mentoring relationships, how much more of an impact could I have if it were documented and broadcast for broader consumption?

I'll readily admit, this appealed to my deep desire to leave a legacy of positive change in the world...something I would laughingly refer to as my "legacy complex." I also have to admit that I knew something of leadership by this time in my professional career, but the idea of a '*Leadership Platform*' was foreign. I remember looking it up in Merriam-Webster's online dictionary at some point and discovering, in the context Lisa was using the term, that a "platform" can be defined as "the particular policies (guiding principles) and promises supporting a position of authority and/or authenticity, which become the basis of all actions and further provide the opportunity for periodic celebration and ongoing evaluation." Blended with the term leadership, I quickly began to see the relationship and understand its importance. I remember thinking: "Wow! Lisa is onto something here." So off I went, not fully realizing what this challenge would require of me, nor that it would ultimately influence my life's purpose, increase my personal potential and result in the summation of what I value, believe, understand and do as a leader. In retrospect, I owe Lisa an incredible debt of gratitude.

Opportunity: *This book can be your guide to realizing success as you continue your leadership journey. Write your own story though the notes you take of what worked and what did not. Don't neglect to include the times when you achieved your intended impact and don't shy away from the times you didn't. Most importantly, capture what you learned in each case that insighted change. Write as you read.*

PLATFORM BLUEPRINTING COMMENCES

Beginning with the first part of Lisa's challenge, I immediately started the design work. Based on the accepted architectural body of knowledge, every basic platform is comprised of a Footing, Foundation and Framing so it seemed fitting as the blueprint/design for a *Leadership Platform*.

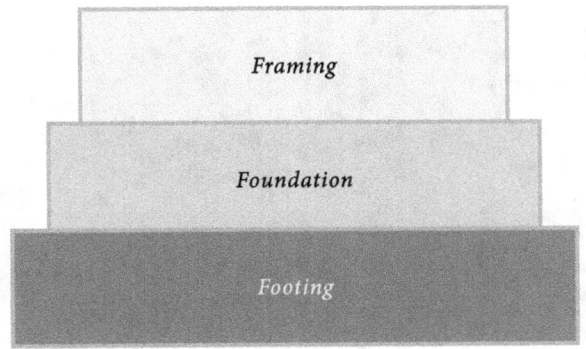

The *Leadership Platform* Blueprint/Design.

As commonly understood in the building process, Footings are set in place first and have the important role of preventing the Foundation from settling as weight is placed upon it. When it comes to *Leadership Platforms*, Footings are based on Vision, Mission, Assumptions and Espoused Values.

From there, the Foundation is attached. The purpose of any Foundation is to distribute the load. Regarding leadership, it constitutes Guiding Principles, Goals and Objectives and Strategic Priorities.

The last step is to work on the Framing itself. The purpose of good Framing in a *Leadership Platform* is to provide a safe, sturdy, reliable and level surface upon which to carry the weight of those who choose to follow, and it includes selecting Managerial Properties, Operational Imperatives and Leadership Traits/Qualities.

Pulling it all together, the personal *Leadership Platform* is built up to the design specifications (i.e., features and characteristics) of who the leader endeavors to be and what type of impact they will have on others.

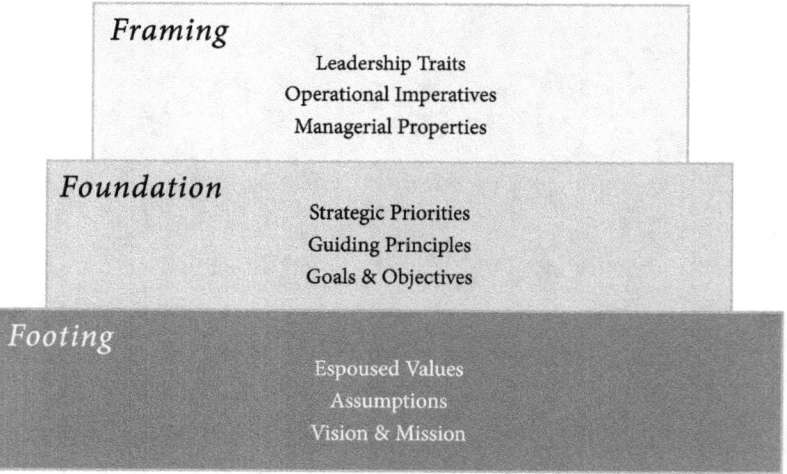

Framing
Leadership Traits
Operational Imperatives
Managerial Properties

Foundation
Strategic Priorities
Guiding Principles
Goals & Objectives

Footing
Espoused Values
Assumptions
Vision & Mission

The personal *Leadership Platform* Design
Features and Characteristics.

In this regard, platforms can be built with the best leadership information available. Safe to say, I've adopted and incorporated leadership theories, models and styles from a host of great leaders and thinkers. In fact, nothing in my *Leadership Platform* is original with me. Over the last 40+ years, we've simply borrowed discriminately from my encounters with *real leaders* on **what to do** and from the fake leaders on **what not to do**. This means, in the most basic terms, that knowing what works in each situation only comes with time and experience, and you need to be prepared for how to respond when it does not work. And in a very real

Dr. D's Reflections

Having openness to learning (spoiler alert: addressed in Part 2) as a leadership contingency does two things: 1) if something doesn't turn out the way you or others expected, it lightens the disappointment for you and lessens the impact for them if it's caught quickly; and 2) it provides an opportunity to pivot with little to no effort...other than the temporary shock to your ego.

sense, operating from contingency will help. I've discovered that the best contingency is often remaining open to feedback and to learning from it quickly, which we'll explore in Part 2 more deeply. In this way you preserve options and can pivot rather than persevere when things go sideways.

PERCEPTION OF THE NEED INCREASES

You may be asking about now: "This is great, but why is it important? Why does it matter? How does it change things?" Okay! Fair questions; so let's answer them.

Opportunity: *Before we give you our answers...write your own in the notes. Then compare your answers to ours. How close do you think we are?*

_____

_____

_____

_____

_____

_____

I'm really not sure when it happened, but there was a point in this iterative process of defining and refining my *Personal Leadership Platform* that I realized something. While there is a lot written on the subject of leadership (e.g., what leadership is, what it does, the difference it makes, et al.) and a good deal of time invested in learning about leadership, there isn't much available in the way of "how" to personalize leadership or why the effort to do so is even important. In fact, it is safe to say that in all the books I had read and courses I had attended, I seldom if ever thought about making anything I learned about leadership personal nor did the idea of creating a personal leadership statement, let alone a platform, emerge as imperative. The closest I came to this may have been in 1992 when I had to write a personal statement for admission to an undergraduate degree program.

Don't get me wrong, it is great to attend courses; read someone else's success stories, review their case studies, study their models, methods and theories; even listen occasionally to a motiva-tional/inspirational speech. But I eventually stumbled upon some-thing that Dr. Lafferty observed in *The Roots of Excellence* (Laf-ferty); none of that does much

Dr. D's Reflections

While we all learn differently, there is power in knowing how you learn. There is also power in knowing how your people learn.

of anything to change the real issue... namely transformation of the individual reading, reviewing, studying, listening, etc. Unless the individual, as a result of having this information—these new points of view—takes it personally and uses that new thinking to produce better results, it follows naturally that little of what he/she learns will change what truly matters. It also follows that little growth will occur and personal and organizational leadership (as well as performance) will remain lackluster.

But there is inherent difficulty in taking new information and applying it. To put it simply, it is not easy. Many who have already tried this know intuitively how difficult it is. And for those still tempted to question the level of difficulty here, consider the following statement in light of all the advancements in, and focus on, health and fitness in our society:

> *We are the best health educated society in the history of mankind but we don't take information and use it to moti-vate us to change our behavior. – Mehmet Cengiz Oz, PhD*

In spite of this, there is hope. While difficult, it is not impos-sible. In fact, Dr. Oz and many others have spent the majority of their careers helping people avoid this trap when it comes to personal health and wellness improvement. Remember you do not have the eat the entire elephant at one time.

When it comes to personal and organizational leadership, there was, in my opinion and my lifetime, no one more knowledgeable than the late Dr. J. Clayton Lafferty. Over 30 years ago, Dr. Lafferty, founder of Human Synergistics International, undertook an initiative with over 300,000 executives to try and measure qualitative differences in how people think. He wondered whether there were consequences to how people thought and, if so, would it be possible to identify some ways of thinking that are associated with a person's ability to handle the challenges of the future and to measure the extent to which it affected their health and welfare or influenced their capacity for professional growth and success. In short, were there ways of thinking about things that added up to the kind of success that most of us are interested in?

What Dr. Lafferty found was that a person's thinking style established the extent to which he/she could change/adapt and how well, as a result, he/she could ultimately perform. In fact, on at least one occasion that I am aware of—and those of us overtaken from death by PowerPoint at times will appreciate this for other reasons—he reinforced this notion by delivering a "live" presentation without the use of visual aids (i.e., MS PowerPoint) or materials (hand-outs or take-aways). He simply announced that the extent to which he wanted to get everyone committed to the outcomes of his presentation was for them to spend the next 30 minutes thinking about the ideas he was about to share with them…just thinking. He felt that if his presentation was successful, the participants would commit to writing those ideas down and then perform some level of self-evaluation against them.

This got me thinking (no kidding, right?). Could the absence of well-defined and well-documented personal and organizational *Leadership Platforms*, which require a lot of thought about the impact leaders intend to have on others vs. the impact they are actually having, account for the widespread fact that there is still a leadership vacuum at all levels of most organizations? And this despite the seemingly countless number of leadership books/case studies that have been written and read/studied, leadership courses offered and taken, leadership speeches given and received, etc. I believe the answer is in the affirmative.

Borrowing from Dr. Oz, I'd like to pose a few questions. **Are we the best leadership-educated society in the history of business? To what extent does that education motivate us to change our leadership behavior?**

Given the sheer volume and rapid acceleration of available information, one might reasonably conclude that the answers are a resounding yes.

Now, let's make it more personal. **How educated are you on the phenomenon of leadership? To what extent does your education motivate you to change your leadership behavior?**

Asking and answering questions like this are a part of our journey. Creating a means to take leadership information and use it to change our behavior and performance is what this book is all about. But if that is our goal, there must be more to the story that just reading about my (or anyone else's) thoughts on leadership. This is certainly a great place to start, and you'll do some of that here. So, what's the "more"? It really comes in four simple yet powerful activities that, when applied cyclically, can produce performance leadership transformation:

1. **Thinking!** The act of just thinking about your leadership and the actual impact it is currently having on others.

2. **Knowing!** Being aware of or familiar with something about your leadership through experience, education, or new information.

3. **Doing!** Making changes in your leadership and the impact it has on others by continually using that new information to renew and improve.

4. **Performing!** Harnessing your leadership to unite people around a shared purpose—while inspiring confidence in themselves and in the outcomes they can achieve together.

This is what it means to **Take Your Lead**. In the remainder of this book you'll have ample opportunities to do just that. And to rethink and reframe what it means to lead in the 21st century is precisely where a personal and organizational *Leadership Platform* comes in.

A PLATFORM EMERGES; PERSONAL AND ORGANIZATIONAL OUTLINES

All this talk about personal and organizational *Leadership Platforms* probably warrants a more detailed illustration. But before getting to the actual outlines, I want to share some conclusions drawn out of the process of creating my own platform.

Platforms are unique in design

The first (and perhaps most obvious) conclusion I drew was, while informed by many others, my platform couldn't have been thought out (i.e., designed, etc.) by anyone else except me. Thinking is a uniquely personal activity, regardless of the subject. Moreover, leading is not an activity that can be performed vicariously. No one else can do the thinking or leading for us. So, when it came to leadership it had to become personal, and that only happens through a process of thorough self-evaluation.

By definition, every person and organization must have their own *Leadership Platform*. In fact, by default they do, whether they realize it or not. They are custom and one-of-a-kind, as unique as the individuals and organizations who design them. The only variables I've found are related to how solid (i.e., right) and stable (i.e., effective) the platforms are, which we'll explore in Part 2. These characteristics depend entirely on the extent to which the impact that we *want* to have on others, as reflected in our *Leadership Platforms*, is the actual impact that we *do* have on others. This approach puts the responsibility directly upon each of us—much as we might like to think otherwise. The responsibility is ours, and it always has been.

We can't hope to *learn as a leader* (or as an organization) until we have designed and blueprinted our platforms. This requires thinking. Tragically, most leaders never spend much time thinking about the impact they intend to have on others, let alone measuring the impact they are actually having. Thinking rightly and effectively about leadership is the first step, but it is not enough. This led to my next conclusion.

Platforms are built by hand

The second (and perhaps a little less obvious) conclusion about my *Leadership Platform* was, while extremely well thought out, it wasn't written down—as pointed out by my mentee back in A.D. 2000—and it had to be in order for me to perform some level of self-evaluation (i.e., how consistent am I living with my life's purpose?, and am I living up to my full potential as a leader?). It had to be moved off the page written by someone else and onto the pages written by me.

Having a *Leadership Platform* that is designed in thought (i.e., blueprinted) but not documented in print (i.e., built) is akin to having goals that aren't written down. Anyone familiar with achievement orientation or Paul J. Meyer's work in *Attitude is Everything* knows a goal that isn't written down to be specific, measurable, attainable, relevant and time-bound (SMART) is just a dream. It's the same with Leadership. The theories, models and styles we want to invoke and emulate as we think about leadership during design should be translated into a solid and stable platform through a personal documentation process. *Leadership Platforms* must be constructed with the materials we have available to us (i.e., pen and paper) before they can be effectively deployed and subsequently assessed against our actual impact on others.

Put bluntly, we cannot hope for worthwhile *change as a leader* (or as an Organization) until we have documented our own *Leadership Platform*. It provides the baseline for future measurement and analysis and brings with it the potential to change in ways that align our actual impact with our original intent. And then it becomes a question of, 'How can I know whether there's a difference?' Here again, this was another great step forward but it still fell short of what I was really after. This led me to another conclusion.

Platforms are tested for strength

The third conclusion was born from the idea of *suitability to* or *fit for* purpose. Ultimately, a *Leadership Platform* is designed and built for a purpose: to carry the weight of those who choose to stand on it (i.e., followers). This is the real test of *Leadership Platform* strength and stability. In fact, some believe that we lead in direct proportion to our willingness and ability to support the weight of those who choose to follow. I agree! After all, of what practical use would a platform be if it were designed and built, but never used?

Strength-testing is the simple process of having others, particularly those who follow, evaluate our impact as a leader. We can only assess our intent as a leader. We need others to give us meaningful feedback about our impact. Without this feedback, our *Leadership Platforms* could be accomplishing the wrong goals or approaching others in extremely ineffective ways, which are common definitions of failure. As the old saying goes: "'I'll handle this myself' is where change goes to die." We must involve others. Or as I recently heard Skip Heitzig say: "First get a grip! Then get a group!"

Dr. D. suggests that, if you are really interested in the hard truth, try posting something on social media and crowd-source the feedback. The benefit from a generalization of reaction is in this way can provide additional reference for direction and for action. The same can play out

Dr. D's Reflections

Do not be afraid to solicit feedback. Feedback can be the difference between turning around after one mile of heading in the wrong direction vs one hundred miles. Feedback provides a vector check on what we are doing and where we are leading. It also comes with some reassurance that we are doing the right things in that situation.

inside your organization on a smaller scale, because it is made of up organisms that have a way of providing a temperature for culture. In this sense, you can elicit extremely valuable feedback and, if you have a vested interest in the success of the organization, you should be providing others with feedback as well. Admittedly, reciprocal feedback gets a bit sticky, generally, and stickier still if you don't have the relationships (built on trust, mutual respect, and shared values as essentials and flexibility on on-essentials) or the culture (constructive vs aggressive/or passive/defensive) to support a design or desire for feedback. What seems to work in just about every situation is prefacing feedback in a way that establishes something most everyone can agree on; namely, that no one wins if we can't confront the brutal facts. But if you really want someone to receive feedback from you, be willing first to receive feedback from them. More than that, ask for it.

Opportunity: *A good leader seeks feedback from all levels of their organization, fully expecting not all of it will be good. That, in and of itself, can be educational and enlightening if you use it in a positive manner to reinforce your platform. If you haven't already, do that now. No diagnostic instruments required, for now. Just ask: "How am I doing?" What you hear in response, and what you don't, can provide invaluable information.*

You may recall that renowned author, researcher and business consultant, Jim Collins, popularized this idea in his book "Good to Great: Why Some Companies Make the Leap...and Others Don't". Confronting the Brutal Facts is a concept, paired with its companion concept The Stockdale Paradox, which asserts that productive change begins when you face the harsh realities. According to Jim, every good-to-great company embraced what he termed "The Stockdale Paradox": you must maintain unwavering faith that you will prevail in the end, regardless of the difficulties, while simultaneously having the discipline to confront the most brutal facts of your current reality, whatever they may be. On an individual, personal level of leadership, it is equally important. This is why "what you hear and don't hear" when asking for feedback is important. If people don't trust you or believe that their honest feedback about your leadership will lead to constructive changes, they won't be candid due to fear of passive-aggressive retaliation or negative consequences. Consequently, you will get filtered and, frankly, inaccurate information that is not suitable for drawing any meaningful conclusions or taking any meaningful actions as a result.

With proven, well established, trusting relationships, people (you included) will tend to give and take the "constructive feedback" pill with less resistance. There are those that will take offense to what you say no matter how you say it and in spite of any reasonable attempts you have made to establish that kind of relationship. These are the ones who believe they are above reproach. They are typically anchored by their position in the hierarchy and/or by an arrogance that produces ignorance, both of which are carefully guarded by hubris that defends their actions and dulls the pain of their stupidity (at least for them). They will interpret your feedback, affirming or critical, as a threat to their ego, power or status. As a result, they will perceive your feedback to be inaccurate and/or disingenuous, no matter what. These same folks, when providing feedback, will offer more noise than signal. Be that as it may, don't let that stop you from asking for feedback or from providing it. By nature, all feedback—like all theories—are valid; some are just more useful than others. It's up to you to determine what's useful from what you hear, and the trick is ensuring your ego doesn't get in the way of receiving and using honest signals, which gets addressed head-on in Part 2.

Measuring the impact we are actually having (as strength-tested) against the impact we intended to have (as-designed/documented) will reduce the potential for failure and/or mitigate its consequences (as-corrected). In the personal context, this equals a 360-degree leadership evaluation. In the organizational context, this is a culture assessment. This simple strategy of strength-testing our platforms will ensure that we are having the impact we personally intended and creating the culture that is organizationally preferred. Furthermore, evaluating our impact will allow us to ascertain whether it constitutes the most effective leadership approach and fosters the ideal organizational culture. If not, there is opportunity for improvement.

We can't hope to *grow as a leader* (or as an Organization) until we have blueprinted, built and strength-tested our platforms. In a very real sense, our personal platforms will be able to carry the weight of those who choose to follow and our organizations will have cultures that are preferred by members. A *Leadership Platform* that accounts for all three (i.e., design/blueprinting, document/building and evaluate/strength-testing) will provide more personal and organizational opportunity to learn, change and grow than any company code of ethics and all of the leadership course(s) and books on the market combined.

MR. D'S PERSONAL PLATFORM ILLUSTRATED

Today, my Leadership Platform is a near-15 page "living" document that encapsulates the best of what I know and intend to apply toward making a positive difference in the outcomes for those I'm privileged to come in contact with each day. Yet the key ideas can be boiled down to a one-page document that I can carry with me for frequent reference. It influences all of my decisions and guides the way I approach others and my work on a daily basis, and it is "living" in the sense that: a) it is continually updated as I learn more about leadership and b) it expands/contracts proportionately with my willingness and ability to support the weight of those who choose to follow. In this regard, I've discovered that by sharing my platform with others (particularly mentors, coaches, direct reports, supervisors, etc.), they are able to help me recognize inconsistency and incongruity between what I designed/built and my actual impact as a leader. They are also able to suggest improvements.

As illustrated under *Platform Blueprinting Commences*, my *Personal Leadership Platform* is divided into three major sections: 1) the Footing, 2) the

Dr. D's Reflections

This book is, of itself, a living document. It is a refresh of two different books published back in 2012. Like everything we've just discussed, it was inevitable that those original works would be updated. Consider this the next iteration but realize that there are some things we didn't change. These foundational items are those that can become a pocket reference guide…one that you can carry with you in the confidence that it was built-to-last and will survive the worst that the business world's torrent can toss your way.

Foundation and 3) the Framing. This is what the prior illustrations look like once filled in with my personal selection of design features (i.e., leadership theories and methods) and characteristics (i.e., leadership models and styles) that inform the kind of leader I am and the type of impact I intend to have on others:

> ### *Support for others/Approach to daily work...*
>
> Leadership Traits (Justice, Judgment, etc.)
> Operational Imperatives (14 Points)
> Managerial Properties (Profound Knowledge)

> ### *Goal/Objectives: create continual prosperity through...*
>
> INNOVATION from human capital
> IMPROVEMENT from structural capital
> GROWTH from relational capital

> ### *Vision/Mission: I endeavor to be...*
>
> I endeavor to be a capable, enthusiastic & committed Servant Leader who continually moves upward & outward with passion, patience & perserverance to create/share extraordinary value for/with others.

Key:

FRAMING ENABLERS (TACTICS):
· Assumptions & Values Alignment   · Change Prioritization & Objectives
· Action Planning & Implementation   · Management & Communication

FOUNDATION STABILIZERS (STRATEGY):
· Strategic Priorities
· Guiding Principles

FOOTING HALLMARKS (DOCTRINE):
· Assumptions of Trust, Personal Accountability & Warning Signs
· Espoused Values

Mr. D's personal *Leadership Platform* Design Specification.

Of note here is that any disconnect between the Footing, Foundation or Framing of the platform, or between the platform and the followers standing on it, provides the leader with an opportunity to improve his/her personal platform. The 360-degree evaluation mentioned earlier helps reveal disconnects between a leaders' intended impact and actual impact, as illustrated with blue lines of separation on the platform below.

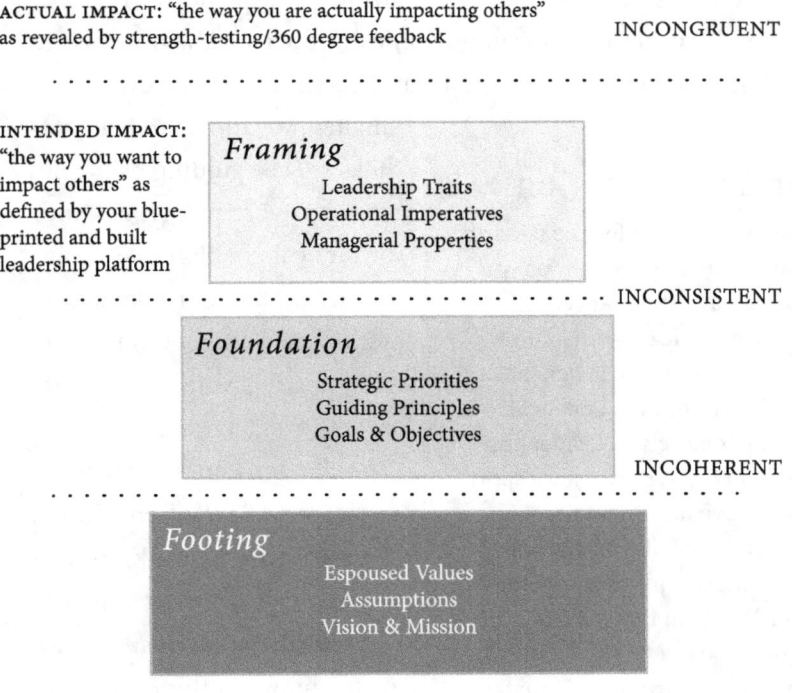

ACTUAL IMPACT: "the way you are actually impacting others" as revealed by strength-testing/360 degree feedback — INCONGRUENT

INTENDED IMPACT: "the way you want to impact others" as defined by your blue-printed and built leadership platform

Framing
Leadership Traits
Operational Imperatives
Managerial Properties

INCONSISTENT

Foundation
Strategic Priorities
Guiding Principles
Goals & Objectives

INCOHERENT

Footing
Espoused Values
Assumptions
Vision & Mission

The personal *Leadership Platform* Disconnect.

One type of disconnect occurs when there is incoherence in the Footing or inconsistency between the platform Footing, Foundation and Framing; all of which defines a leader's **intended** *impact*. If the substance of our leadership Footing (i.e., vision/ mission, doctrine) isn't coherent or our Foundation (goals/ objectives, guiding principles) and Framing (support for others/ approach to daily work) are inconsistent with one another or the Footing, the compromising effect is no different than what occurs structurally when a carpenter builds a wooden platform with incompatible materials. The structure weakens and must be reinforced; otherwise leadership eventually breaks down and the followers being supported will abandon the platform. This type of disconnect can occur any time our doctrinal hallmarks (i.e., espoused values and assumptions) get misaligned or, even when aligned, we adopt strategic stabilizers (i.e., guiding principles and strategic priorities) and/ or tactical enablers (i.e., management and communication, action planning, etc.) that are incompatible with one another or with the doctrinal hallmarks. The danger here is that these disconnects are often hidden deep within the thinking style of a leader and harder to detect.

Another disconnect can occur between the *Leadership Platform* and those whose weight is being supported (i.e., followers), which determines the **actual impact** the leader is

Dr. D's Reflection

Leadership is not for the faint of heart. You either want it or you don't. I have experienced the fair-weather leader where they do what they think is beneficial at the time, but the beneficiary is usually themselves. Leadership is not a me sport, it is a we sport. If you stive for others success, your success will come along with theirs. A lot of companies put a "One" in front of the company name to show that we are all in this together. If that is the case, leadership will reflect that and they will recognize and reward the successes of all.

having on others. Incongruity at this level is more obvious and easier to detect, but equally as devastating to the leaders' impact because it can keep followers off-balance. One way this shows up is when our support for others or our approach to daily work shifts on a regular basis, such that our followers are never quite able to figure out which leader is showing up each day.

This is where strength-testing plays a key role; using measures and measurement instruments to ensure that we are actually having the impact we intended. With the aid of 360-degree feedback, a leader can perform more extensive self-evaluation to uncover incoherence and inconsistency and repair hidden compromises. Followers can more readily tell when there is incongruity and our leadership gets off-balance. All we have to do is care enough to ask or actively listen when they volunteer the information.

ORGANIZATIONAL PLATFORM ILLUSTRATED

As stated earlier, once you have your personal *Leadership Platform* in place you are ready to positively impact and improve upon your organization's platform. I've had the privilege of consulting directly with three organizations on how to successfully measure and improve their cultures, increase managerial effectiveness and improve outcomes through well-designed, sturdily-built and strength-tested *Leadership Platforms*. I have also worked successfully at building numerous constructive sub-cultures for the teams I've led and the organizations I've served.

It may come as a surprise, but things aren't really that different regarding the organizational platform than what was discussed about personal *Leadership Platforms*, and we shouldn't expect them to be. We simply move from addressing leadership at the personal level to addressing it at the organizational level; from measuring the impact on individuals to measuring the impact across the entire organization, or its culture, through the decisions made and strategies adopted by its senior leaders.

> *Culture can be defined as the thinking and behavioral styles that might be implicitly or explicitly required for people to "fit in" and "meet expectations" in an organization...the ways in which all members of an organization...are expected to approach their work and interact with one another.* (Cooke and Szumal, Using the Organizational Culture Inventory to understand the operating cultures of organizations)

Human Synergistics International has created a robust Theoretical Model for understanding leadership, its relationship to organizational culture and how it all really works. Using their model for *How Culture Works*, here is a basic illustration of the organizational *Leadership Platform* within the construct of a Footing, Foundation and Framing Blueprint/Design with full design specifications (i.e., features and characteristics):

CURRENT CULTURE: "what is expected of members around here"
as revealed by strength-testing/Cultural Assessment

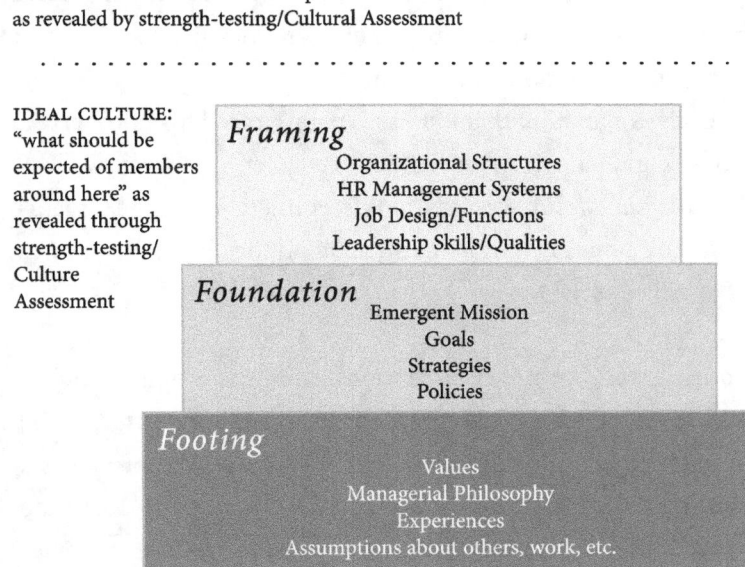

IDEAL CULTURE:
"what should be
expected of members
around here" as
revealed through
strength-testing/
Culture
Assessment

Framing
Organizational Structures
HR Management Systems
Job Design/Functions
Leadership Skills/Qualities

Foundation
Emergent Mission
Goals
Strategies
Policies

Footing
Values
Managerial Philosophy
Experiences
Assumptions about others, work, etc.

The Organizational *Leadership Platform* Design
Features & Characteristics. Research and development
of the model *How Culture Works* by Robert A. Cooke,
Ph.D. Copyright © 1997 by Human Synergistics
International. Adapted by permission.

As the organization matures, it is impacted by various internal factors that eventually reinforce organizational values, norms and behaviors. As a result, the Ideal Culture (or what should be expected of members to increase effectiveness) is likely different than the Current Culture (or what is currently expected of members to 'fit in' and succeed) (Cooke and Szumal, Using the Organizational Culture Inventory to understand the operating cultures of organizations). The need to understand this difference underscores the importance of strength-testing the organizational *Leadership Platform.* It is through the process of evaluation that we identify critical differences between current and ideal cultures. Only then can we begin to move from the current toward the ideal through meaningful adjustments to the Footing, Foundation and Framing.

Each explanation that follows is paraphrased from Robert A. Cooke's and Janet L. Szumal's (2000) chapter in the *Handbook of Organizational Culture and Climate,* entitled "Using the Organizational Culture Inventory to understand the operating cultures of organizations".

Footing and Foundation– The vision of the organization, as well as the underlying assumptions and values espoused by the founders and molded by senior leaders, over time, produces a culture within the organization. This is intended to adapt the organization to the external environment and produce outcomes that are consistent with the organization's goals and objectives.

The particulars of their managerial philosophy, assumptions about people, espoused values and history—past experience with "the tests of time"—form the Footing of the Organizational *Leadership Platform.* Then, from the onset, founders and senior leaders make choices regarding mission, goals, policies and strategy that they believe will help the organization be successful. These choices form the Foundation and are influenced by the aforementioned underlying assumptions and espoused values. Not only is all of this a natural part of an organization's maturation and development process, but each plays a role in determining the organization's culture.

Foundation and Framing– As the organization pursues goals, deploys policies and executes strategy (i.e., Foundation), the founders and senior leaders enact or adopt certain Structures,

Systems, Technology, and Skills/Qualities (SSTS) to distinguish, organize, and manage different aspects of the environment:

- **S**tructures (e.g., role definition, distribution of influence, decision-making authority),

- **S**ystems (e.g., training, appraisal, reinforcement, goal setting),

- **T**echnology (e.g., job designs/specific functions, variety, feedback, interdependence) and

- **S**kills/Qualities (e.g., leadership, communication, bases of power)

The SSTS initially enacted/adopted become antecedents of organizational culture and directly influence the ways people relate to one another...the ways that feel right and seem to work. Those believed to help the organization accomplish its goals are retained, others get discarded or may be modified and a few new approaches may even be added along the way. Either way, in and of themselves, they become Framing mechanisms that reinforce culture by a) reflecting and communicating organizational values and b) shaping norms and expectations for specific types of task-oriented and people-oriented behaviors. Over time, they get collated into the comprehensive framework or "the way we *are* expected to do things around here"—referred to as the organization's Current Culture in the Human Synergistics International *Organizational Culture Inventory*® (OCI®) literature. The extent to which this way of doing things is eventually recognized and shared by members of the organization reflects the intensity of the organization's Current Culture.

If you'll note, the most proximate and immediate impact of this fleshing-out process is on what is valued by the organization, and this may be largely different than the original, espoused values. This is precisely why the Footing is so important. In spite of the current expectations, as the organization continues maturing and growing, all members can articulate what leaders should expect of them in order to maximize individual performance and the long-term effectiveness of the organization. Simply stated, this can be understood as "The way we ***should be*** expected to do things around here", and it is referred to as the Ideal Culture in OCI® literature. To the extent these members widely and strongly share the same underlying assumptions and espoused values, there will be a lot of consistency across the responses of all members.

Dr. D's Reflections

Interesting enough, this shared set of values that originates from the beginning of the organization and evolves with the organization is reliant on the members of the organization to maintain and improve the culture. The challenge of leadership is ensuring the values of the new personnel brought into the organization over time are aligned. Unfortunately, you seldom see a values section on a job posting and lessor still, a way of testing for that alignment prior to a hiring decision.

As with personal *Leadership Platforms*, differences between the Current (i.e., Operating) Culture and Ideal (i.e., Preferred) Culture highlight those platform areas where leaders should focus the organization's change and development efforts. In other words, once we understand something about where we're at (Current Culture) versus where we want to be (Ideal Culture), we can develop a plan to close the gap.

Finally, since you've read the Preface, you'll recall there

is a clear Leadership-Culture-Performance connection built into the Human Synergistics International *How Culture Works* model. This connection gets hardwired through the impact that founders and senior leaders have on the culture of the organization. We'll further decompose this idea in Part 2. For now, just know that they have also created a 360-degree feedback assessment designed to help senior leaders evaluate the impact they have on the organization through the strategies (Prescriptive vs. Restrictive) they adopt and behaviors they actually promote. It's called *Leadership/Impact®*, and it is germane to a complete understanding of organizational *Leadership Platforms*.

THE GAP BETWEEN PLATFORMS AND ENRICHMENT

Blueprinting, building and strength-testing my platform was really tough at first, but it solved some major problems and closed more than a few gaps in my leadership. At some point in the effort of moving through design, document, etc., it dawned on me that *Leadership Platforms*, like all living documents, must be continually renewed through ongoing leadership enrichment. If they are not, they can become weak and begin to exhibit signs of warping, dry-rot and other structural damage…no longer suitable to carry the weight of those who would otherwise follow.

Over time I had secured a well-designed/blueprinted, documented/built and evaluated/strength-tested *Leadership Platform*. But at what point would it be "good enough" or "strong enough"? Moreover, what happens if I wanted to have a bigger impact than

I was having? It would inevitably mean that I'd have to expand my current platform. Problem was, by the time I finished the first iteration of blueprint—build—strength-test, I had so much time invested that my natural tendency was to lock it down and never change it. In fact, I saw this happen a lot with quality management systems (QMS') like ISO 9000 or 14000 over the years. In my work as a quality management practitioner, I quickly discovered that once organizations invest so much money just to implement ISO and secure the accreditation, the last thing they wanted to do was change it. So the QMS became anachronistic, which is precisely why I was forced to contend with the temptation of locking my personal *Leadership Platform* down. Thankfully, while I was tempted, I couldn't allow that to be the epitaph of my leadership.

Now it was just a matter of working through the method of continually renewing and improving my *Leadership Platform*. As I thought more about it, the reality of how leadership development (i.e., enrichment) is typically approached lends itself to anything but an upward and outward pattern of continual renewal… nothing close to the one W. Edwards Deming illustrated in the plan-do-check-act (PDCA) learning cycle. Instead of steadily improving our impact through continual renewal, leadership enrichment tends to resemble short-lived spurts, exhibiting patterns of peaks (a little enrichment) and valleys (a little decay) that appear as something many have called *knowing-doing gaps*. As if this weren't bad enough, we actually run the risk of leadership enrichment fading away entirely and our platforms falling prey to the 2nd Law of Thermodynamics (i.e., entropy). When this happens, our platform can return, like all living systems without new information, to a state of equilibrium (i.e., performance returns to the same level we were at before temporary enrichment elevated our thinking). Once we're out of new information, we're obviously unable to use it to continually improve our leadership performance. Let me explain.

The knowing-doing gap for leadership is subtle, but one of the ways it creeps in is when a leadership course is attended (either because it was "required" by the job or because there was legitimate interest in learning about leadership) and, even though some knowledge was transferred, it produces little systemic growth and never quite makes its way back into the workplace; into action. Then, over time, the old eraser goes to work and we forget (or treat with disregard and inattention) the very knowledge we once gained, returning to our prior level… just as if we never attended the course in the first place. There are a couple of primary reasons for this, which we'll address at length a little later.

For now, it is important to understand there are both personal and organizational limiters that promote the gap between leadership knowing and leadership doing. On the personal side, there are thinking styles that produce an oppositional and avoidance orientation in the learner, both of which result in lower acceptance of what was just learned and, as a result, little if any of it gets applied toward making worthwhile changes. On the organizational side, there are cultures established by the senior leaders that inhibit, demotivate, or dis-incentivize the learner from applying the new knowledge.

Regardless of the limiter, the knowledge gained is eventually forgotten (i.e., treated with disregard or inattention) or rejected by the learner and never applied, and the mind of the leader (and organization) returns to a prior state of ignorance without the benefit of growth. And, without question, this is a tragedy because the mind is truly one of the most wonderful of all God's creations. It literally has an infinite capacity for progress, by design, but only if it is left free to roam. The former was of God's volition and it is perfect, the latter is of our volition (i.e., free will) and we frankly haven't done that well.

One need only think back to the last century for the evidence needed to support this claim. In fact, near the latter part of the 20th century, where the growth of knowledge is reported to be equal to the height of the Washington Monument against that of 3 inches (1845-1945) and 1 inch (beginning of time to 1845), my good friend and mentor, Tom Smith, was fond of levying the following indictment on American business: "nearly 100 years unhampered by progress." He was referring specifically to the fact that managers in the last decade of the 20th century had yet to replace the theories and ideas of Frederick Taylor (e.g., scientific management) and Skinnerian Behaviorism with the more useful theories of W. Edwards Deming (e.g., system of profound knowledge and 14 points) and Alfie Kohn (e.g., motivation and human behavior). Imagine if we still practiced medicine based on what we understood at the beginning of the 20th century.

Dr. D's Reflections

I acknowledge first-hand, this knowing-doing gap can be very frustrating when it inhibits, demotivates, or dis-incentivizes you. But as the old saying goes, when one door closes another opens. Trick is, you've got to find it. Do not get disenfranchised from these situations, instead look for that open door and don't walk but run through it. We all face these situations, but we can't let them define us if we want to be leaders.

Difficult isn't it? So why are we still holding onto the management theories of a century past?

Great question! And it deserves an answer. Part 2 of this book is dedicated to helping leaders remove the personal and organizational limiters that result in undiscovered leadership, as well as addressing the knowing-doing gap currently holding progress back in our 21st century endeavors toward leadership enrichment.

A quick note and challenge before we continue. You may not have heard this from your leadership, but you have an inherent right to choose to be happy with what you do in life. After all, you are going to spend at least on third of your time in life doing it. If you are not happy, it is incumbent on you to make the change. If you are in an organization that doesn't value your input or, worse yet, actually enables obstacles to successful work or creates problems that only "management" can solve,

Dr. D's Reflections

The effects that an unhappy person can have on an organization can be devastating. Don't be that person. Pastor Chuck Swindoll once quipped: "Life is 10% what happens to you and 90% how you respond to it." You control that 90 percent; you decide how you act or react. Choose wisely!

you are in the wrong place. Eventually, it will wear on you as your expectation of negative outcomes eats away at your attitude, behavior and performance.

Opportunity: *It may be time for you to take stock and accept the realization that no one, no matter how gifted, will perform well as a leader in your organization. As my old mentor, the*

---

late Thomas A. "Smitty" Smith used to say: "The system creates the behavior". If this describes your situation, start looking for another company and better leadership now. For what it's worth, I've personally left over $40K/year on the table to escape the caustic leadership of my manager. It was worth every penny.

_____

_____

_____

_____

_____

_____

YOUR PLATFORM OPPORTUNITY

In the simplest of terms, Platforms are steeped in the central idea presented throughout Part 1: **Rethinking Potential when it comes to Personal and Organizational Leadership**. But to convert Rethinking into Reframing and our Potential into Performance requires specific and deliberate effort. To that end, I propose the Pathway to Leadership Enrichment in Part 2. And to make the transition from Part 1 to Part 2, the following illustration is provided to tie the old and familiar with the new and unfamiliar.

Years ago, there was a popular movement in business toward inverting the organization chart; placing the CEO at the bottom and all the workers at the top. Do you remember that? I remember thinking at the time that this "management fad" actually had merit—I'd seen more than my share come and go because of flawed assumptions or faulty execution. While the assumptions about the relationship between leader and follower were sound (e.g., leaders should serve and support the weight of those who choose to follow), this movement eventually failed because its execution was faulty. In execution, nothing really changed in the organization except the chart. Let me explain.

Inverting the typical hierarchical organization chart created the image of an inverted pyramid; easy and fair enough based on the Rethinking of leadership assumptions driving the effort. Without the effort of Reframing, however, it creates an extremely unstable structure upon which to place workers, which is why many saw right through it and defected—opting instead to treat it as just another "flavor of the month" and something they could simply wait out. The real reason this management movement failed and became

Dr. D's Reflections

The reality is that people in appointed positions are afforded power, decision authority and other abilities they are not so willing to give up. Be it pride or just the gluttony of power over others, the relinquishment of anything comparable requires humility. How many people in authority do you know who are willing to give up what they perceive to be something they worked hard to earn and, therefore, deserve. It is possible, but by human nature not very probable.

fad wasn't because the idea (i.e., Rethinking) was flawed, it was because very little of the leadership function actually changed during execution (i.e., Reframing) leaving little support, strength or stability in the new structure. These well-meaning senior managers simply overlooked a basic principle of organizational development: to carry more weight above the surface, on top of the Platform Framing, you've got to have a solid Foundation and firm Footing.

If the leaders would have executed better and made the type of specific and deliberate effort to enrich leadership proposed in Part 2, the new organization chart would have started to look like the image below (much different than an inverted pyramid).

The *Leadership Platform* Organization Chart.

In this image, the Manager, now at the bottom because of Rethinking her assumptions about leadership and those who follow, is actually Reframing her *Leadership Platform* with a more stable Foundation and Footing. She is moving well beyond mere potential to better performance in order to carry the weight of more workers, now positioned at the top.

Our sincere hope is you'll also move your leadership beyond merely Rethinking personal and organizational potential (presented in Part 1) to Reframing personal and organizational performance (offered in Part 2). If you do, you'll naturally find more opportunities to lead and develop as a leader. And when you do, the Leadership Enrichment LIFE-cycle (LEL-c) in Part 2 will be your guide to solid and stable *Leadership Platforms* that produce better outcomes for you, for others and for your organization.

For those of you who dare to believe you can make a positive difference in this world through your leadership, Part 2 is for you. But as you move through the opportunities therein, keep this in mind. We talked about leadership in terms of your willingness to consider the opportunity as we moved from the Preface into Part 1. Now, in Part 2, your **commitment** will be required. And you'll see this word used frequently in the following pages, discovering more about what we mean by using the term. For now, we'll leave you with something to ponder:

> *Movement without commitment is not progress...it's dabbling. It's dipping the toe into destiny while keeping one foot anchored in [the past]. You must destroy the exit if you want to force destiny to open the door ahead. (Napoleon Hill)*

This is very appropriate for what awaits you. After all, movement by appointment is the history of leadership and the opportunity—dare we say "destiny"—in front of you. To the extent you were willing, Part 1 was designed to help you unlearn some of what you once thought true about leadership. Now, your commitment will be essential to resisting the temptation of reverting to old ways of thinking, knowing, doing, and performing. Metaphorically, my sincere hope is that, like Cortés, you'll burn the ships that would otherwise tempt you to abandon your pursuit of *Real Leadership*. Earlier I introduced you to my late friend and mentor, Smitty, in one of the 'Opportunities'. He'd often say that the new ways are incompatible with the old and can't be reconciled. You simply cannot make progress if your energy is split between advancing and retreating.

To your leadership destiny, continue to Part 2 and seize your opportunity to...

PART 2

The Pathway to Leadership Enrichment

[Written by Mr. D with reflections by Dr. D.]

Here again, you will find that Dr. D has made some incredible contributions. His thoughtful reflections, added with a dash of humor, will help to ease you, the reader, into new ways of thinking, knowing, doing and performing as a leader. Dr. D's sense of humor was vitally important to me when republishing and updating my first two books as a single work. Reason is simple; because my professional, personal, and social experience with lackluster leadership has left scars where deep wounds were once inflicted. As a result, in writing those initial copies, I took the substance matter very seriously. Dr. D is a past-master at breaking the seriousness down, reducing the shock of challenging topics, and layering in opportunities to laugh along the way. Becoming a leader worth following is a journey, so you might as well enjoy it. Our sincere hope is that you enjoy Part 2.

A S I BEGAN thinking more about the process of blue-printing, building and strength-testing personal and organizational *Leadership Platforms*, I realized how much I had already invested and, as a result, how much I wanted to avoid the knowing-doing gap or reaching a point of equilibrium. The problem was I didn't know how I had brought my platform from concept to completion and, as a result, how to continually renew and improve it. Moreover, not having a *Leadership Platform* held me back from becoming a *real leader*, but now my challenge was to figure out how I could HELP OTHERS and ORGANI-ZATIONS build and renew their own *Leadership Platforms*. I distinctly remember thinking at some point that Lisa really was onto more than (at least I had) originally thought when she challenged me not only to document my platform, but to also document the process I moved through over the years to establish the Footing, Foundation and Framing. While I hadn't really thought that much about it, I figured that since I had gotten to this point at least once, perhaps I could figure out how and capture it for the benefit of others.

Working through the process, I recalled something from my short stint as a Recruiter Aide with the U.S. Marine Corps back in 1989. It was from a boot camp video we would show to the young men and women who made the commitment to enter our delayed-entry program. The scene was a familiar one to anyone who has ever earned the title: U.S. Marine. A new platoon of recruits meets their Senior Drill Instructor (SDI) at Marine Corps Recruit Depot (MCRD) for the first time. As the SDI for each platoon is introduced by their Series Commander, with all military bearing and a commanding voice each delivers this same short but highly inspirational/motivational message:

Our mission is to train each one of you to be a Marine. A Marine is characterized as one who possesses the highest of military virtues. He obeys all [lawful] orders, respects his seniors and strives constantly to be the best in everything he does. Discipline and spirit are the hallmark of a Marine, and these qualities are the goals of your training here. Above all else, you must never quit or give up. We cannot train you or help you unless you are willing to become a Marine; unless you are willing to give your very best. We offer you the challenge of recruit training and the opportunity to become a United States Marine. (United States Marine Corps)

I thought about my response to that challenge and my own transformation in those short 3 months at MCRD in San Diego, CA. Based on this starting point, I began to outline the basic leadership enrichment process.

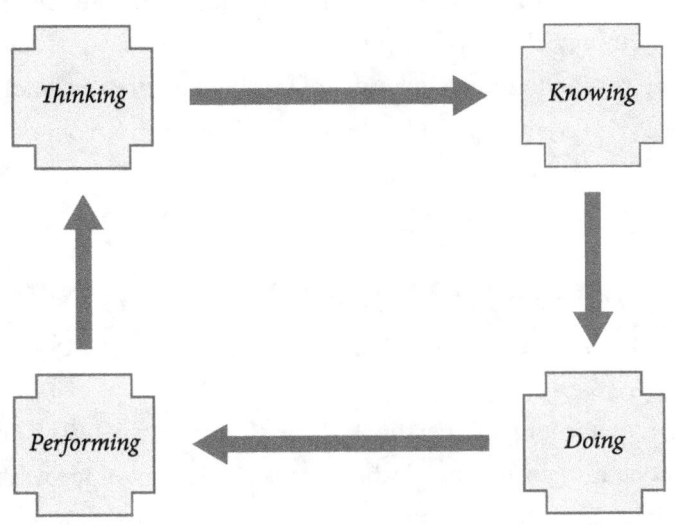

The Leadership Enrichment Journey Map.

This is a process that I could recall moving through, to some extent and with varying degrees of success, numerous times as a long-term student of leadership. What I ended up with was a map of the recursive journey I had undertaken between thinking and knowing, between knowing and doing, between doing and performing and between performing and the next level of new thinking that resulted.

This initial journey map captured the high-level process I had been using to convert new thinking into better performance over time. The next step was to associate this process with the attributes that characterized the pursuit and ultimately formed the major stages of my own Leadership Enrichment. After some deep digging and a lot of hard work, I eventually landed on four attributes/stages and codified them in the acronym LIFE. And because my actual Leadership Enrichment journey had been recursive, I quickly attached the suffix "-cycle" to the end of this acronym to denote that it was a process of continual renewal and improvement. What finally emerged was a Leadership Enrichment LIFE-cycle (LEL-c) model, which is explained in detail throughout the remainder of this book. Before advancing, however, I want to provide a little more backdrop as context for your journey, should you accept the challenge.

LEADERSHIP ENRICHMENT LIFE-CYCLE (LEL-c) BACKDROP

Though it is a highly personal process/journey, the LEL-c does not occur in a vacuum. Nothing strikes the spark of leadership enrichment better than personal contact with a *real leader*. *Real leaders* beget *real leaders*. And by now you know how my life and leadership was forever changed by the commitment of a few who were not only interested in my development as a leader, but were willing to put their time, talent and treasure behind it. You've seen their names in Part 1, and you'll see them here as well. And there's good reason for that.

The first reason is rather obvious. I mentioned back in the *Platform Blueprinting Commences* section that nothing in my personal *Leadership Platform* was original with me. And you would expect this given the essence of leadership is impact or influence. I was influenced by a lot of great thinkers and leaders, so I gave credit where it was due. It is no different with the LEL-c. Everything you'll read in the following pages I've gleaned from personal contact with great leaders. Now this doesn't mean these aren't my words or that the LEL-c isn't based on my decomposition, clarification, or unique application of what they originally introduced. It simply means that I recognize and want to honor the profound impact that these leaders had (and continue to have) on me.

Dr. D's Reflections

This is in direct correlation to the previously discussed humility in leadership and an inherent desire to serve others. It also speaks to the fact that feedback can go in one of three directions: down, up or laterally. Telling your leaders about the impact they had on your life provides validation that what they invested in you was of value. I have had several individuals over time tell me that I had a significant impact on their life. That incited an emotion of satisfaction and reassurance. Don't get me wrong, I don't do anything with the expectation of receiving something in return, however I just want to point out that it felt good for someone to say I had a positive impact on their outcome.

The second reason is that I want you to have the same opportunity I had to renew and improve leadership, personally and organizationally. This means exposing the exact information available to me from those who were most influential. These are the authors and thought-leaders I learned from and, without them, this book wouldn't exist. In fact, the success of this book largely depends on you seeing some value in, and making some use of, my ideas as you build your own *Leadership Platform*. To that end, I've included personal vignettes in order to highlight my interaction with this new information. My goal is to provide an illustration from my own progression through the LEL-c in order to aid your progression. And you may decide to incorporate someone else's along the way. That's perfectly okay; it's all part of it. In fact, it's encouraged. The point is to keep nurturing your own leadership.

The final reason is, in many cases, these thought-leaders are far better at explaining and underscoring the importance of certain components in the LEL-c than I might be. As the old saying goes, "If it's not broke, don't fix it!" So, for the reader's benefit, where I felt it was more important to pass on information with a level of detail in accuracy, clarity and completeness only an original author can provide, you'll find a direct reference along with a citation. Otherwise, I will simply point out the reference material and direct you to the author for more information in order to keep the length of this book manageable. My sincere hope is you won't find the references distracting or overused, and you will find their insight as useful as I did. The best outcome would be that you use this book as the pocket guide it was originally intended to be, continually referring back for guidance when times get tough…and they will.

Having said all that, I want to be upfront about something else. There will be work for you to do along the way. While personal contact with leaders may strike the spark of enrichment, we are the ones who must kindle the coals through personal transformation if we are ever to brandish the torch of organizational transformation. To that end, each stage of the LEL-c will require you to perform some "platform work" if you are to enrich your leadership in a practical way, applying what you are about to read. It is THE goal, after all, of Part 2; to help you take this new information on leadership and use it to improve personal and organizational performance and, over time, to yield mastery.

One final thought before getting on with it. I never set out to create the LEL-c. I simply wanted to understand the history of how I had created a personal *Leadership Platform* so I could help others create and maintain one. I also wanted to reveal the hidden value of an organizational *Leadership Platform* so those with a personal platform could have a greater impact. It was only after I had already established the performance waypoints that the concept evolved and matured as detailed shortly. I suppose it was also inevitable that I would have insisted that the round-trip journey be repeated over time, which explains where the suffix "-cycle" comes from.

THE LEL-c MODEL

As previously introduced, the LEL-c is comprised of four stages—captured by the acronym LIFE—that serve as the basis for leadership enrichment. The illustration below reveals these

Enrichment Stages within the context of the original journey I mapped.

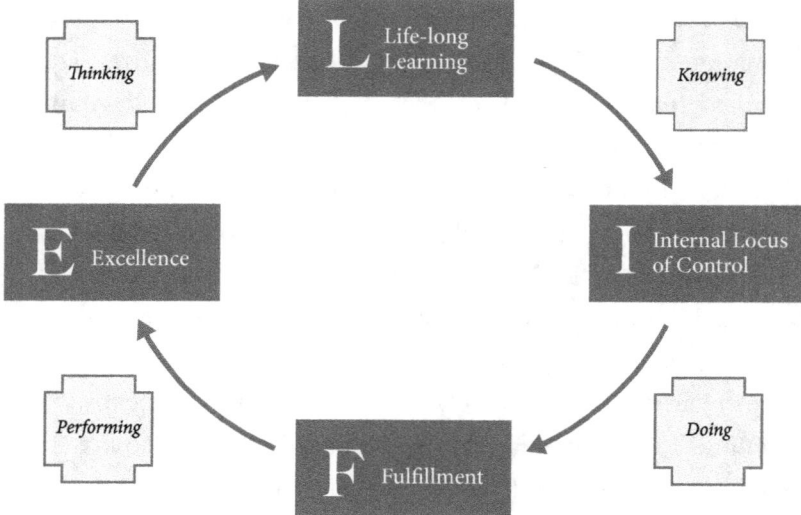

The LIFE-cycle Enrichment Stages.

And here's how it correlates to the creation of my personal *Leadership Platform*—with corresponding alignment to the Plan-Do-Check-Act (PDCA) cycle as an illustration that ties the new and relatively unfamiliar LEL-c with something old and familiar:

1. Enrichment Stage #1 - Defining and designing my platform through **Life-long Learning** (i.e., thinking about and carefully blueprinting the design)—PLAN;

2. Enrichment Stage #2 - Building and modifying my platform through an **Internal Locus of Control**

(i.e., documenting and updating the as-built; most likely an enhanced version of the original blueprint)—DO;

3. Enrichment Stage #3 - Validating my platform through **Fulfillment** activities (i.e., strength-testing by evaluation and assessment)—CHECK; and

4. Enrichment Stage #4 - Leveraging my platform through **Excellence** in achievement (i.e., carrying the weight of those who chose to follow)—ACT.

The Enrichment Stages are *sequential*, meaning the LIFE-cycle always begins with Enrichment Stage #1: Life-long Learning and ends with Enrichment Stage #4: Excellence. They are also *progressive*, meaning each Enrichment Stage builds upon the previous one(s) and, as previously mentioned, the suffix "-*cycle*" indicates that it must be repeated on a continual basis for sustained enrichment.

This LIFE-cycle also applies equally to groups as it does to individuals—organizations just don't exist apart from organisms (i.e., people) and, as a LIFE-cycle, it is *irreducible*; meaning all four Enrichment Stages must be completed for leadership to be enriched.

With this understanding of the four Enrichment Stages, the last step I took was toward detailing out each of them with a specific performance target (because it is important to give every stage in the overall LEL-c an aim), and a primary emotional enabler (because it was essential for movement through the LEL-c). Consistent with the journey map theme, I classified the performance targets as "waypoints", and the emotional enablers as "connectors" as depicted in the image below.

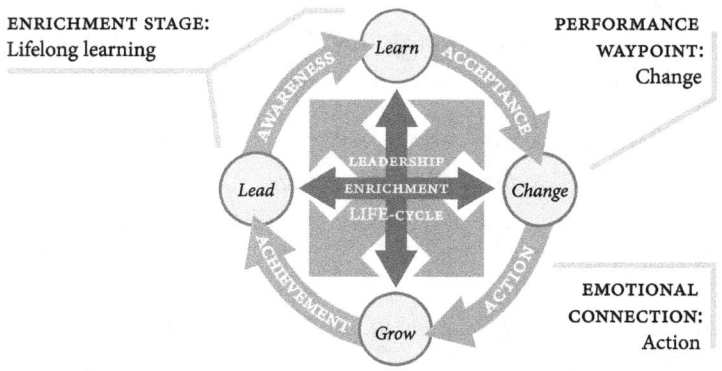

The Leadership Enrichment LIFE-cycle (LEL-c).

I realized after analyzing my own Leadership Enrichment journey that multiple performance waypoints proved essential because they broke the LIFE-cycle into smaller, more manageable parts. The emotional connectors proved equally vital because they served the essential function of providing the energy in motion (i.e., emotion) that helped me: a) get started and b) control my speed of movement through the LIFE-cycle.

The effort to arrive at this point in understanding my own journey of Leadership Enrichment was absolutely incredible. It was incredibly exhausting. It was also incredibly rewarding. The image below pulls the entire model together; showing the relationship of my original journey map to the four Enrichment Stages and the individual Performance Waypoints and Emotional Connectors contained in the recursive process of renewing and improving leadership.

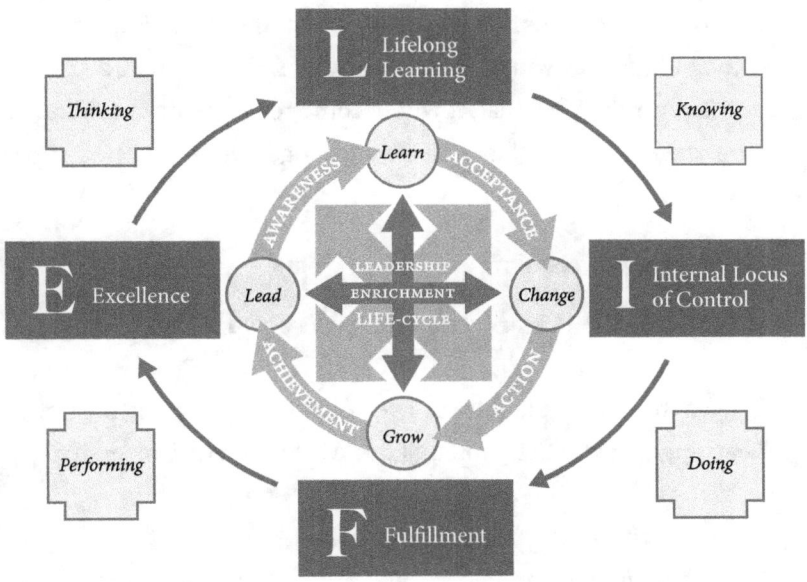

The LEL-c Model.

This LEL-c Model provides the roadmap for blueprinting/ designing, building/documenting, strength-testing/validating and continually renewing and improving personal and organizational *Leadership Platforms*.

If you are interested in the idea of leadership, in your growth as a leader, in developing the leaders around you, or in leading your organization to a whole new level of performance, I propose the challenge of Leadership Enrichment as offered by the LIFE-cycle. With it comes the potential to become the best leader version of you and the opportunity to improve the leadership in your organizations.

And as you embark on your own fascinating journey, don't forget to take along the *LEL-c Navigation Aid* at the back of the book. I created it to help you get started and track your progress.

I encourage you to print off a copy before heading out. It will come in handy as you move through the LEL-c the first couple or three times. After that, it will become reflexive and you'll no longer need it. With that, let's advance together.

ENRICHMENT STAGE #1 - LIFELONG LEARNING

One of the best explanations I've come across for this idea of "learning" is from the United States Air Force, Air University:

> *Learning is the process that conditions us to react to a given situation or process a given set of information in a certain way. Learning helps us to gain an understanding of right and wrong and helps us to respond accordingly.* (Air Force Insitute for Advanced Distributed Learning)

It follows naturally that, if we want to start and hope to continue improving personal and organizational leadership, we need to ensure we are focused on doing the right things. Remember, one definition of failure is "succeeding at the wrong things."

Doing the right things, however, emerges as a consequence of thinking rightly... about ourselves (e.g., concept of self: portrait, ideal, esteem); about the world (e.g., worldview: perspective from which we see and interpret fundamental aspects of reality); and about ourselves in the world (e.g., interaction with things, interdependence with others, interrelatedness and interoperability of systems, etc.). Thinking rightly requires that we develop knowledge through a deep desire for, and openness to, learning.

W. Edwards Deming, the world-renowned statistician, professor, author, lecturer and business performance consultant of the 20th century, once said: "acting without knowledge, the effect is to make things worse." Dr. Deming developed what many consider to be the best system for transforming individuals and organizations; Profound Knowledge, which incorporates an appreciation of systems, knowledge of variation,

Dr. D's Reflections

I struggled with learning early on—barely passing high school, likely because I was the class clown and headed for the Air Force. There, I was diagnosed with ADHD, and I had to learn how to learn. Discovering Dr. David Kolb's Learning Style Theory helped me realize that I simply learned differently—and that was okay. Now, as a university professor, I believe education would improve if more teachers understood the diverse ways students learn. Lifelong learning starts with knowing how you learn best. That's the key to unlocking your potential.

theory of knowledge and psychology, and its practical application through the "Fourteen Points." In fact, so fundamental to transformation was learning that Dr. Deming advocated the Plan-Do-Check-Act (PDCA) cycle as a great way to learn in business because he understood a lot about the inelegance of our learning and, therefore, the need for forgiveness in the learning process. Moreover, he impressed upon everyone the usefulness and necessity of "operational definitions" when it came to accuracy, clarity and completeness of communication for learning. Lastly, Dr. Deming firmly believed that transformation begins with the individual:

The first step is transformation of the individual. This transformation is discontinuous. It comes from [learning] the system of profound knowledge. The individual, transformed, will perceive new meaning to his life, to events, to numbers, to interactions between people. Once the individual understands the system of profound knowledge, he will apply its principles in every kind of relationship with other people. He will have a basis for judgment of his own decisions and for transformation of the organizations that he belongs to. The individual, once transformed, will:

- *Set an example*
- *Be a good listener, but will not compromise*
- *Continually teach other people*
- *Help people to pull away from their current practice and beliefs and move into the new philosophy without a feeling of guilt about the past* (Deming)

If you want to improve the effectiveness of your organization or team (i.e., transformation…), focus first on enriching your leadership (…begins with the individual). If you want to enrich your leadership, build a personal Leadership Platform as the basis of transformation. Once you are transformed, you will be able to help others transform as you set the example, listen, teach and help, ultimately building a better organizational Leadership Platform. This is not easy, but it is essential. As the old quote from Leo Tolstoy goes: "Everyone thinks of changing the world but no one thinks of changing himself." As if this weren't hard enough, in order to change we have to be committed to learning. I love the quote from Stuart Emmett: "When I learn, I have to do something—therefore—I Change." Remember this as we move through the first two Enrichment Stages.

Improving our personal and organizational leadership requires then, on the front end, this idea of openness to learning, which includes three components: acute alertness (paying attention to life), a keen awareness (knowing what to look for or where to focus our attention) and an insatiable curiosity (a strong desire or willingness to discover more and continually question accepted knowledge). All three are internal processes

Dr. D's Reflections

In the next stages you will start to actually begin to make changes and practice what you are learning. I encourage you to try different things throughout this process and remember that "the only thing you can't do is what you have not tried".

that routinely look outward at life and the world in which we live, actively seeking new information about ourselves and our situation and/or condition, and then, through the learning process, skillfully turning that new information into knowledge for application—the definition of wisdom. Simply put, the key to knowledge is learning and central to learning is this idea of Awareness.

But before digging in, let's fully establish the correlation between leadership and learning. A systematic literature review of 105 studies by (Lundqvist, Wallo, Coetzer and Kock) found statistically significant relationships between leadership and learning at the individual, group and organizational levels. Leaders who actively promote learning—through coaching, feedback and creating a learning culture—tend to foster more adaptive and high-performing teams. Now, let's get after the emotional connector *Awareness*.

Emotional Connector – AWARENESS

The first of four emotional connectors, and the most important, Awareness means one knows what to look for and where to find it... in ourselves, in others and in the world around us. Awareness of self involves knowing who we are and getting comfortable in our own skin. It involves understanding our personality, our present limitations, our future potential and our learning preferences and tendencies (i.e., how we prefer to learn). Awareness is enabled by alertness and emboldened by curiosity.

In its simplest form, alertness is nothing more than paying attention to life with all the sense(s) we've been given. Its importance has been underscored by practical warnings like: "don't fall asleep at the wheel" and characterized by some along the lines of mental color codes or conditions (i.e., white, yellow, orange, red and black) with the color/condition determined by your ability to successfully detect certain stimuli. Alertness is an essential ingredient to awareness. If we are not paying attention, we'll miss it... whatever "it" is, even if we know what to look for. In contrast, even if we are paying attention (e.g., we are alert), without awareness (e.g., knowing who we are and what to look for), "it" stays hidden, even while "in plain sight." Why? Because we remain blissfully unaware. Put another way, if we aim at nothing, we'll probably hit it. Worse yet, if we aim at the wrong thing, we're likely to hit that also. Alertness ensures we keep both eyes open and on-target.

Awareness ensures we are able to understand our situation, identify the right target/goals and achieve learning on purpose. The more we learn on purpose, the more we have heightened our sense of awareness. You will start to look for things you had not thought of looking for in the past, if you stay alert. Dr. Jeff Myers, in his video series *Secrets of the World Changers*, helps reinforce the idea that alertness is dissimilar to, but necessary for, awareness by clarifying the difference between "seeing" (i.e., to physically get an impression using the sense of sight... what we call Alertness) and "perceiving" (to mentally understand using the powers of reason... what we call Awareness). The natural— albeit unintended—consequence of alertness void of awareness (or vice-versa) is missed opportunities. These misses restrict our movement from a state of unconscious incompetence (e.g., I don't know that I don't know) to a state of conscious incompetence (e.g., I know that I don't know), short-circuiting any opportunity to choose learning right from the beginning.

But sometimes we only have a theory about what to look for and where we might find it. This is where the idea of insatiable curiosity (and the scientific method) comes in to embolden awareness that leads to learning. We understand Leonardo D' Vinci was characterized by this incredible attribute. Curiosity advances our theory by asking the right questions in transit to learning, such that our awareness (i.e., knowledge of what to look for and where to find it) is either validated or rejected. An insatiable curiosity also renews our awareness because, as our understanding increases by asking, and seeking answers to, the right questions, we gain more confidence in the discovery by inquiry approach and can't stop ourselves from becoming even more curious... wanting to know more. This becomes self-evident

Dr. D's Reflections

Learning is not just driven by the desire to learn but can also be enjoyable and I would say at times fun. There are so many ways to learn now. Gamification has changed the way the military trains a lot of their members. Personally, I learn best in micro doses. Small incremental bits of information that culminate into a desired outcome. I actually enjoy learning something new, especially if it is going to help me accomplish a task I have not done in the past. With what we have access to, there is a you tube video or tutorial on how do almost everything. This is usually my first stop when tackling something new. Why recreate the wheel? Remember what I said before, the only thing you can't do is what you haven't tried. "Can't do!" is a mindset, something you tell yourself. So is "Can do!" You chose when that happens next.

later in the LIFE-cycle as we move through Achievement into greater levels of Leadership. It is also where we deal head-on with this idea of learning... where we begin to deal personally/internally with what our alertness (paying attention to life) and curiosity (questioning with boldness) has revealed to us.

On that note, consider Dr. Phil's first life law: "Be someone who gets it." This requires a thorough self-examination to begin understanding why you do things or don't do things. Only then can you decide whether to change, what to change to, or how to change it. One method of self-examination is to ask and answer tough questions. In this regard, be guided by theory... not by experience or intuition alone. Experience may provide some of the right *answers*, but it is theory that will get you closer to asking the right *questions*. This is important because even correct answers to poorly framed questions can lead to unproductive outcomes—or worse, they can actually lead you to draw the wrong conclusions about yourself. By the way, this also happens to be the basis of making artificial intelligence (AI) work: theory-guided questions. And just a quick aside on AI, since it is available for everything, everywhere, all at once. Here are a few ways in which asking questions when interacting with AI helps cut through complexity to derive better answers:

- **Surfaces Assumptions and Gaps:** Good questions can reveal hidden assumptions or missing information in a topic, allowing the AI to address them directly or prompting you to reconsider your approach.

- **Personalizes the Response:** Questions help the AI tailor its answers to your specific context, goals, or level of expertise, making the information more actionable and relevant.

- **Enhances Engagement and Critical Thinking:** Asking thoughtful questions encourages a more interactive and reflective dialogue, helping you think critically and explore ideas more deeply.

Now, it is true that bias must be accounted for and mitigated in either case, but asking tough but open ended questions of yourself is akin to asking AI without prompt engineering, selective labeling, or adversarial inputs… you'll simply get better answers. This is why I reference and recommend throughout this book the use of statistically-valid diagnostic instruments, because they are designed to control for bias in self- and organizational-assessment. And there will be a time to involve others in the process, which we'll address in the Platform Work section in a few pages. For now, since it really starts with you, you can be the only one answering at this point. That also means, however, that the bias will emerge in answers as a natural reflection of your own experiences, thinking styles, and worldview. Nevertheless, the goal is to respond honestly and, when a part of the self-evaluation exercise, to stay within allotted time limits. To that end, borrowing from and adapting Brian Tracy's "Seven questions we must answer…" outlined in *Psychology of Achievement* (Tracy), here are a few worth considering as you begin self-evaluation, personally or organizationally:

- What are your 5 highest values (i.e., what's most important to you)? Write them down and then place them in order of priority. [60 Seconds]

- What are your three most important goals right now? [30 Seconds]

- What would you do (i.e., how would you spend your time) if you learned today that you only had three months to live or three months before your organization was going out of business? Assume that they would be three healthy and productive months. [45 seconds]

- What would you do if you won a million dollars cash, tax free, in the lottery tomorrow or some philanthropist gave your organization a billion dollar grant? How would you change your life/ business? What would you buy? What would you start doing? What would you stop doing? What would you do more of? [You get 2 minutes to come up with 10 things, and if you can't come up with at least 10 things written down you don't get any of them.]

- What have you always wanted to do but been afraid to attempt? [30 Seconds]

- What do you most enjoy, what gives you your greatest feelings of self-esteem and personal satisfaction? What is your organization most passionate about? [60 seconds]

- What one great thing would you dare to accomplish if you knew you absolutely could not fail? [30 seconds]

Opportunity: *Don't race past this. Take time now, get your stop watch and a piece of paper to jot down your answers—in your leadership journal, perhaps—then complete the exercise. I think you will discover that it's not as easy as it sounds, but it does get easier.*

The purpose of this simple exercise is to provide you with new information about yourself. I recommend repeating the exercise at least once a week for 7-10 consecutive weeks. It will ensure that the best and most accurate information emerges. It will also account for the fact that we may respond differently on the basis of what kind of day we are having. And as mentioned, stick to the timing on this exercise. It will truly help you determine, over time, what is important... what deserves your attention... what your values really are... where your treasure is... where your heart is.

Like all new information, the results of this exercise carry with it an intended effect: RESPONSIBILITY. Jan Carlzon, CEO of Scandinavian Airlines System (SAS), once quipped: "An individual without information cannot take responsibility; an individual who is given information cannot help but take responsibility." Our first responsibility with the new information about ourselves and our organizations, as revealed through the emotional connector of awareness, is to do something with it. In the LEL-c, that means we are to LEARN from it and use it to establish the Footing of our platforms.

Performance Waypoint – LEARN

The term 'learn'—unfortunately and undeservingly—carries with it a negative stigma and has become for many a big yawn (at best) or something to be avoided (at worst).

Let's talk about the "big yawn" first. A lot of us, if we're honest, don't view learning as a series of opportunities brilliantly disguised as daily work or play. But the truth is, learning opportunities are everywhere! In every environment we may find ourselves, at each moment throughout the day, there is an opportunity to learn if we are willing. And if we are to enrich our leadership, we need to be able to break away from the mental trap that suggests "old dogs can't learn new tricks." The net effect of this trap is we start believing the lie that "we already know it all," so curiosity diminishes and, eventually, we stop learning. And, our inclination to believe this lie grows with our position, age or education, which is a real danger. In fact, I remember hearing one man say: "It took me four years to get a college education and forty years to get over it!"

While this may not require a lot of explanation, permit me to unpack it a little. What we learn in college can lay a foundation for learning, but the education system itself may disincentive

Dr. D's Reflections

The operative term here is "**can't learn**". The reality is, this is no less a choice than "can learn" or "will learn.".

this. First, it promotes the idea that once you have your degree, at whichever level you decide to stop, the learning stops along with it. Second, it places the student in the unfortunate position of being passive recipients of information, stifling their creativity and critical thinking. There isn't space to unpack farther, but I'd encourage the reader to investigate the work of Alfie Kohn in "The Schools Our Children Deserve, where he advocates for a more student-centered curriculum that fosters lifelong learning and intellectual curiosity through a focus on understanding and engagement rather than rote memorization and test preparation.

Now let's talk about learning as something to be avoided. It is how most of us feel when it comes to actual 'learning' events. If your organization is like mine, we're told to show up at training on a certain date/time and at a certain place, so we do. Then we proceed to park our brain at the door, sit down, sign the attendance roster and wait to go back to work. This type of response to most learning events is not unwarranted. Recently, my 6 year old first grade daughter was asked by her 23 year old sister what her favorite part of the day was at school. Her answer was: "Recess!" I think that's expected. She was then asked what her second favorite part of the school day was, and she replied without hesitation or reservation: "going home!" I think that's honest. We've all felt that way and in most cases, we offer what seem to be compelling reasons for why we didn't learn anything:

- The lesson plan wasn't put together well;

- The instructor (or author) said something I disagree with;

- The subject matter was boring;

- The preacher couldn't preach.

But these reasons ultimately equal excuses, and it is our first big mistake when it comes to leadership enrichment. Learning isn't always going to be "fun" and you are never going to agree with everything said or taught. We need to come to terms with that. In fact, in the case of enriching our leadership, learning is going to prove darn difficult at times yet ultimately rewarding if we can exercise the stick-to-it-iveness required.

Most of what we're learning at this point about our personal leadership or the level of leadership in our organizations is going to be presented in the form of unflattering information. This is hard enough to accept, so we'll talk more about this in the next Emotional Connector: ACCEPTANCE. What we're addressing here is how difficult it is to learn as leaders and this translates into how open we really are to learning as we grow smarter and get older. According to Kathlyn and Gay Hendricks at The Hendricks Institute, an opportunity to learn is continuously available to us.

Dr. D's Reflections

Remember, you can learn just as much from the content you don't agree with than from that with which you are in violent agreement. Learning is learning, whether or not you agree—at first—with what you learned. A key in my learning journey has been to suspend my disbelief long enough to give any new information about leadership, particularly my own, a chance to be given full consideration, even if I've disagreed with it at first. You may choose to reject it, just don't excuse it away. For every one of our legitimate leadership shortcomings, we have a choice to make. We can make excuses, but that doesn't excuse our choice to remain unconvinced and unchanged.

Willingness to learn from each moment—as opposed to defending ourselves by stonewalling, explaining, justifying, withdrawing, blaming—is much more important than factors like IQ, family background, race or degrees. The great advantage of openness-to-learning is that you're in charge of it at all times: it's always within your control to shift out of defensiveness into genuine curiosity. Another great advantage: it can't be faked. You can feel instantly whether you're genuinely wondering or clinging to a defense. (Hendricks and Hendricks)

As you become aware of new information regarding your leadership and the leadership in your organization, I encourage you to refer to the Openness – to – Learning scale at The Hendricks

Institute to evaluate where your thinking is currently positioned along the scale. It will help you make the transition/commitment moves that shift your learning toward higher openness. It may be helpful to draft a personal learning commitment statement at this point. Taking stock of the fact that you may already know a few things about leadership, identifying that to which you are committed to learning more about…then recording it.

Opportunity: *A personal learning commitment statement can be approached in many ways, but the physical task of writing (or typing) it out will reinforce a design and desire for lifelong learning. It will help you overcome the initial shock of unflattering feedback about your leadership, moving you from the educational process and into the practitioner process. Take time here to record a Personal Learning Commitment Statement.*

With that established, there are a few more challenges with which we must contend to successfully reach and move through the LEARN waypoint, whether personally or organizationally:

1. **We learn in one of two ways:** a) by experience—a poor teacher because it removes forgiveness from the learning process; forcing us to take the test before revealing the lesson or b) by experiment (PDCA)—a great teacher because it provides forgiveness in the learning process, allowing us to safely formulate a theory and test a hypothesis (and our assumptions against the facts) by asking the right questions... about ourselves, the world and ourselves in the world... our "situation." The former is akin to learning the hard way or, as Dr. Deming put it: "doing our best without knowledge." The latter is akin to doing our best WITH knowledge or, as Dr. Deming often suggested: being "guided by theory." In both cases we are doing our best; the real difference is in the "process" of learning, in the actual lessons we learn and in the toll those lessons take on us. I prefer the latter in almost every life circumstance that is actually controllable (i.e., where I have a choice of what to learn and how/ when to learn it). This isn't to suggest we should jettison experience altogether. That would be equally foolish and rather impossible. Just remember, experience may help us find the right answers, but it won't help us ask the right questions.

2. **Awareness reveals personal and organizational problems.** Referring back to the ideas that: a)

leadership is our responsibility, no one else's, b)
new information brings with it the intended effect
of responsibility and c) the openness-to-learning
chart reveals that claiming full responsibility for
problems is the highest shift toward openness
on the scale; it is easy to get the impression that
responsibility here is key. But taking or claiming
responsibility for problems is not the same as
learning from it. Einstein was right; these specific
problems cannot be solved by the same patterns
of thought that created them. But this does not
mean that problems can't be solved by the same
person or organization that created them, as is
commonly believed today. If so, this would imply
that people/organizations are incapable of learning
from their mistakes, which we know isn't true.
We aren't helpless at solving our own problems;
there are just a few challenges to overcome before
our thinking can be elevated and our patterns of
thought changed. One of the challenges is "seeing"
(or identifying) the problem and the other is
"perceiving" (or defining) the problem correctly...
particularly when it comes to our own reflection.

   a. Seeing Problems. I love what John W.
    Gardner had to say: "Most ailing organiza-
    tions have developed a functional blindness
    to their own defects. They are not suffering
    because they cannot solve their problems
    but because they cannot see their problems."
    Awareness, as just defined, gives us the
    opportunity to open ourselves up to learning.

So, at this point, seeing the problem isn't the challenge; perceiving and/or defining the problem are.

b. Perceiving Problems. Complicating the matter is the fact that most of us actually think we are good problem solvers. This means that even if we become remotely aware of an existing problem (i.e., development opportunity), we jump directly to the answers/solutions, without bothering to ask the right questions, understand the essentials, or properly define the problem. But this is basic to learning. It was H.L. Mencken who observed: "For every complex problem there is an answer that is clear, simple and wrong." He also happens to be right, at least on this particular point. Reality suggests that a problem properly defined is a problem already half-solved. If we are to learn, we must be willing to invest the time and energy required to understand the new information...to understand the problem and avoid jumping to wrong conclusions. This will help us immensely in the next Enrichment Stage, where the performance waypoint is CHANGE.

3. **Our tendency is to pick low-hanging fruit** (i.e., acute problems that seem easy to solve or issues that are easy to face) and then divine what Tom Clason calls "left-hand simple solutions" in his book *Fast Cycle Production*. This means we avoid learning about the real, chronic problems that are

causing us the most trouble and never move to the other side of complexity for a workable solution to the seemingly easy issues we decide to solve. As one person said, we have fallen into the trap of "rearranging the deck chairs on the Titanic." No doubt we stay busily engaged while only superficially addressing the real issues. As a result, the old, original, easy problems/issues come back (actually, they were never solved in the first place) and new problems/issues emerge from the poor solutions we implemented. If you are serious about learning, commit to developing the courage to go after the real problems/issues and the scholarship to truly solve/face them.

4. **Learning is often blocked by old paradigms.** I won't go much farther on paradigms than to say that Joel Barker, in Chapter 3 of his work on *Paradigms*, defines them as: "...a set of rules and regulations that does two things: a) it establishes and defines boundaries and b) it tells you how to behave inside those boundaries to be successful." Joel goes on to describe paradigm shifters in Chapter 5 simply as: "...the folks who change the rules." Some rules ought NOT be changed, like the ones that form the Foundation (e.g., the moral law, virtues and values that set ethical boundaries of thinking, behavior and performance) of our *Leadership Platform*. Some rules should be changed, like the ones that keep us from learning. Commit to pushing the boundaries of your limitations/

potential and tearing down the barriers to your own learning.

Leadership (Lifelong Learning) Vignette

I was a slow, extremely inelegant learner for most of my early years, up to and including secondary education. In spite of being parochially trained and attending some of the finest schools in Metropolitan Detroit, halfway through my junior year of high school I was still falling into just about every learning trap there was; at least everyone listed above and probably a few others. In fact, I tried a number of ways to escape learning, and if you saw my overall high school GPA you'd know this was a firm reality statement. Then something shifted in me as a result of three "non-neutral" learning events, all of which occurred over a very short period of time from 1982 to 1984. They were all non-neutral in the sense that they forced me to make a commitment move… to decide in that moment whether I was going to learn or remain in ignorance.

The first occurred with my Mom in late 1982, the beginning of my junior year. By this time, she had been breaking her back for 8 years following my Father's premature death to cancer, working full-time to provide the kind of education I was squandering. But I didn't care about that, until one fateful evening. I finally came home from another night of killing brain cells and another day of recovering at a friend's house to find my Mom in the basement doing laundry. It was a Saturday, and I remember she was very tired from having worked at the bank all week and now almost half of the weekend just keeping up with things around the house. In fact, I was returning home to do some laundry myself, which is why this non-neutral learning event occurred in the laundry room. Stranger places, right?

Anyway, this was not unusual. We each pulled our own weight around the house. It was part of growing up in a single-parent home, and a natural consequence of my Father's legacy, which included the idea: "If you don't work; you don't eat!" It also was not unusual for me to lie to my Mother about where I had been or what I had been doing. So we went through our normal routine of her asking and me lying. Situation normal!

Then the unusual happened, and it speaks directly to how inelegant a learner I truly was at the time. My Mom became visibly broken by my words. I can't remember what she said, but I'll never forget how I made her feel. In that moment I began learning about myself. Oh! I had been self-aware for some time, but seeing my Mom like that opened me up to learning things that were not so gratifying or flattering. And as a proud German with perfectionist leanings, this was a literal breakthrough. In spite of all my defenses—and, believe me, I had built some doozies—my Mom's quiet brokenness penetrated the exterior and found its target in my innermost being. I was 15 going on 16 that November, and my self-centered adolescent existence came screeching to a halt. Thank God! My Mom's response helped me to see what I had allowed myself to become, and to want something better. It was the first of many non-neutral learning events that would open me up to a whole new level of learning about myself, my leadership and the impact I was having on others. My Mother is a Saint!

The second non-neutral learning event occurred a few months later in the Spring of 1983, and it served to reinforce my first lifelong learning lesson. By the latter half of my junior year, I was getting better grades, holding down a part-time job and still working around the house. Having played well in Junior Varsity Baseball the year before, I decided to try-out for Varsity. Sure enough, I made the Varsity team and almost immediately began thinking that I had somehow arrived at a level of proficiency in the sport that I no longer needed to learn. After all, isn't that why I was selected to play Varsity Baseball? Much to my initial surprise and ultimate chagrin, baseball got much harder for me...not easier. The practices were longer, the plays more sophisticated, the signals and signs from the base coach more elaborate. But that wasn't what got to me. The Varsity Baseball Coach was what got to me. He was tougher and far more critical of my playing than anyone had ever been.

Dr D's Reflections:

Recall again, we all learn differently. I mentioned earlier that Dr. Kolb introduced us to Learning Style Theory. What I didn't mention is that he initially identified five learning styles. Later he added four more. Although there is a lot of controversy surrounding the limitation of learning styles into nine different categories, and one could argue that as individuals, we all learn differently, there is power in knowing how you learn. There is also power in knowing how others learn.

I remember reaching a tipping point in my playing career with him. About half way through that Varsity Baseball season, I had reached my rope's end and was extremely discouraged. I was in a batting slump, my defense was suffering and I was "riding pine" more often than not. But like all great coaches, this did not escape Mr. Heil's attention. He pulled me aside during one practice to ask how I felt about my current effort on the field. It was a question he already knew the answer to, but I suppose he needed to set the stage for what came next. When I finished answering, he replied with another question...one that he intended to answer. And the dialogue went something like this:

> [Mr. Heil] "Do you know why I'm so hard on you?"
> [Me] "I don't, but sure would like to know!"
> [Mr. Heil] "Because I know you are not playing up to your potential."

I kind of suspected that, given what I had just learned from the prior non-neutral learning event with my Mom. But then he went on to say: "When I stop being tough you'll have reached your potential."

Okay! That was a shocker! I remember thinking, "How is that going to help me?" What I didn't understand at the time was that his tough, uncompromising approach to my game (not THE game) was putting me into a position where I'd have to recognize my own potential, if I was ever going to learn more and perform better. Instead of arriving at a level of proficiency that meant I could stop learning and start performing, I had to start learning in order to remove the barriers that were actually hindering my performance at that level. It may interest you to know, never once did he let up on me. Never once did he give up on me. What a great coach!

The third non-neutral learning event was like the first two, only on a much larger scale: Marine Corps Boot Camp in the summer of 1984. For Marines, this goes without explanation. For others, you may never be able to fully appreciate the impact it had on my commitment to learning and its contribution to my personal transformation and leadership enrichment.

These three non-neutral learning events forever altered the course of my life and my commitment to learning. They struck the spark of lifelong learning before I was 18 and helped me to realize my responsibility in kindling the coals of personal transformation. And the difference it made was remarkable. Like my Brother, Dr. D, after barely graduating from high school (2.667 GPA), I went on to earn an Associate in Arts Degree with a 3.8 GPA, a Bachelor of Science with a 4.0 GPA (cumulative GPA of 3.9) and I'm presently carrying a 4.0 GPA in Graduate School. In the years since 1984, I've continued to benefit from long-term relationships with many coaches and mentors, completed dozens of psychometric assessments and inventories and adopted simple techniques like "management by walking around" in order to continually elevate my awareness and increase my learning through multiple points of view.

Yes! There is incredible power in non-neutral learning events when we are *ready* to recognize when they occur and then are *willing* to take advantage of them on a regular basis. But there is an inherent challenge with this. Because non-neutral learning events often place us in a vulnerable position before others, we can easily choose to ignore them, leaving us in the doom-loop of oscillating between "getting ready" and "being unwilling." When I've been ready and willing, every non-neutral learning event has contributed in a unique way to personal intimacy (a.k.a., into-me-see). This may seem like a strange term to use, but "personal intimacy" easily translates into self-familiarity, self-understanding and self-confidence, all of which are essential to enriching leadership. By my estimation, they've **contributed in measurable ways** to enriching my personal *Leadership Platform*, and I have the year-over-year assessment results to support this assertion.

Dr. D's Reflections

A word of caution: LIFELONG LEARNING doesn't mean chasing every new trend. We all know that rarely works. But understanding current trends can be valuable—it gives insight into where others are in their thinking, which better equips you to lead them. I'm also not a big fan of certifications. Let's be honest: sitting through a week-long course designed to help you pass an exam isn't the same as learning. And it certainly doesn't prepare you to be a leadership practitioner.

Still, many of us have pursued those initials behind our names—whether required for a role or to boost credibility. But in the end, nothing delivers a better return on investment than real-world experience.

More importantly, they have **contributed immeasurably** to the impact I'm having on others and the difference I'm making on a daily basis at home and work, and in the community.

Platform Work ... Blueprinting/ Defining and Designing Your Platform

Now let's see how this plays into your platform design work. The goal here is to understand more about your current level of thinking and begin defining your leadership within the framework of a personal *Leadership Platform*. There are many opportunities to elevate your awareness and increase your learning when it comes to leadership, all of which can help you design a strong *Leadership Platform*. One way, already discussed in the introduction, is through formal or informal coaching and mentoring. Many coaches and mentors will recommend adding diagnostic instruments that are designed to provide you with vital feedback about your leadership. I happen to be one of them and have had a lot of success using them for myself and clients/ mentees over the years.

There are literally hundreds of assessments available on the market, including Career and Vocational Exploration, Coaching and Leadership Development, Personality and Personal Skills Assessment, as well as Self-Development; many of which are offered in 90^0, 180^0, 360^0 and 540^0 feedback variations. Some of the more popular include those that address personality (e.g., Myers-Briggs Type Indicator/MBTI®, DISC®, etc.), thinking styles (e.g., Human Synergistics International *Life Styles Inventory*™), personal skills (e.g., Performance Assessment Network/PAN®), competency (e.g., The Leadership Circle®, SumTotal®, etc.), performance (e.g., SuccessFactors™), or effectiveness and engagement (e.g., Kenexa®).

Dr. D's Reflections

Knowing yourself is a crucial part of growth. Remember: the only thing you truly can't do is what you haven't tried. Understanding your limitations isn't a weakness—it's the foundation for building a stronger platform. These limitations don't make your platform any less solid; they simply highlight areas where you might need to supplement with new strategies or support from others. Leadership is never a solo act. You're allowed—and encouraged—to bring in help.

Personal Platform

All of these assessments are valuable and can provide some level of new information about your leadership and how it is affecting others as you approach your daily work or recreation. If you are uncertain as to where you should begin, consult with a coach or contact the assessment companies directly. They often have staff that can assist in the diagnostic selection process, as well as in the administration, reporting and analysis. As you review feedback from the assessment(s), focus on your level of thinking about it so you'll remain open to learning. To the extent you remain open, the feedback will enable you to immediately question why you respond or act the way you do, and to take pains with the assumptions and values driving those responses. Both are basic to enriching leadership. You'll also be able to start understanding your personal leadership vision and get an early read on whether the mission, goals and strategies that emerge are really consistent with your values and vision. Most importantly, they will provide you with a great starting point for the next Leadership Enrichment Stages, where you'll make a commitment to changing your level of thinking, building an action plan around those worthwhile changes and ultimately building your *Leadership Platform* and documenting the "as-built".

Organizational Platform

My primary focus until now has been on the individual who wants to develop as a leader because, as established, organizational transformation begins with personal transformation. But Dr. D and I realized a long time ago that there is a tendency on the part of leaders—especially those new to the company or role—to start making organizational changes before any meaningful personal change occurs or before gaining any practical understanding of their new situation. Often this shows up by way of quickly assessing the organizational landscape, identifying friend or foe and immediately making changes to ensure you are surrounded by folks you can trust. We get it! The pressures to perform well and deliver results can be immense, and they are never higher than when you start to Take Your Lead in new ways. And we know how vulnerable you can start to feel when progress appears slower than expected. I'll introduce a different kind of "progress trap" later on, but this one—driven by myriad pressures, both internal and external—is particularly insidious. While trust between leaders with different management accountabilities is important, it's important to remember that it takes time to build. Equally important, before making changes to your team— whether in structure, function or person—take the time to thoroughly understand the current management team, the culture of the organization and the people at least one level up and a skip-level down in the hierarchy. Sometimes it's necessary to make changes and often this comes in the form of new talent from outside (or elsewhere in) the company; new talent chosen because they have a proven track record with you. Avoid rushing the process.

Dr. D's Reflections

Bringing in external talent can be essential at times, but it may also give the impression of what's sometimes referred to as 'Empire Building.' When I first encountered this, I assumed it meant leadership was overlooking internal talent. However, as I progressed in my career, I came to understand that when you're in a position of responsibility, it's critical to surround yourself with people you trust. That said, trust shouldn't be confused with surrounding yourself with people who think and act exactly like you. While that might feel comfortable, it won't drive sustainable, long-term organizational effectiveness. True leadership embraces diverse perspectives and complementary strengths.

If you're experiencing something similar, know that building trust with leadership is key to your own growth. And if you're the one building your 'empire,' make sure your team understands the 'why' behind your decisions. Transparency and inclusion go a long way in fostering trust and collaboration."

When you do decide to move forward, be sure to communicate clearly and thoughtfully with those affected by the changes.

Now, toward understanding more about current group styles, operating culture and levels of organizational effectiveness, there are many assessments that can help. Among them are the inventories from the Human Synergistics International Integrated Diagnostic System: the *Group Styles Inventory*™ (GSI), the *Organizational Culture Inventory*® (OCI®) and *Organizational Effectiveness Inventory*® (OEI) previously introduced. Here again, there are many other instruments on the market, including the Denison Organizational Culture Survey (DOCS). All are valid assessments, but they are only useful to the extent that you and your organization are willing to learn. In fact, I'm often asked: "What's the best survey for this?" or "What's the best methodology for that?" My answer is invariably: "The one you're willing to use." I recommend and continue to use for my own development and with my clients the assessments from Human Synergistics International, simply because of the statistical rigor they apply toward validating inventories, their ease of use and the level of customer service you receive in the process.

Perhaps one of the most important pieces of feedback you can receive at this point is what members of your organization say that your Ideal Culture ought to be. Remember, this is the culture that is based on the shared values of organizational members, so it is important for you to have this perspective for comparison to the Current Culture, which is more likely driven by the current structures, systems and skills/qualities put in place by senior leaders. We'll dig deeper into the structures, systems, etc., in the next Enrichment Stage. For now, just note the Human Synergistics International OCI® gives you both perspectives on culture with associated levels of intensity (i.e., consistency across members), and it is one of the most powerful ways I've found to understand the extent to which values are consistently shared by members of the organization.

If you are a senior leader—and this may come as a shock to you—the reality is that your actual impact on the organization may be different than what you intended. This is where the Human Synergistics International *Leadership/Impact®* (L/I) comes in handy. While we're addressing the organizational rather than the personal side in this section, they are linked. Your strategies—prescriptive vs. restrictive—as a senior leader influences the thinking, behavior and performance of those in your down-line and, ultimately, the culture of the entire organization. So it is vitally important that you learn something about your impact at this stage of the LEL-c. Undoubtedly, the frequency and style of your communication play a significant role in shaping those outcomes. But that's not all. Chances are, you're also influencing the

Dr. D's Reflections

Remember that game in kindergarten where the teacher whispered a message to the first student, who then passed it along the row until it reached the last person? By the end, the message was often completely different from the original. The same thing can happen with communication in leadership. Just because a message is sent doesn't mean it's received—or understood—the way you intended. That's why seeking feedback is so important. It helps confirm not only that your message was heard, but that it was interpreted in the right context. Lastly, be open to the possibility that your communication may not have landed as intended. You might need to clarify or reframe your message. This is where humility in leadership becomes essential—because you won't always get it right the first time, and that's okay.

structures, systems, technologies, and skills/qualities within your organization in ways that have unintentionally shaped a culture that diverges from the ideal. As a result, this misalignment may be driving outcomes you never intended or truly want. This is where the Human Synergistics International OEI mentioned a little earlier is both necessary and useful. I mention it here again because it is important that you collect the feedback that this inventory provides as part of Enrichment Stage # 1. It will become extremely valuable in the next Enrichment Stage, so be on the lookout for it.

Regardless of whether you are operating at the personal or organizational level, when it comes to assessments, feedback, etc., you must be willing to take pains with it head-on. All feedback, like all theory, is valid. Some is just more useful than others. It is up to you to determine its usefulness. This means that when you receive feedback about your leadership (i.e., your impact on others), regardless of the delivery mechanism, you must be willing to recognize it as extremely valuable, take responsibility for it and use it to validate or refute any assumptions your holding about things, people, the world, etc., as well as what's really important (i.e., your values) so you can learn about how to establish and continually reinforce your Personal or Organizational *Leadership Platform*.

This is where Enrichment Stage #2 – Internal Locus of Control enters the LIFE-cycle to carry feedback about personal and organizational leadership forward to the point of identifying worthwhile changes, and it's where we are headed next. From here on out the relationship between personal and organizational are so interconnected that they will be combined when it comes to *platform work*.

Summary – Enrichment Stage #1: LIFELONG LEARNING

Awareness leads to learning!

Thesis: Conscious Incompetence. If you want to start and hope to continue improving personal and organizational leadership, you need to develop knowledge through a deep desire for, and openness to, learning. Awareness is the essential emotional connector (measure of progress); Learning is the essential waypoint (measure of effectiveness).

Antithesis: Unconscious Incompetence. We still don't know that we don't know what we don't know or, worse yet, intentional incompetence... we know that we don't know and we don't care.

Dr. D's Reflections

You've heard the saying, "Ignorance is bliss!" But is it really? In the context of organizational culture, the impact is revealing. While ignorance might feel blissful to the one who's unaware, it often creates frustration, confusion or even dysfunction for everyone else around them. In leadership, what you don't know—or choose not to see—can hurt more than just you.

Enrichment Stage #2 - INTERNAL LOCUS OF CONTROL

Locus of control refers to a person's belief about what causes the good or bad results in his or her life, either in general or in a specific area such as health or academics, and the extent to which they believe that they can control events that affect them. Individuals with a high *internal* locus of control believe that events result primarily from their own behavior and actions... that their individual efforts count. Those with a high *external* locus of control believe that powerful others, fate or chance primarily determine events... that their individual efforts don't really matter much.

Spend any time in or around the high-performance/high-precision world of defensive tactics for law enforcement or military applications, and you'll inevitably learn that there is a common belief that, in a crisis situation, no one rises to the occasion; rather everyone defaults to the level of their thinking and training. As a result of this belief... this worldview, they spend a lot of time developing mental toughness and the right combative mindset through adrenaline stress conditioning and force-on-force (i.e., live-action, reality-based situations) training in order to be fully prepared for the worst that their missions regularly throw at them. In fact, the U.S. Marine Corps believes in this idea so firmly that it surfaces in the very terms they use to encour-

Dr. D's Reflections

In law enforcement, the unspoken ethos has always been simple: every cop makes it home at the end of the day. That requires a preparation mindset that includes training is what's required to look out for yourself, for your fellow LEO's, and for the welfare of the public. This is foundational. There is no higher calling than to protect and to serve others. That's how you earn the peace of laying your head down on the pillow each night with no regrets—only lessons learned. Because no matter how much you prepare, life (and mission) rarely goes exactly as planned. Preparation doesn't eliminate uncertainty, but it does reduce its impact."

age this training: "pain is only weakness leaving the body" and "the more you sweat in peace, the less you bleed in war." They aren't called our Nation's "force in readiness" without reason, and their level of thinking and training captures the essence of individuals with a high internal locus of control. Marines (and others with high self-efficacy) remove the words "luck", "fate", "chance" and "magic" from their vocabulary.

Those with a high internal locus of control have better control of their thoughts and behavior, and they are more likely to attempt to influence other people than those with a high external locus of control. They are also more likely to assume that their efforts will be successful. This is paramount later on, as the Performance Waypoint "Lead" emerges from the Emotional Connector "Achievement" when it is pursued with and for others.

In the first LIFE-cycle Enrichment Stage, we addressed the idea of alertness, awareness and curiosity producing ever increasing levels of knowledge through a commitment to Lifelong Learning. At this second point in the LIFE-cycle, if you want the knowledge you've gained through awareness/learning to CHANGE anything in a worthwhile way (i.e., in order to REALLY grow), make sure you are focusing now on ACCEPTANCE, the emotional connector, to help move you through this next stage. This step is tough because we can still come up with myriad reasons for our current thinking, behaviors and performance. What we need to realize is, reason equals excuse when we don't admit to others or to ourselves that we have a problem, that we are not living up to our potential. Whether it is an addiction, a bad habit, a character weakness or a fear that haunts you, the first step is to admit it and then to fully accept it. This means we see ourselves as not only responsible for our thoughts, behaviors and performance, but fully capable of changing them.

> **Opportunity:** *Rotter's I-E Scale (Internal-External Scale) is a psychological tool developed by Julian B. Rotter in 1966 to measure an individual's locus of control—that is, the degree to which people believe they have control over the outcomes of events in their lives. Take some time to find this scale and answer the forced-choice questionnaire. This will indicate where you currently fall on the internal-external continuum. Document the outcome here and date it so you have a baseline from which to compare future assessments.*

Emotional Connector – ACCEPTANCE

With genuine and complete acceptance comes the potential for real worthwhile change. This is perhaps the most compelling reason you should readily acknowledge what is not working in your life and for your organization. An alternative is to continue lying to yourself in two ways: 1) you can tell yourself something that is not true, or 2) you can leave out the details you don't wish to acknowledge. Either way, you gain nothing by deceiving yourself. Acceptance builds off the idea that you either get it, or you don't. If you lie to yourself, you are guaranteed not to "get it" and you will take either the wrong action, resulting in change that is not worthwhile, or you will take no action at all on real worthwhile changes.

According to Hale Dwoskin, in his book *The Sedona Method; Your Key to Lasting Happiness, Success, Peace and Emotional Well-being*, a simple process of releasing limiting emotions was originally inspired by Lester Levenson, a physicist and entrepreneur. Levenson believed that limiting emotions like *apathy, grief, fear, lust, anger and pride* must be released in order for our unlimited potential to be activated by emotions like *courage, acceptance and peace.* In short, these nine emotional states are already inherent in all of us, and courage and acceptance are the *unlimiting* emotions that remove the inhibitors to change. To underscore this point, Dwoskin shares the following story:

> *In 1952, at age 42, Lester was at the pinnacle of worldly success, yet he was an unhappy, very unhealthy man. Among his health problems were depression, an enlarged liver, kidney stones, spleen trouble, hyperacidity and ulcers that perforated his stomach and formed lesions. So unhealthy, in fact, that after his second coronary, his doctors sent him home to die. Instead of giving up, he determined to go back to the lab within himself and find some answers.* (Dwoskin)

What he discovered firsthand is that: "...we are all unlimited beings, limited only by the concepts of limitation we hold in our minds." To Levenson, these concepts of limitation were not true. Furthermore, because they're not really true, they can easily be released or discharged through a simple technique. According to the accounts recorded by Dwoskin in the "official" book, in 1973, he formalized this technique into a system called *The Sedona Method* so that others could teach it.

Dwoskin goes on to suggest that the reason so many of us frequently get stuck is that we don't know when it is appropriate to let go and when it is appropriate to hold on, and most of us err on the side of holding on—often to our detriment. When this happens, we more often than not "...suppress our emotions, rather than allowing ourselves to experience our feelings fully in the moment they arise", so they linger and make us uncomfortable. Through avoidance-based suppression, we prevent our emotions from flowing through us, either transforming or dissolving, and it doesn't feel good.

To provide an answer to this dilemma, *The Sedona Method* includes a handful of Basic Releasing Questions that can produce the courage that leads to full acceptance. And **releasing** isn't difficult. In fact, there is a roadmap to emotional freedom built into *The Sedona Method*, and Dwoskin proposes the roadmap flows through the nine emotional states mentioned earlier.

The states flow in increasing gradients of energy and action as you move from the most energy-limiting (i.e., *apathy*) to the most energy-releasing (i.e., *peace*). I'd encourage you to look at *The Sedona Method* closely, and as you review the scale of energy you'll note that the higher energy emotions of courage and acceptance ultimately lead to peace, but they are buried under all the limiting emotions (e.g., Apathy, Grief, Fear, et al.). As we let go, we begin uncovering those higher energy emotions, which actually hold the potential for worthwhile change. While it is gradual, every time we work through the process of releasing—no matter where we start—we'll find that courage can move us toward acceptance, which is essential for change. Any way you look it, the best we can expect from limiting emotions is the status quo which, according to the old southern preacher, is Latin for "the mess we's in."

This may seem more intuitive from a personal perspective, but the process of uncovering potential for worthwhile change and the consequences of failing to do so are the same on the organizational side. Looking first at the releasing process, any executive faced with the challenge of change will need to have the courage to accept what they've just learned about their leadership and culture if they are ever to move their organization forward. And we need look no further for consequences than that of Fear, a limiting emotion at the organizational level. Without much effort, we can easily recall what Dr. Deming said about fear more than 30 years ago in *Out of the Crisis*. In Point #8 of his 14

Dr. D's Reflections

Don't view letting go or releasing as if it were a "...two-ton heavy thing". Some of you will get that reference (thanks Queensrÿche, Empire). It is only heavy if you continue holding on to your own limiting emotions. In every problem there is opportunity. Challenging your initial perception (our default lens is a negative one that sees insoluble problems) and replacing it with a positive one that sees real opportunity will take conscious effort. Consider this: falling down is easy… it takes little to no effort at all but it really hurts. Getting up on the other hand is hard and can hurt even worse. This is why it requires courage. Make a conscious decision that, no matter the pain, you are determined to get up (in this case, release), recover and move past whatever caused you to fall in the first place.

Points to Management, he insisted we must: "Drive out fear." He also warned managers that FEAR was a natural consequence of Deadly Disease #3: "Evaluation of performance, merit rating, or annual review." Yet for all the supporting evidence we still haven't accepted these as firm reality statements and, as a result, Point #8 is overlooked and Deadly Disease #3 remains prevalent in most organizations.

Now, let's address the two key emotional states of Courage and Acceptance, where I really want to focus our attention. The first thing to say here borders on the obvious: if we're stuck in any of the limiting emotions, we'll lack the courage to accept what we have learned about ourselves and/or our organizations and remain incapable of changing it. If we can stretch ourselves through the roadmap to Courage, we will have made much progress.

> **Courage–** *When we experience courageousness, we have the willingness to act without hesitation. We can do. We can correct. We can change whatever, whenever needed. We have the willingness to let go [of what's holding change back] and move on....Our energy is high, available and clear. Our minds are much less cluttered than in pride, and a lot less noisy. We are flexible, resilient, and open. Our pictures and thoughts are about what we can do and learn, and of how we can support others in the same way. We are self-motivated and self-reliant while still being willing for others to succeed. We can laugh out loud, even at our own mistakes. Life is fun.* (Dwoskin)

Dwoskin goes on to say that, every time we say 'yes' to the releasing questions, we automatically tap into the energy of courageousness. This isn't easy! I'll readily admit this because I've pained through the releasing process. But it is possible, if we are willing, and it is essential if we are to move through the emotional connector of Acceptance to arrive at the performance waypoint of CHANGE.

> **Acceptance–** *Our bodies have a lot more energy than in courageousness. That energy is mostly at rest, yet available if we need it. Our energy is light, warm, and open. Our minds are much less cluttered than in courageousness, and mostly quiet and content. Our pictures and thoughts are in love with the exquisiteness of what is.* (Dwoskin)

I realize this may seem a bit odd, but the idea of acceptance doesn't mean we **have to** change anything, it means we **can** change anything. It means our energy is available to us, when we need it, to change what we want about ourselves and our organizations.

Human Synergistics International offers a few ideas on acceptance in the *Life Styles Inventory*™ (LSI) *Self-Development Guide;* guidelines they suggest are essential to our change-ability:

1. Acknowledge and accept all aspects of yourself. Remember, the question is not "Am I a good or bad person?" but rather "What is preventing me from being more effective, and what can I do to improve?"

2. Recognize that your sense of self-worth is not connected to your scores. You are worthwhile because you are a human being—tying your self-worth to outside factors can limit your ability to make positive changes in yourself.

Releasing limiting emotions to uncover courage and accept our underlying strengths and weaknesses can make a tremendous difference in whether we are able to change based on what we've learned. Courage promotes a new outlook on new information and enables us to accept who we are and what we've learned about our leadership from self-evaluation and the feedback of others. Both are essential to leadership enrichment because they help us to arrive at the performance waypoint: CHANGE.

Performance Waypoint – CHANGE

Change is difficult. In fact, it has been said that "no one likes change except a wet baby." – Anonymous. Regardless, change is inescapable if we are to enrich our leadership.

In order to understand what enables change, we need to address the antecedents. There are a few different things that can precipitate change. Among them are necessity, which is a forcing function that reduces our intrinsic motivation to operating from desperation; and contingency, which is a freeing function that enables us to operate from inspiration. Sometimes, it may be a matter of both. As William Pollard observed, "Those who initiate change will have a better opportunity to manage the change that is inevitable."

In this stage of the Leadership Enrichment LIFE-cycle, we are planning worthwhile changes based on what we have learned and accepted about our current level of leadership thinking, behavior and/or performance. This means we are operating from contingency, not necessity, which is better motivation. But initiating and planning for change also requires that we build a solid case for change.

Dr. D's Reflections

Remember my earlier reflection on Leadership Contingency? Change is easier when you have thought about contingency. Continually thinking about the "as-is" state affords you more opportunities to consider alternatives. These alternatives can help you to communicate the possibilities that lead to change and at that point the change was anticipated, vetted and is more likely to be accepted.

To this end, I love the simple *Formula for Successful Change* that Human Synergistics International sets forth in the OCI® *Leader's Guide*. This formula produces a compelling case for change and can help you avoid the common problems that inhibit change when these basic components aren't addressed. For example, if the Level of Dissatisfaction with the way things are is currently too low or not present (see first line of the model), we will not feel the need for change. Working down the model; if a Clear Vision of Change is missing, a lot of anxiety and confusion will result from the change effort. Simply put, the formula helps us reflect on whether the benefits are greater than the cost of change so we can be successful in the effort. Here is a crude representation to get the idea over so we can spend some time decomposing the major components:

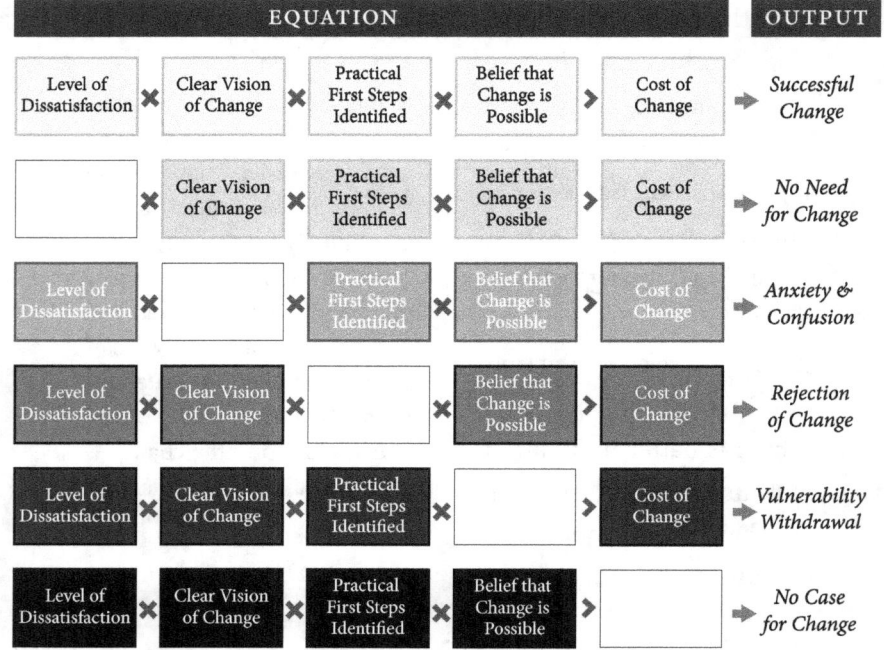

EQUATION					OUTPUT
Level of Dissatisfaction **×**	Clear Vision of Change **×**	Practical First Steps Identified **×**	Belief that Change is Possible **>**	Cost of Change **➡**	*Successful Change*
×	Clear Vision of Change **×**	Practical First Steps Identified **×**	Belief that Change is Possible **>**	Cost of Change **➡**	*No Need for Change*
Level of Dissatisfaction **×**	**×**	Practical First Steps Identified **×**	Belief that Change is Possible **>**	Cost of Change **➡**	*Anxiety & Confusion*
Level of Dissatisfaction **×**	Clear Vision of Change **×**	**×**	Belief that Change is Possible **>**	Cost of Change **➡**	*Rejection of Change*
Level of Dissatisfaction **×**	Clear Vision of Change **×**	Practical First Steps Identified **×**	**>**	Cost of Change **➡**	*Vulnerability Withdrawal*
Level of Dissatisfaction **×**	Clear Vision of Change **×**	Practical First Steps Identified **×**	Belief that Change is Possible **>**	**➡**	*No Case for Change*

This model is based upon the notion that effective change is a combination of leadership, direction and the implementation process (Huse & Cummings, 1985; Zaltman, Duncan and Holbek, 1973). – From the OCI® *Leader's Guide*, Plymouth, MI: Human Synergistics® International. Adapted by permission.

Now let's look carefully at each of these major components.

Level of Dissatisfaction (LD)– The starting block for planning change is the level of dissatisfaction we have with the way things presently are. Openness to learning and full acceptance of what we have learned has left us with energy that is available for making changes, but WHAT we choose to change, in large part, is determined by the areas where we have the highest level of dissatisfaction. Evaluating all the opportunities you have to improve your leadership (and by now you will have a number of them) by this single factor will help prioritize what you should be working on. To get started, ask: What aspect of my leadership am I least satisfied with today?

Clear Vision of Potential (CVoP)– The next block for building a case for change is having a clear vision of how

Dr. D's Reflections

The question of satisfaction is not to be taken lightly. In fact, you should ask yourself this question on a regular basis. Write it down. Keep that as part of your platform build. Just like asking yourself about what you wanted to be when you grew up... this question provides vector towards your leadership outcome.

things ought to (or could) be. Now that we know what to change, we can decide what to change to. This is incredibly important because without a known destination in mind it will be impossible to add the next block. To gain the advance, ask: What could this aspect of my leadership look like in the future?

Practical First Steps (PFS)– Getting to our change destination will require that we lay out only a few practical first steps. Recognize at this point that we don't have to have the entire journey mapped, just a general idea of how and, more importantly, where we'll start. Like the familiar quote from "A Journey to Silver Mountain; the story of one man's pursuit of excellence", sometimes "you can't get there from here." Find the best starting point for your journey and plan out a few practical first steps to get you moving toward your CVoP by asking: Where will I start and what practical first steps will I take to get there?

Belief that Change is Possible (BCP)– This block comes from the idea that our beliefs determine expectations of outcomes, and these determine our attitude, behavior and performance. This single block becomes a powerful multiplier when it comes to taking the first steps and staying the course. To confirm your beliefs, ask: Do I truly believe that this change is possible and will leave me better off than where I am today?

Cost of Change (CoC)– All of the previous blocks produce a benefit perception that, in the final analysis, must still be compared against our perception of the cost of change. If the perceived cost outweighs the benefit, we will likely never start and, if we do, we'll abandon the pursuit after the first set-back. To begin the comparison, ask: What are the perceived costs of this change?

Thinking back on a recent change I made in my career where the monetary cost of the change was a $42,000/year reduction in salary simply to find and follow a better leader, I can tell you with certainty that it was the output of this formula that made my decision to pursue that particular change both clear and compelling. For your take-way, however, you will want to quantify or qualify each component of the formula; if the outcome is positive, then you've built a successful case for change and are prepared for the next Enrichment Stage.

Dr. D's Reflections

These kinds of changes, although seemingly backward, are the vector changes I mentioned above. Sometimes, forward progress requires a few steps (or more) backwards to change your starting point and alter the course toward a more positive outcome in the future.

Barriers to Change

As you would expect, there are consequences when any one of the formula values is not present in the change formula. Human

Synergistics International suggests the following outcomes of omission:

- NO felt need for change: lack of MOTIVATION

- NO clear vision: FRUSTRATION

- NO belief that change is possible: INDIFFERENCE

- NO practical first steps: CONFUSION

These outcomes can certainly be avoided when each of these values is qualified/quantified. The formula for successful change even appears weighted on the side of the change enablers (e.g., four components get multiplied together (LD x CVoP x PFS x BCP) and only have to be greater than one component: CoC). That said, there is still a high risk of change failure. While CoC is only one component of the formula, it is extremely easy to elevate this value above the result of all the others. How is that? Why is that?

Well, we introduced earlier the personal and organizational limiters that promote the gap between knowing and doing. In Part 1, we established that there are personal thinking styles that produce an oppositional and avoidance orientation in the learner. In acceptance we outlined quite a few limiting emotions that keep us from acceptance and constrict our energy for change. Likewise, on

Dr. D's Reflections

The experience-driven "comfort zone." Are you in it? Can you get yourself out of it? You can! It comes at a cost… a significant investment in your own leadership stock. That's what this book is all about. Don't stay out of the market on this. Remove the reasons for resistance because they can become little more than excuses for why you don't want to change.

the organizational side, we outlined systemic issues that inhibit, demotivate, or dis-incentivize the learner and short-circuit acceptance. All of this adds up to an extremely high CoC value in the change formula when the leader tries to make the case. Subsequently, they aren't able to and nothing changes.

Again, I'll go back to something I first heard from my mentor, Smitty, and modify it only slightly: "Most managers would rather get a root canal than change [themselves or] the system." Personal and organizational leadership has not been tried and found wanting; it's been found difficult and left untried. Why is that? On the personal level, why do we continue holding onto experience-driven leadership styles or models when more effective ones have been firmly established by the evidence? Why do we continue to apply useless and outdated theories about people or how we ought to approach each other and our daily work in lieu of far more useful and modern ones? Why do we fail to change even when we know we ought to change? On the organizational side, why do we create structures and systems that make it so difficult for our members to change and improve their leadership?

Opportunity: *Take note of your thoughts on this. Answering these questions will provide insight into how you view change. As you read on… see how they compare with what's presented.*

_____

_____

_____

_____

There are explanations for these personal and organizational behaviors. Let's address the personal side first, because transformation begins with the individual.

Personal Resistance to Change

On the personal side, there are three elements that often misalign to create an inadequate change response: Science (MATTER or Existence), Philosophy (MIND or Intellect) and Spirit (HEART or Volition). One reason we resist change and hold on to the old way of doing things is because, *scientifically*, we aren't guided by theory. As a result, we simply cling to what we know by experience, which we already established is a poor teacher, and resist any new information that runs contrary. I've discovered in my own development and in the development of others that our tendency to cling to experience when confronted with new information is extremely hard to overcome, which brings us to a few more reasons.

The next reason we resist new information for worthwhile change when it comes to leadership enrichment is because, *philosophically*, the change is incompatible with our worldview/paradigm (e.g., core values, presuppositions, beliefs, biases, etc.)… our level of thinking about the world, things, people, etc. And because the heart cannot fully rejoice in what the mind does not comprehend, *spiritually*, it creates an internal conflict with our personal interests/desires (e.g., comfort, convenience, expedience, etc.), and our will to change is compromised. In fact, it is altogether possible for us to accept the scientific evidence that demands a change verdict yet still refuse to adjust our thinking because of the philosophical implications or do anything different because we don't have the heart for it. Unfortunately, this occurs more often than we know or may be willing to admit. In fact, this is why we won't change our mind in the presence of facts that suggest we ought, and it underscores why it is so important to adopt the openness to learning that we discussed in the last Enrichment Stage: LIFELONG LEARNING. It also explains why we don't abandon or reverse bad decisions once they are made, which we'll address again in the next Enrichment Stage: FULFILLMENT.

Opportunity: *Take a few moments to reflect on this. Does the thought of having to make some changes leave you feeling like there is something wrong with you or that to do so would require that you compromise who you've always thought yourself to be? Or perhaps you are questioning whether it's really worth it... will it really make a difference? Write down your questions and concerns about personal and organizational change in first person singular terms using the most potent emotions these concerns conjure up. This will help you take stock of where you are now as you endeavor to **Take Your Lead**... a proposition that remains perpetually before you.*

Leadership Enrichment, perhaps like no other development pursuit, cuts to the core of this extremely personal area. And as you might imagine, when we start to push our mind and heart, they push back…HARD! This makes change extremely difficult, so it either remains untried or goes unrealized. As discussed earlier in this Enrichment Stage, deceiving ourselves (e.g., exchanging the truth of what we've just learned with the lie that it is really false, or intentionally leaving out details we don't want to acknowledge) overrules acceptance.

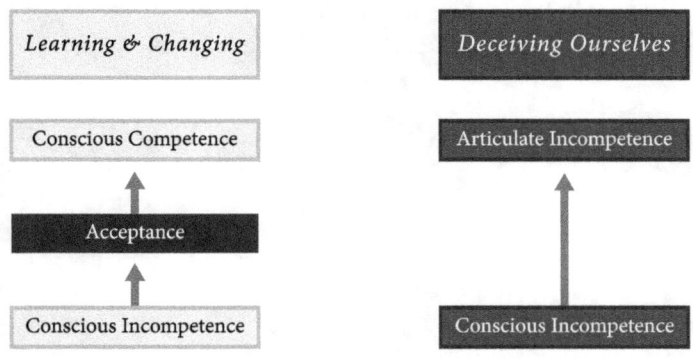

When Self-Deceit Overrules Acceptance.

As we learn and change, we progress toward a state of conscious competence. Contrarily, by deceiving ourselves, instead of moving from conscious incompetence to conscious competence, we end up in a state of intentional incompetence that, over time, produces an articulate incompetence. In the simplest terms, articulate incompetence is the outcome of our ability to rationalize why we rejected the new information (and the case for change) in spite of the evidence. Eventually, we become extremely articulate in our reasons (i.e., excuses) for not changing, even though we know better, and this ultimately short-circuits our ability to do anything different (i.e., the knowing-doing gap). It is important that we understand how hazardous this is to Leadership Enrichment and how often it really occurs.

Opportunity: *To what extent are you willing to challenge the status quo... to think outside your current boundaries for the betterment of the group and/or organization? This is a centering question because we cannot expect the organization to change if the leaders are unwilling.*

Organizational Resistance to Change

Let's not forget the other side of this flawed coin. As people, what we end up doing reflects our core values... consistent with our beliefs and presuppositions. But how does this work on the organizational side? How do organizations end up reflecting their core values, assumptions and beliefs? It may go without saying, but organizations don't behave rationally because people don't always think rationally. On the organizational side, there appears an image of this irrational explanation for change responses that result in systemic knowing-doing gaps: the Leadership—Culture connection.

Human Synergistics International defines the essence of leadership as the impact that a person has on the thinking and behavior of others and the culture that he or she ends up creating as a result (Szumal). Based on a large cross-section of data collected during applications of their *Leadership/Impact*®, *Organizational Culture Inventory*® and *Life Styles Inventory*™, they have concluded that a delta often exists between an organization's Ideal culture and Current culture because of the gap between how senior leaders want their managers/leaders to behave (i.e., knowing) and the behaviors that managers/leaders say their senior leaders actually promote (i.e., doing). For example, senior leaders say they want their managers/leaders to set challenging goals, be creative, be supportive and encouraging to others and to work co-operatively, but then actually promote the opposite through the use of exhaustive rules to justify actions, a strict adherence to standard operating procedures, doing things only to be seen and noticed and being indirectly critical of others. This results in the self-protective, critical and fault-finding, comparative and vying, controlling and forceful and risk-averse behaviors that employees routinely see their managers/leaders using. So, instead of a preferred culture with the behaviors those senior leaders believed would best help the organization achieve its goals, we end up with an operating culture where employees behave in critical, demanding and uncompromising ways, avoid blame, reinforce competition and follow procedures at all costs.

Bottom Line– If we are genuinely committed to closing the leadership knowing-doing gap at the personal level, we must reject the lies that we are tempted to tell ourselves and call into ques-

Dr. D's Reflections

I've always said that if you expect nothing, then everything is something. I'm not suggesting you should have no expectations or settle for less—only that your expectations should be level-set around incremental change. This mindset helps reduce the fear of failure that often accompanies change. Remember, trying and not succeeding isn't failure—it's a lesson learned. As Alfred, Lord Tennyson wrote in *In Memoriam*, "Tis better to have loved and lost than never to have loved at all." So go ahead—try new things, take risks, and move forward with no regrets... just lessons learned.

tion our long-standing values, presuppositions and beliefs. If we are committed to closing the leadership knowing-doing gap at the organizational level, we must recognize the leadership—culture connection and incorporate both elements in our change strategies (systems approach).

Our acceptance of ourselves and commitment to change in this Enrichment Stage builds off of what we established in the last Enrichment Stage: LIFELONG LEARNING and is intended to get us ready for the next Enrichment Stage: FULFILLMENT. Problem is... we know that not all change is worthwhile! Ellen Glasgow was noted as saying: "All change is not growth, as all movement is not forward." If we expect change from this stage to yield growth in the next stage, basing it on what we learned in the last stage is an important first step. But we're not out of the woods yet. The next step is going to enter through the very action we take to grow... the means we engage in the change effort (i.e., how we pursue change) and the motive we have for doing it (i.e., why we pursue change). This is why we'll spend some time on the 'how?', which is important, and the 'why?', which is critical.

Leadership (Internal Locus of Control) Vignette

I remember it well. In fact, I'll never forget the day I became a true professional. The date was August 31, 1984, and I had just graduated from Marine Corps Recruit Depot in San Diego, CA. Over the next decade, I had numerous opportunities to practice acceptance and increase my potential for worthwhile change. For the Marines, it's simple: "Mind over matter!" If you mind, it will matter. If you don't mind, it won't matter. If you are willing to accept the challenge, change is inevitable. Simple? Yes! Easy? No! While change is inevitable, pain is not optional if you intend to secure outcomes that are worthwhile. There are no pain-free shortcuts to worthwhile change.

We've all heard the body-sculpting phrase: "No pain; no gain!" But Marines are also taught things like "Pain is only weakness leaving the body!" and "Pain is only temporary, pride is forever!" This helps us to manage our own expectations and level-set around the fact that there is no free lunch. Someone has to pay. And for Marines, it begins Day One of receiving barracks at MCRD and becomes immediately personal. If you want to be a United States Marine, you have to personally earn The Title. It is never given; it is only earned. Then, once

Dr. D's Reflections

As an Airman, I can say the mindset forged in basic training is universal across the military—what differs is the level of pain endured. Approach building your leadership platform with that same grit: open-minded, feet forward. Those who succeed in the toughest challenges don't focus on the finish line—they focus on the next step. So each morning, ask yourself: What's my next step?

transformed, you are accountable to carry (and pass) on the traditions. The change is worthwhile, and it lasts forever.

But then my wife and I made the extremely difficult decision in 1994 to transition from The Corps so that I could start my career as a "civilian-Marine." Our goal was for me to spend more time at home and take a larger part in raising our first two girls who were five and seven at the time. And we reached our goal. After spending a little time in retail management and as a letter carrier for the U.S. Postal Service, I finally landed my first "professional" job as a civilian in 1995, and it didn't require travel. It was at a large Midwest pork producer. My position: Safety & Security Manager. My facility: Fresh Pork Division (code for "slaughter house").

Now it may be hard, but try to imagine jumping from the discipline, esprit de corps and camaraderie of the Marine Corps to a slaughter house in Detroit's inner city. Talk about culture shock. It was hard enough to take the Marine uniform off—perhaps one of the hardest things I've ever done. But to find myself in the chaotic torrent that pervaded this particular work place at the time was a non-neutral learning event in the extreme. To give you an idea of what it was like, we "processed" 13,000 hogs a day—from 'Kill Floor' to 'Cut Floor'—with 1100 employees (most of whom were strapped with a knife or wielding a saw of some kind) standing arms-locked in a 1.3M square-foot facility. And that wasn't the most interesting part. The most interesting aspects I don't want to reveal because you may never eat pork again but suffice it to say I was not very popular with the IPs—indigenous personnel. As a safety manager, I was expected to be the "the cop", ensuring everyone wore their personal protective equipment (PPE). As the security manager, I *was* the cop. When the *new guy* is perceived as the *new sheriff in town*, things are about to go haywire…and they did.

As expected, there was immediate push-back. Everyone on the floor was told by their supervisor that I was the new enforcer, so you can imagine how popular this made me with the United Food and Commercial Workers (UFCW) Union. At a plant where few actually wore PPE, you can easily imagine the first impression they had of me as a leader. And this was in spite of the fact that over 113 out of every 100 employees paid the price for it in injuries and illnesses each year. Yes! You read that correctly. When I came to that facility, they had an incidence rate of 113, which meant that, over the course of one year, the equivalent of every employee (i.e., 100 out of every 100) would be injured once, and 13 out of every 100 would be injured twice. It was, putting it mildly, what Peter Scholtes would call "train-wreck management" at its finest.

So what was I to do? I could *accept* my new situation and work toward identifying ways to *change* it, or I could ignore it and hope it would get better or go away on its own. Being the Marine that I am, I opted for the former and immediately began working with senior leaders, floor managers and union stewards in a way that many "managers" never did. I met them where they were at…on the plant floor.

First and foremost, I wanted to work on changing the impression that the hourly workers had of me. There was no way I could win a hearing with them if they didn't believe their effort in talking to me was going to pay off…if I didn't understand how they viewed my role or what their needs were. So I spent a lot of time on the Kill Floor and Cut Floor with them. I worked side by side with the workers in the Gambrel Room, where the temperatures exceeded 100 degrees Fahrenheit every day, peaking at 120 in the summer. I worked with them in the Chillers, where the temperatures were maintained at a bone-chilling 20 degrees year round in order to bring the temperature of the fresh pork down to 32 degrees in 12 hours for further processing. This gave me the unique opportunity to "walk a mile in their shoes" or, as the Japanese would say, to spend some time at the *Gemba* (the real place).

As a result of this simple leadership strategy, I heard repeatedly that product movers (e.g., hi-lo's, pallet trucks, etc.) were extremely unsafe and hazardous. They were seldom serviced and often responsible for worker injuries. And, wouldn't you know, after a little investigative work, I discovered they were right. So I did what every conscientious leader and great safety manager would do; I proceeded to remove the unsafe hi-lo's and mark them with red tags (meaning they couldn't be used until maintenance fixed the safety issue). I knew what this could mean and, sure enough, it had the effect of shutting the entire plant down because they didn't have enough product movers to keep up with production.

Within a half hour, the VP and General Manager entered my office. His first question: "What am I paying you for?" The second thing out of his mouth: "Come with me!" I'll leave much of what happened next to your imagination, but essentially I spent the next half hour at "six and center" off his desk getting educated on "how things really work around here" and "who's really in charge". Finally, at about minute 29, he charged me with removing the tags so they could get production going. It was at this point I had to make a choice. Was I going to exercise *courage* to accept the implications of my actions and push for the worthwhile changes that needed to be made or was I going to succumb to *fear* and allow that limiting emotion to rule the hour?

I chose courage and used it as an opportunity to "educate up". You see, the VP didn't practice *management by walking around*, so he simply didn't know how bad-off the workers were when it came to their own safety. He also didn't realize the financial impact from productivity losses each month being caused by the high rate of worker injury. After positioning both consequences in front of him, he reluctantly agreed that the worst product movers should remain tagged for safety maintenance. I then agreed that the best of them should return to production.

To my up-line (i.e., those whom I reported to), what started as an impediment to production actually increased productivity because I had the courage to change the point of view about the relationship it had with safety. To the workers, I went from being "the cop" to becoming their champion because I had the courage to change their point of view about a relationship with me. Tough? You bet! But worth every ounce of pain I suffered— recall the etymology of leadership includes passion, patience and suffering—that day.

Platform Work ... Building/Modifying and Reinforcing Your Platform

Now let's reflect on how all of this plays into your platform development work (i.e., building or modifying the Personal or Organizational *Leadership Platform*).

If this is your first time through the LEL-c begin with the Footing and, to the extent it is helpful, follow the outline of my *Personal Leadership Platform*. Once you have documented your personal Vision and Mission, as well as any Hallmarks (i.e., promises, assurances, guarantees, guards, etc.)—rooted in assumptions about yourself, others and your interdependency, as well as espoused values—move on to the Foundation and Framing. Recall that the Foundation and Framing of your *Leadership Platform* are what will actually distribute and carry the weight of those who choose to follow your personal lead...those who are members of your organization.

Be very discriminate here. As discussed, the best platforms are ones that have a positive impact on others by leading upward and/or outward, and they pursue goals (ends) in the right way (means), for the right reasons (motives). These will emerge from your Platform Footing. And when it comes to the materials for your Personal (i.e., Goals/Objectives, Strategic Priorities, Guiding Principles, etc.) and Organizational (i.e., Emerging Mission, Goals, Strategies and Policies) Platform Foundation, carefully select the ones that you believe will actually help achieve your desired impact, personally, or preferred culture, organizationally. All are not equally useful in this regard or suitable to this purpose, and you now know more about the difference.

Platform Framing is also crucial here, as we established in Part 1 that personal choices—such as leadership traits, operational imperatives, and managerial qualities—as well as organizational decisions regarding Structures, Systems, Technology, and Skills/ Qualities (SSTS), have both immediate influences on others and long-term effects on organizational culture through your impact as a leader. In both cases, the Framing can be built to ensure the impact is what you personally intended or what is organizationally preferred.

At this point, it may seem odd to address Artificial Intelligence (AI) as part of organizational STSS decisions, but it's now more a firm reality than it was back in 2012 when my first books were published. Moreover, every company is scrambling to harness its power for competitive advantage—but not without a measure of trepidation. A conversation with Dr. D underscored this in my mind. Someone in his network had recently expressed fear over Artificial Intelligence (AI). That fear—like many we've worked to dispel—often stems from a lack of understanding, so I'm including Dr. D's thoughts here as he originally shared with me:

> *As with any transformative technology, AI will inevitably impact organizational culture. Gartner recently reported that AI influences 77% of the average person's day—often without them even realizing it. That's a significant level of impact, whether people are aware of it or not.*
>
> *When Elon Musk was asked if AI would replace people, he replied, "Not if they know how to use it." That's the key. The technologies leaders choose to adopt will shape their organizations—for better or worse. Technology is never neutral; it's steeped in ethics and law. It can be used to empower or to harm. From a leadership perspective, lifelong learning means exploring what's possible. Adopting new technologies requires a social and cultural litmus test. Done well, it can fuel growth. Done poorly, it can leave lasting damage.*
>
> *Remember the old IT saying: "Garbage in, garbage out"? It still applies. Today's AI/ML and Model-Based*

Systems Engineering are only as good as the data they're fed. That's why two things are critical:

- *An Authoritative Source of Truth (ASOT) – Verified, clean, and unaltered data that drives reliable outcomes.*

- *Trust – Human oversight is still essential to ensure the data and its interpretations align with expectations.*

I think we should all follow Dr. D's lead and acknowledge that AI isn't something to fear—it's something to understand, guide, and use responsibly. Sounds a lot like it falls in the domain of leadership, doesn't it?

Dr. D's Reflections

I am not suggesting here that everyone needs to be an expert in the latest technology to be an effective leader. This gets back to understanding your limitations and finding the right people to mitigate or overcome them.

Now, back to your personal *Leadership Platform*. If you've already built it and this is your second or subsequent iteration through the LEL-c, consider how your it can be modified to better enable fulfillment of your vision and completion of your mission. Furthermore, to the extent you have learned more about your assumptions/values in the LIFELONG LEARNING Enrichment Stage and/or are now committed to changing as a result of what you just completed in this Enrichment Stage, you can revisit the Footing of your platform to work on Vision, Mission and Espoused Values.

Personal and Organizational Platforms

The effort here is largely the same when it comes to personal and organizational platforms. You are now at the point of using what you learned in Enrichment Stage #1 for the purpose of deciding what to change, and defining what to change to, as part of Enrichment Stage #2. If this is your first time through the LIFE-cycle, you'll need to identify core values and select goals that enable your vision/mission, as well as the SSTS that you believe will help you accomplish those personal or organizational goals based on your current level of thinking. This will largely be driven by experience as opposed to theory, unless you committed to being guided by theory prior to your first run through the LIFE-cycle. This is okay because you just learned a lot about your current thinking through the mentoring relationships and assessments in Enrichment Stage #1, and you can now make a commitment to change any one of them to something more useful and suitable.

Alternatively, if you've already moved through the LIFE-cycle a few times and have a well-built *Leadership Platform*, each repetition offers an opportunity to renew and improve. You are now guided by theory. If you recall, applying Deming's PDCA cycle was a great way to learn and, to the extent you've applied it toward the SSTSs you last selected, it will prove extremely valuable in confirming usefulness and adopting the most suitable. In other words, you already selected SSTSs your last time through Enrichment Stage #2, and then strength-tested them on a small scale in Enrichment Stage #3. If they improved the positive impact of your personal leadership on others or the impact organizationally on your culture, you began leveraging them on a broader scale through Enrichment Stage #4. No need to change this now unless you've actually found something better or feel the need to modify an existing SSTS, which is altogether possible as you begin repeating the LIFE-cycle. If something previously selected for your platform didn't work, you can now commit to using what you learned the next time through the LIFE-cycle. This is important because, in this regard, the LIFE-cycle can be repeated more rapidly with each new iteration. Any learning gained through strength-testing (Enrichment Stage #3) and leveraging (Enrichment Stage #4) can be used to expedite the process of arriving at the CHANGE performance waypoint. Lastly, when you repeat the LIFE-cycle, you really aren't starting over, you're simply reinforcing or remodeling what is already there.

Summary – Enrichment Stage #2: INTERNAL LOCUS OF CONTROL

Awareness leads to learning *and, through acceptance, releases your potential (energy) for worthwhile change, which must be carefully selected and planned.*

Thesis: Learning produces the potential (energy) for worthwhile change only through acceptance. Essential emotional connector is ACCEPTANCE! Essential performance waypoint is worthwhile CHANGE!

Antithesis: Denial, projection, or reaction formation, as effective defense mechanisms against acceptance, secure Intentional

Incompetence... the choice to remain where you are rather than risk worthwhile change. Over time, Articulate Incompetence sets in – more savvy, though less rational, arguments for remaining unchanged.

ENRICHMENT STAGE #3 - FULFILLMENT

The previous Enrichment Stage (i.e., Internal LoC) addressed the WHAT of Leadership Enrichment. But knowing "what" is not the same as knowing "how". This third stage will address the equally if not more important aspect of HOW. If we want to take and sustain ACTION on CHANGES that produce real, long-term GROWTH, we need to make sure we are focusing on changing the RIGHT things, (which we identified and committed to change in the first two Enrichment Stages) in the right way and for the right reasons. In other words, choosing an ethical way forward. This will ensure that we stay on track as courage and acceptance release the positive emotion (energy-in-motion) needed to propel us toward the goal of our leadership enrichment in the third Enrichment Stage of Fulfillment. Here's why: self-improvement as a goal is of itself a good thing, but to pursue it in the wrong way, by the wrong means or for the wrong reason is certain to get us off-track and corrupt/pervert the results. As Robert Wood Johnson of Johnson & Johnson once said: "Life has an overall purpose. Men must judge their conduct, not merely in terms of personal gain or convenience, but also as right or wrong."

Opportunity: *Take a moment to craft your Personal Purpose Statement. You can find mine in the Personal Leadership Platform section at the back of this book. Though I first wrote it long before Simon Sinek wrote about discovering and articulating your 'Why' in his 2009 book: Start with Why: How Great Leaders Inspire Everyone to Take Action, it follows a similar pattern to his Golden Circle model:*

Why – Your purpose, cause, or belief

How – The process or values that support your Why

What – The result of your Why (products, services, actions)

Emotional Connector – ACTION

A.W. Tozer once said, "Aimless activity is beneath worth and dignity of a human being. Activity that does not result in progress toward a goal is wasted." There is a proven action-sequence (i.e., a sequence of activity that precedes any action to ensure the change you are trying to make results in the growth you are looking for) that I'd like to introduce at this point. This approach—captured in the following graphic—is simple, extremely powerful and absolutely essential for action:

The Action-Sequence Model.

Step #1—Virtues as Values: You defined these in the first two Enrichment Stages, and now you must consult them to ensure your action will be consistent with the core values that are shaped by your highest virtues.

This is critical for a number of reasons. First, it allows you to remember what is really important in your life. Second, it gives you the opportunity to recall any changes you had in your thinking before you begin planning action. In all likelihood you made some adjustments. Finally, it ensures that motives which precede action, and implications which follow action, are carefully considered before you engage the means that promote action.

Every action we take along the way places us in the direction of right or wrong not just based on ends (i.e., expected outcomes or the goal of change), but on means (i.e., actions, how we pursue change) and motives (i.e., the reasons why we pursue change). Before acting, ask yourself "for what purpose am I doing this?" "What reasons do I have for wanting to make this change?" While achievement psychology teaches the more reasons we have for doing something the more likely we are to do it, it's not just a matter of quantity; it's a matter of quality...of having enough of the right reasons. While reason quantity provides emotional potency to propel us faster toward our enrichment goals, reason quality provides constancy of purpose around the goal itself.

A common motive today is "self-actualization" and, according to Maslow's extremely popular Hierarchy of Needs, it is the pinnacle of our potential and mental health. But this particular motive when taken to extremes can be prohibitive to true leadership enrichment for two primary reasons:

1. Self-actualization is a monistic view that considers only the natural or physical aspect of one's leadership qualities and defines one's ultimate potential in this world as such. Importantly however, it ignores the supernatural or spiritual altogether. In contrast, a dualistic view of enrichment is more holistic, considering both of these aspects and resulting in better development opportunity and richer leadership experiences.

2. Self-actualization places a primary passage of reference on self when, in fact, the best reason we could have for enriching our leadership is OTHERS.

For starters, this dualistic view secures what psychologists refer to as "unity of identity." Without room for details, this simply refers to our intuitive awareness that our identity remains undisrupted throughout the course of development or, in this case, leadership enrichment. The duality of the physical brain and the spiritual mind is a good illustration of this and, in Understanding the Times, Dr. David Noebel provides an explanation of what Dr. Paul Weiss, 20th Century scientist of distinction, originally wrote in Beyond Reductionism:

...since the physical substance of the brain is constantly changing, no unity of identity could exist if consciousness were a condition wholly dependent on the physical brain. Something more than the physical brain, something supernatural, must exist. (Noebel)

Advancing this idea, Dr. Noebel goes on to cite our human capacity to remember (i.e., memory), the distinct differences in mind vs. brain development/decline throughout life and the reality of free-will as ample scientific evidence supporting full acceptance of our dualistic nature. And along with it comes the realities of intellect, moral freedom and personal aspiration, all of which are required to act on worthwhile changes. As Michelangelo once quipped, "When the spirit does not work with the hand there is no art."

We see leaders get off-course a lot when the pursuit of self-actualization is taken to extremes. We'll see this again in our next Emotional Connector: ACHIEVEMENT, and we'll talk about some of the terrible consequences. For now, just remember the best examples of successful leaders that we have are those who first worked to become someone worth following and then created something of value for and with others. Our participation in the LIFE-cycle of Leadership Enrichment ultimately moves us from *something* toward *something* as we give ourselves away in order to inspire confidence in the ability of others to achieve great results. But first it tracks from *someone* toward *someone* as we become leaders capable of garnering followers and corralling them around a common purpose.

Indeed! Motives are good antecedents of selecting the right means/actions, so it is important to spend some time thinking about them (i.e., internal contemplation). And since the ends often impact others directly or indirectly, it is equally important to contemplate the implications of our actions before we take them. To do this, try using the voice of trusted others as an aid in coming up with the right motives for your actions or to assess their implications. This is best accomplished through informal feedback mechanisms like coaching/mentoring relationships, management by roaming or friendships. Regardless of the mechanism, a conversation with someone you trust is just as important as contemplation, and both can make a big difference in the motives for, and ends of, actions you take.

Dr. D's Reflections

This reminds me of what Stephen Covey described as "making deposits in the emotional bank"—actions that build trust, respect and goodwill in relationships. These emotional investments foster confidence in your leadership, and that confidence can help ease the fear that often accompanies change.

A recent study on ethical decision-making by Brian C. Gunia, Long Wang, Li Huang, Jiunwen Wang and J. Keith Murnighan from Northwestern University's Kellogg School of Management offers incredible insight into the value of contemplation and conversation when it comes to making right choices and acting on them. Their research revealed that "…84% of the participants who experienced a [3-minute] contemplation period or had a truly minimal moral conversation" acted ethically. In contrast, "…53% of the participants who made their decision without contemplation" or received unprincipled counsel during their minimal conversation acted unethically. They suggest, and I agree, the implication for leaders and organizations is clear: "… how people choose can have a dramatic impact on what they choose....Encouraging people to think and talk about their tough decisions can have remarkably positive consequences."

Now let's introduce the second step in the action-sequence:

Step #2—Vision & Strategy: Building off the level of dissatisfaction you have with certain areas of your *Leadership Platform*, the clear vision of future potential you've envisioned for yourself and the practical first steps you identified earlier in the Case for Change exercise from the last Enrichment Stage, this is where you develop a complete plan, including long-term strategies and short-term actions to accomplish your Vision of Potential. In this step of the action-sequence, all actions are planned, timed, set in motion and measured against specific targets along the way. In other words, this is goal-setting for goal-getting, the latter of which we'll expand on in the next Enrichment Stage.

At this point, it is important to remember that while creating a better version of you through self-improvement is a great, worthwhile and intrinsically good goal to have, that end of itself does not justify all the means of getting there, nor does it make it right (i.e., just because you have the power/ability to do something, doesn't mean you should do it). In other words, don't expect that you can actually begin DOING good without first BEING good. Put another way, shape the lens of your VISION for personal and organizational potential on virtues that inform your VALUES. As Dr. Jeff Myers puts it: "A person's view of the world determines the meaning that he gives to the things he sees; a vision-driven person works to see and perceive the world as it really is [Morality], and also the way he wants it to be [Ethics]."

Once you have ensured that your virtues inform your values and your vision of potential has become a strategic plan, you are ready to advance through the next steps in the action-sequence. Both individuals and organizations must also have a good understanding of the essential components for acting on the Case for Change previously created; otherwise, nothing ever gets accomplished.

Step #3—Support Structures: Ensuring the right systemic and structural fundamentals are in place to support the strategy and ensure your actions are effective and efficient is what this step is all about. This includes abandoning what doesn't (or won't) work as much as it means adopting new approaches. I find the failure to abandon ineffective habits, practices, methods and models, as well as useless theories more difficult, almost to a person. We tend to get hidebound to our own way of doing things and this holds us back. The awareness we gained during the first Enrichment Stage, if fully accepted during the second Enrichment Stage, has already enabled you to change your mind and commit to worthwhile changes. This is where, in specific terms, you get to decide on what you must stop doing (or do less of) in order to be successful.

Step #4—Skills: If you don't have the right knowledge to act on the changes you intend to make, stop here and do what it takes to gain that knowledge. Identify those around you or in your network who also have the skills you need or have made a similar journey and get them engaged in the process. In a very real sense, this will improve your starting point before you take widespread action and will ensure all follow-on activities are successful.

Now you are ready to act. This is as simple as "getting it done." Depending on the size or scope of the endeavor, you may want to take advantage of various tools that are designed to help manage work (i.e., work breakdown structure) and monitor effort/outcomes (i.e., work plan and schedule).

Following this approach will help you avoid the negative consequences of failing to think the process through before working it out. These consequences include false starts, delays/ rework, confusion, frustration, anxiety, et al. When you know you are doing the right things for the right reasons and by the right means, there is intrinsic value in, and motivation for, the work itself. It also enables both joy and pride in the effort. Joy produces strength; pride produces higher confidence (from the Latin words: *con* and *fideo*, meaning "with Faith"). Both are essential sustenance for long-term, systemic growth. If you question that, think about the last time you experienced a false-start or got off-track during the pursuit of some goal. Chances are, the goal itself was worthwhile and intrinsically good but, because your motives were off (i.e., you had the wrong reasons) and/or the means were off (i.e., you chose the wrong method), the action stalled or the effort derailed. This reinforces the idea that real growth seldom

> ## Dr. D's Reflections
>
> Remember this is not something you have to do alone. No one takes their lead without the help of others.

happens rapidly and reminds us that, if we persevere and stick it out, we will grow. Patience and perseverance are necessary for leadership enrichment to occur.

Performance Waypoint – GROW

Webster's first definition of this intransitive verb is: "to spring up and develop to maturity." Likewise, his last definition includes the following: a) "to pass into a condition"; b) "to have an increasing influence"; and c) "to become increasingly acceptable or attractive." I believe all of these are applicable to our use of the term "grow" here and, when viewed in light of this definition, I can't imagine why we wouldn't want to grow.

Ironically, I have to contrast this with the firm reality that we tend to fear growth or simply don't want to grow at all. There is an old Chinese Proverb that states: "Be not afraid of growing slowly; be afraid only of standing still." Even more tragic, we all seem to fall under the indictment levied by Johann Wolfgang von Goethe: "Everybody wants to be somebody; nobody wants to grow."

The fact is, growth is a natural process, but the type of growth we're after often doesn't come easy. The LEL-c is specifically designed to make growth as *real leaders* easier and more systematic. From our first iteration of the LIFE-cycle, it requires that we adopt what Carol Dweck calls a Growth Mindset. According to an editorial review on Amazon by Publishers Weekly, "Dweck proposes [in her new book: Mindset: The New Psychology of Success], that everyone has either a "fixed" mindset or a "growth" mindset. A fixed mindset is one in which you view your talents and abilities as... well, fixed. In other words, you are who you are, your intelligence and talents are fixed, and your fate is to go through life avoiding challenge and failure. A growth mindset on the other hand is one in which you see yourself as fluid and adaptable; a work in progress. Your fate is one of growth and opportunity." I would replace the words 'fate' with 'future' but, other than that, on the basis of how Publishers Weekly describes Dweck's proposal of a fixed vs. growth mindset, I couldn't agree more. And having read or progressed this far in the LEL-c, I'm sure you feel that you'll definitely begin adoption of a growth mindset as you iterate through the LEL-c and develop your *Leadership Platform.*

Growth in the context of enriching our leadership means we have acted on worthwhile changes and, as a result, have grown in appropriate ways....in maturity, influence, acceptability and attractiveness. It also implies we are able to achieve more than before and lead in ways never before imaginable, which we'll discuss in Enrichment Stage #4. But here again I want to pause for a quick cautionary note. Remember the quote from Stuart Emmett introduced in the first Enrichment Stage: "When I learn, I have to do something—therefore—I Change." Well, change produces growth because the actions we take are suitable to that purpose. Our growth is locked in a cause-effect relationship with the energy we cultivate through our actions.

I realize we've already spent a lot of time on motives, means and ends related to the actions we took to grow, but I just want to reinforce the idea that not all growth is desirable. Edward Abbey once quipped: "Growth for the sake of growth is the ideology of the cancer cell." He is spot-on. We've likely all had occasion to observe in ourselves and in others, undesirable growth. If we cultivate the wrong things in the wrong way and for the wrong reasons, things will continue to go wrong and we'll grow in ways that do not enrich leadership. So, as previously mentioned, ensure that you are focusing on changing the right things in the right way for the right reasons and you will stay on course.

Leadership (Fulfillment) Vignette

By 1997 I had come a long way as a civilian-Marine. The 2-plus years I spent at that Fresh Pork Facility between 1995 and 1997 were years of incredible leadership enrichment, both personally and organizationally. But it was time to move on. My next position took me to the automotive industry where I would spend the next seven years moving through a few career fields and a number of different roles to go with each. Early on, I was faced with a challenge that required action on a scale I'd never experienced with the promise of personal and organizational growth never before available to me. In the fall of 1997, I was promoted to a corporate position and given the responsibility of leading the development of a global safety management and operating system for a company that was just formed through a merger of three distinct international organizations. No small task.

I immediately discovered, like most in a post-acquisition integration effort, that there were actually many "ways of doing things" in the newly formed business units (BU's), often in conflict with one another. Shared services organizations were yet to gain popularity in business, so each unit was given the responsibility of managing safety in a way that seemed best to them. So my challenge was not only to find a common ground so safety could be standardized across all BU's where it made good business sense, but also to gain buy-in from each BU leader in the effort.

The first steps were to learn everything I could and identify what needed to change and how in regard to safety—something we spent a lot of time on in the first two Leadership Enrichment Stages. By early 1998, I had adopted a new theory for safety management that was going to transform the organization and enable each BU to standardize its approach, save money and increase productivity. All I had to do now was figure out how to implement it. The right kind of action was required if this type of growth was going to occur.

The next steps are what made all the difference. Following the Shewhart-Deming PDCA approach and invoking the action-sequence outlined above, I gained approval from senior leaders to conduct a pilot at one of the facilities impacted most by injury and illness, and I worked through the General Manager of that facility to win a hearing with his up-line. There were a lot of skeptics. Few could see the usefulness or necessity of safety management in their operations let alone the distraction imposed by a pilot activity designed to improve the situation. Nevertheless, because I was able to find an operational champion amongst their peer group, they were willing to "indulge" me.

Needless to say, the safety pilot was a success. But for those of us who have been around for a while, we know that doesn't mean very much for the organization as a whole. If you're like me, you've seen many successful pilot programs never reach their full potential. In fact, there was another initiative I undertook with a different business unit in this same company a few years later that proves this point. Essentially, I worked with the senior leader of that BU to charter a self-directed work team around designing and implementing a formal mentoring program. It too was successful but for reasons I'll have to save for another book (hint: they have to do with disruptions in the action-sequence), it never advanced beyond its success at the BU level.

The challenge with the safety pilot had shifted from proving the concept in a pilot to selling the concept in a boardroom. Borrowing some insight from Neil Rackham in *SPIN Selling*, I laid out the situation, problem, implication and need related to a global management and operating system for safety. I first tied values with vision, vision with strategy, strategy with structures and resources and resources with skills and qualities. Then I laid out an action plan for organizational roll-out. It was not easy. In fact, it took all of the things we've been talking about up to this point in the LIFE-cycle. It took increasing my *awareness* of the vision, challenges and obstacles in order to *learn* about the current and desired future state of safety within the organization (e.g., Enrichment Stage #1). It took courage to *accept* the situation as it was, gain this acknowledgement from the organization and work with others to design a *change* solution that fit and solves the problems (e.g., Enrichment Stage #2). It was now going to take wide-spread *action* from a lot of people to *grow* safety performance (e.g., Enrichment Stage #3).

Entering the boardroom, perhaps the biggest skeptic of them all was the Senior Vice President...the one who sat at the head of the table. Many of the GM's had already gotten to him during the pilot and were successful at convincing him that this change wasn't worthwhile or it couldn't be done. I remember feeling a high level of trepidation walking into that room, but I did it anyway. It really wasn't about me; it never was. It was about making a positive difference in the lives of many workers being injured every day.

About two thirds through the presentation, the stoic SVP at the head of the table stopped me abruptly. I thought: "Darn! This is where he's going to tell me how ridiculous this is and ask me to stop wasting his and everyone else's time!" But that didn't happen. Instead, he looked around the room at all of his GM's and asked: "Do all of you understand what Richard is saying? Do you know how vital this is to our future…to our bottom line?" From that moment on, it was "all systems go".

This meeting represented a growth event in my own enrichment as a leader because it forced me to move through the three Enrichment Stages (as referenced above). As a result of my commitment to the LEL-c and that SVP's commitment move in the conference room that day (e.g., management speaks its commitment through making resources, money, time, etc. available), the pilot was successfully expanded across the organization. As a result, the incidence and severity rates of the company were on a precipitous rate of decline from baseline performance, and this ultimately reduced workers' compensation cost and increased net profit on sales. In fact, our global management and operating system was successful enough to earn benchmarking visits by Wyeth-Ayerst Pharmaceuticals (part of American Home Products) and Callaway Golf.

And in case you are tempted to say: "Not bad for the son of an under-educated cotton-picker from Arkansas," please know that it was a team of folks who were responsible for this ultimate ACHIEVEMENT…not one individual…and we're going to spend some time on what this means from a personal and organization perspective in the next Leadership Enrichment Stage: EXCELLENCE.

Platform Work ... Strength-testing/ Validating Your Platform

At this point, we need to spend some time on understanding how much we've grown… how far we've reinforced our *Leadership Platforms* through strength-testing. We'll need our baseline results from earlier personal (i.e., thinking style) and organizational (i.e., culture, effectiveness, or leadership impact) assessments for comparison so we can, in essence, validate our *Leadership Platforms* through the voice of those who are impacted by it on a daily basis. Remember that gaining feedback is key to ensuring that the impact we are actually having as a leader matches the impact we intended to have. If not, now is the time to make changes to our platform.

Repeating the same assessments first applied during the Lifelong Learning leadership Enrichment Stage will refresh the data to show progress, as well as uncover any future development opportunities. The results will either support the fact that you have learned, changed and grown successfully (i.e., you really are thinking in new ways) and effectively (i.e., you are having the impact you intended to have, as documented in your platform). In other words, it will help confirm that you are leading in ways consistent with changes to your personal platform and that your organization's Current Culture is becoming more like its Ideal Culture. If so, Leadership Enrichment, whether related to Footing, Foundation or Framing, can be validated and the platform strength-tested.

Personal and Organizational Platforms

Again, you'll see relatively the same effort for both personal and organizational platforms. Begin by asking a couple of basic questions aimed at the same target. Personally, have you elevated your thinking styles to the point that you are now more constructive in your approach to others and your daily work, as reflected by changes you've made to your *Leadership Platform*? Organizationally, have you moved your Current Culture closer to the Ideal Culture by changing the cultural antecedents to the point that they reinforce espoused values or by improving your impact as senior leaders?

Consider again this critical element of leadership etymology as captured in my personal *Leadership Platform's* Vision/Mission statement: "move upward and/or outward." This is a vital part of leadership, and it requires that you continue to grow vertically (i.e., up) in your thinking and horizontally, (i.e., out) in your core values and SSTS. Anything that takes away from this **is not** leadership enrichment. Anything that undergirds and supports this movement **is** leadership enrichment.

Summary – Enrichment Stage #3: FULFILLMENT

Awareness leads to learning and, through acceptance, releases your potential (energy) for worthwhile change that must be carefully selected and planned. *Potential is fulfilled through taking action on worthwhile change in the right way and for the right reasons (for others), which produces real growth.*

> **Thesis:** Action around worthwhile change is empowered by intrinsic motivation…if you have enough of the right reasons and follow the right methods—you will enable growth. Essential emotional connector is ACTION! Essential performance waypoint is GROW!

> **Antithesis:** "The Disciplined Pursuit of Less" - Greg McKeown

ENRICHMENT STAGE #4 - EXCELLENCE

The third Enrichment Stage of Fulfillment ultimately brings us to a final Leadership Enrichment Stage: EXCELLENCE. The LIFE-cycle began with Enrichment Stage #1: LIFELONG LEARNING, and along with it came the discovery that there is a new and better way of thinking about us, our situation, others and our world when it comes to Leadership. This new information about our leadership elevated our awareness and resulted in the opportunity to learn more about our current thinking, behavior and performance... what is working and what isn't. Since it was never intended that we should stop here, we moved onto Enrichment Stage #2: INTERNAL LOCUS OF CONTROL. This enabled us to fully accept what we had learned and plan worthwhile changes in our leadership thinking, behavior and performance... changes that can have a direct impact on others through personal and organizational leadership. Enrichment Stage #3: FULFILLMENT touched us through the emotional connector of Action so we could challenge ourselves to arrive at the performance waypoint of Grow, and it was the hardest to move through. It was also the only way to actually enrich our leadership in a practical, pragmatic way to prepare us for personal and organizational excellence, which is where we are headed next.

Before getting there, however, it is critical to pause and give added reference to something that's been presented throughout this book. Having labored to this point, you've already seen the word "others" seventy-seven times, and it will be eighty before the end of this paragraph. You've read it enough to know that your leadership has as much to do with someone else as it has to do with you, and that it is *for and with* others where we actually begin to increase economies of scale when it comes to our impact. You also know that leadership is personal first as we become someone capable of leading, then it becomes organizational through *movement by appointment* as others choose to follow. This intense, unwavering focus on both self and others when it comes to leadership is not accidental.

Nowhere else in the LIFE-cycle of Leadership Enrichment does our focus on Self in relation to others become more important than at Enrichment Stage #4: EXCELLENCE, for a couple of reasons. First, it is extremely easy to forget our intrinsic worth and value in the Leadership Enrichment equation and thus to place too much reference on others in the wrong way. Second, it is equally easy to lose perspective and place insufficient reference on others, forgetting that they are central and basic to moving upward and outward with passion, patience and perseverance, whether the movement is personal or organizational.

We'll need to keep a wary eye on both as we pursue Excellence as a part of Leadership Enrichment, which includes the emotional connector of Achievement, and the subsequent performance waypoint Lead.

Emotional Connector – ACHIEVEMENT

This idea is as misunderstood and misattributed as the phenomenon of leadership itself. So, it would help to spend some time defining it in terms of the LEL-c.

When I think of achievement, three primary contributors come to mind: Dr. J. Clayton Lafferty (*Roots of Excellence*), Brian Tracy (*Psychology of Achievement*) and Dr. Jim Loehr (*Mental Toughness*). I've made investments in, and successfully reaped rewards from, each one of these phenomenal works over the years. And I still find myself referring back to them for a refresher from time to time.

But for tracking achievement from a personal thinking style to group styles to organizational culture and effectiveness, no one had it figured out like Dr. Lafferty at Human Synergistics International. Clay, as he was known by many, believed "Personal Effectiveness Builds on Achievement." After years of research, he found that thought sequences in achievement (i.e., our achievement-orientation) correlate strongly with personal effectiveness. Individuals who think in achievement-oriented terms are:

> ...*more effective, reach higher salary levels, experience less stress and physical illness, and are generally more respected by their peers as having accomplished something.* (Lafferty)

As a matter of fact, organizations that contain higher levels of achievement are also more effective and perform better than the competition. And to help organizations measure and improve performance along the continuum, Dr. Lafferty and Human Synergistics International created a Circumplex (reflects both the current and intended/preferred states for individuals, others, groups and the organization) and knitted them together in an Integrated Diagnostic System to track improvements from personal to organizational levels.

For all of this, perhaps the most significant contribution to my leadership development and my approach to elevating organizational leadership were a handful of ideas about achievement that Dr. Lafferty shared in *The Roots of Excellence* (Lafferty), a video that truly changed things for me and the organizations I serve [exposition added]:

1. Passion for Personal Excellence [not winning at all costs or perfection]

2. Belief in Cause and Effect [the opposite of luck, fate, chance and magic]

3. Belief in the Idea that Individual Efforts Count [self-set goal-getting, not just goal-setting]

4. Moderate Risk Taking [small, incremental improvement; no stretch targets or BHAG's – Big Hairy Audacious Goals]

5. Desire and Design for Feedback [from others and the system, regardless of form or delivery]

The 1987 video is extremely rare and hard to obtain, since it is no longer being produced. You have to personally know someone like me who has a copy on VHS. This is why I'm going to dig a little deeper into each of the ideas listed above to give you an opportunity to benefit as much as I did. I've decomposed and clarified them on the basis of how they were applied toward building my *Personal Leadership Platform.*

Idea # 1 - Passion for Personal Excellence

Of all the things the human brain can preoccupy itself, it can preoccupy itself with winning. But a preoccupation with winning without paying attention to excellence in performance doesn't mean very much. If you don't have

*the skills and aren't excellent at what you do, the desire
to win is empty.* (Lafferty)

What we've learned from the research of Dr. Lafferty, Dr.
Jim Loehr and a host of others is: the more preoccupied we are
with winning, the more likely we are to lose. In fact, Dr. Lafferty
discovered this idea of Excellence (i.e., being good at what we do)
correlates at 0.54 to the outcomes in athletic events. This means
that more than 50% of the variance in athletic performances can
be explained by a preoccupation with getting good... A PASSION
FOR EXCELLENCE.

PASSION is, in a very real sense, *a constructive or healthy
preoccupation with, or attachment to, something.* In this case:
EXCELLENCE.

Earl Nightingale, Dennis Waitley, Brian Tracy, Zig Zigler,
Tony Robbins, Tom Peters and a host of others have written
and spoken exhaustively on the subject of personal excellence.
In fact, we spend a lot of time defining "Excellence", and we
have more than a few examples that prove how we think about
it truly matters. But for all that has been said, it boils down to
one thing: hard work! Excellence is a tough, uncompromising,
never-ending journey or pursuit that must engage every area of
our *Leadership Platforms* in order to continually produce results
or gains. And it must be pursued with the same conditions for
motive, means and ends that we discussed in Enrichment Stage
#3: FULFILLMENT...or we know how it can degenerate.

EXCELLENCE, in a very basic sense, is *doing what is right, no
matter the cost, to continually renew and improve who we are
and what we do.*

Putting it all together, **a Passion for Personal or Organizational Excellence means having a healthy preoccupation with the tough, uncompromising, never-ending pursuit of doing what's right in order to get better at who we are and what we do.**

But how do we avoid turning this into a "win at all cost" pursuit? It may not yet be intuitive, so this may be a good place for a cautionary interlude in our understanding of achievement. Our passion for personal excellence as a part of achievement must never be construed as an individual effort. John W. Gardner writes about this challenge for America during the Industrial Revolution in "EXCELLENCE: Can We Be Equal and Excellent Too?"

> *It soon became apparent that emphasis on individual performance can be pushed to extremes; and we now know that there are hazards in such extremes. "Everyone for himself and the devil take the hindmost" is a colorful saying but an unworkable model for social organization. No society has ever fully tested this manner of organizing human relationships—for the very good reason that any society which carried the principle to its logical conclusion would tear itself into pieces.* (Gardner)

Gardner goes on to write that, although our laws against such things are designed to prevent such mayhem, even within the bounds of that law extreme emphasis on individual performance "...as a criterion of status may foster an atmosphere of raw striving" that ultimately results in what the law was trying to prevent. This is why I mentioned earlier that our leadership can't be built around a company "code of ethics" and that leadership, as attained and applied through the Leadership Enrichment LIFE-cycle, is intended to be constrained (i.e., governed) by righteousness or "the moral law", otherwise motive, means and ends get perverted and bad things naturally begin to follow.

Moreover, C. S. Lewis reminds us of an extremely sobering and humbling aspect of our impact on others in his closing to *The Weight of Glory* [emphasis added]:

> It may be possible for each to think too much of his own potential glory hereafter; it is hardly possible for him to think too often or too deeply about that of his neighbour. The load, or weight, or burden of my neighbour's glory should be laid on my back, a load so heavy that only humility can carry it, and the backs of the proud will be broken. It is a serious thing to live in a society of possible gods and goddesses, to remember that the dullest and most uninteresting person you can talk to may one day be a creature which, if you saw it now, you would be strongly tempted to worship, or else a horror and a corruption such as you now meet, if at all, only in a nightmare. **All day long we are, in some degree, helping each other to one or other of these destinations.** It is in the light of these overwhelming possibilities, it is with the awe and the circumspection proper to them, that we should conduct all our dealings with one another, all friendships, all loves, all play, all politics. There are no ordinary people. You have never met a mere mortal.... it is immortals whom we joke with, work with, marry, snub, and exploit—immortal horrors or everlasting splendours. (Lewis, The Weight of Glory)

Based on what we know about leadership, what truth is C. S. Lewis pointing out? Every day we are leading, whether we know it or not. It is my contention that we are using both our potential and performance as leaders to control outcomes for ourselves and influence outcomes for those around us, and he is right to remind us of the gravity of the situation. If we are leading upward and outward, it will aid others toward everlasting splendors. If we are leading downward and inward, it will aid in unimaginable horrors. As it is said of sin itself… it will take you farther than you want to go, keep you longer than you want to stay and cost you more than you want to pay.

Opportunity: *Consider how quickly something can happen— just seconds or minutes. Yet we often dwell on it far longer. A moment like being cut off in traffic might ruin someone's day—or, in extreme cases, lead to life-altering consequences through road rage. If less than 5% of life is what happens to you, and 95% is how you respond, then you hold more control than you might think.*

Take a moment to reflect: How are you letting the 5% of what happens at work influence your ability to lead? Are you guiding others upward and outward—or downward and inward?

To avoid the negative consequences described by Gardner and Lewis, I believe we need to continually remind ourselves that our pursuit of Excellence—the effort toward getting better at who we are and what we do—translates best through the concept of **participative enrichment.** The idea here is to find others to partner with us in the journey... the coaches and mentors mentioned earlier, as well as those who choose to follow our lead. In fact, this very idea fueled the selection of Dillard Partners LLC as the name of my first consulting firm. As partners in the journey, coaches, mentors and consultants can help us build strengths, uncover blind or weak spots, identify new opportunities and avoid threats/dangers lurking unaware (i.e., traps which are hidden in plain sight) to ensure we stay the course and continue to achieve in ways that maintain a resolute focus on others.

But we need to be careful here, as we could easily place so much reference on others that our own self-worth gets tied to whether or not they "approve" of us. Returning to Dr. Lafferty once again, he believed that we can easily fall into the trap of getting preoccupied with this. Commercials on TV and radio and in print inundate us with the notion that our sense of self-worth is tied to others' approval of us...if we'd just buy the right products or wear the right clothes, somehow we'd be more worthy. And in case you think that this is a benign issue, consider that the former director of marketing for Tommy Hilfiger, Gordon Pennington, estimates: "Western society sees over 60,000 audio and visual advertising images daily."

On the other hand, Dr. Lafferty also thought that we could get preoccupied with power, prestige, influence, status and control; and somehow we'd begin to see all of these as measures of personal worth when, in fact, "...they are hollow, they don't change the issue and they bear no relationship to personal effectiveness." Here again we find the extreme emphasis on performance as a criterion of status, just like Gardner warned.

A Passion for Personal Excellence through participative enrichment is important because, when it's not there, these other things begin to substitute for it and the result is an increase in passive thinking and behavior (i.e., approval orientation) or aggressive thinking and behavior (i.e., perfection, competitiveness, or the desire to "win at all costs"). Either way, it is defensive thinking and precisely the point at which compromise creeps into our value system. When this happens, it shifts our leadership focus and energy from a pursuit of excellence in achievement *for and with* others toward one of two defeating directions: (a) the *approval* of others as a matter of our self-worth or (b) the *dismissal* of others out of self-advancement or self-preservation.

To put this into perspective as it relates to participative enrichment, the only cell in our human body that lives for itself is the cancer cell…every other cell in the body lives to enable all the other cells. This means that we must recognize we have intrinsic worth and value—that we are healthy cells—before we can live to enable others. It also means we must choose cooperation over competition if our goal is personal or organizational excellence in achievement.

The extent to which excellence is pursued through participative enrichment and not viewed as a measure of personal worth or a means to self-advancement will determine the extent to which our leadership performance can be characterized as "outstanding." Put another way, excellence pursued simply because it can be done, for and with others, characterizes outstanding personal and organizational leadership performance. But for the best way

Dr. D's Reflections

Preoccupation with what others think of you breeds doubt—and self-doubt can quietly crush a leader. If your definition of achievement is based solely on others' validation, you'll never reach excellence. You'll chase it endlessly, only to settle for their marginalized version of you, which is mediocrity. So, **Take Your Lead**!

of stating it, I defer to one of Dag Hammarskjöld's writings, published posthumously in the book *Markings* and cited by Dr. J. Juls in *From Theology to Mystagogy*:

> *Hunger is my native place in the land of the passions. Hunger for fellowship, hunger for righteousness — for a fellowship founded on righteousness, and a righteousness attained in fellowship.*
>
> *Only life can satisfy the demands of life. And this hunger of mine can be satisfied for the simple reason that the nature of life is such that I can realise my individuality by becoming a bridge for others, a stone in the temple of righteousness.*
>
> *Don't be afraid of yourself, live your individuality to the full — but for the good of others. Don't copy others in order to buy fellowship, or make convention your law instead of living the righteousness. To become free and responsible. For this alone was man created, and he who fails to take the Way which could have been his shall be lost eternally (cf. 1988:62.).* (Huls)

Since the days of Alexis de Tocqueville (1820s), we've been warned that a pursuit like this would not characterize many in our society unless extreme individualism was curbed by higher virtues as described by Hammarskjöld. It is no different today. Imagine what could be accomplished if we found a way to capitalize on this idea of pursuing excellence through participative enrichment. Well, we can, but only if the passion for excellence is tamed by virtues that place others squarely in and with the pursuit in an appropriate way. Remembering this will come in handy when we begin looking at the servant model of leadership in the upcoming Performance Waypoint: LEAD.

Idea # 2 - Belief in Cause and Effect

Continuing his ideas on achievement is a belief in cause and effect, and Dr. Lafferty offered a very simple explanation:

> *This concept has a very long history. Things are caused. If you want to figure out what took place at point Y, then you have to find out something about what preceded it. At many points in history, people concluded this. But we are perhaps living in a time that is not unlike the decline of the Greeks. The decline of the Greeks was characterized by a belief in luck, fate, chance, and magic [the Opposite of Cause and Effect] and, if you haven't already noticed it, our belief in luck, fate, chance, and magic as a society is growing by leaps and bounds. In fact, there are studies that show it characterizes a large part of our current socio-economic scale in America. All I have to do is get 'lucky'. Sure isn't my effort that makes any difference.* (Lafferty)

One way Dr. Lafferty believed Cause and Effect thinking surfaces in individuals is through goal-setting. Science shows that we have an extremely high self-set goal characteristic that can be measured as early as 4 and 5 years of age. We are, in fact, Teleological by nature...meaning we do things by design not by accident...by choice not by chance. We are, in this sense, goal-seeking mechanisms. Science has also suggested that the network of cells at the base of our skull called the reticular activating system (RAS) may be responsible for our individual motivation to set and achieve goals. We are told the RAS serves to block out all the noise that would otherwise get in the way of achievement.

That sounds fantastic, doesn't it? But if Dr. Lafferty is right on his next point, about half of you reading this would have to admit that you are holding yourself accountable for (or worrying about) things you do NOT personally control related to their accomplishment. Setting a goal and then holding yourself accountable for things outside of your control translates nicely into a very sophisticated game of personal "Gotcha!", and it is just as damaging as having no goals at all.

On that note, something tells me that every person has at some point in the past lived without goals, or you have set them and, as quickly, forgotten about them. What happens? Without goals, we are left with the Status Quo. And when we take our mind off the goals we've set, fear quickly appears as an obstacle to hold us back. I like the way one person put it: "when you take your mind off the goals, you become the obstacle." Think about that.

Another place that cause and effect thinking helps us is in how we handle our own mistakes or errors, and it should come as no surprise that we will continue making mistakes as we move upward and outward with passion, patience and suffering to pursue excellence and create value for and with others. Unfortunately, a mistake is made and the fashionable thing is to hide; and if that isn't possible, to find someone else to point a finger at and play the blame game. If you question that, go back and read the 3rd Chapter of Genesis. We hide, and then we hurl. And if we're not careful, we can quickly move in the other (internal) direction, which produces self-blame. Either way, it degenerates to another sophisticated game of "GOTCHA!"

Unless I miss my educated guess, all of us have toyed with the notion that we are to blame for things, and we have shamefully kicked ourselves in the seat of the pants every chance we got with the foot of regret over things we could have/should have done differently and, if we only had done this or that, perhaps we wouldn't be where we are today. I believe Dr. Lafferty was right:

Dr. D's Reflections

Ironically, we're taught this from a very young age: "Keep your eye on the ball." "Stay the course." "Keep your head in the game." These simple sayings all carry the same message—don't become your own obstacle. Focus isn't just about goals; it's about discipline, clarity, and staying out of your own way.

> *These tendencies to hold ourselves accountable for things outside of our control and/or engage in self-blame is so entrenched in our psyche that studies have shown upwards of 25% of executives are so up to their ears in self-blaming characteristics that they are just terrific on an executive team. In fact, they save the company a heck of a lot of time. When a mistake happens and the senior executive walks into the room and wants to know who screwed up, about 25% of the managers feel*

so guilty that they will volunteer even though they had nothing to do with it. (Lafferty)

We need to be aware that self-blame produces self-refuting/self-defeating thought processes, which ultimately stifles human potential, as well as any progress.

Of course, if the focus is on fixing the blame (internal or external), it is not on excellence (getting better at who we are or what we do). We need to remember the Serenity Prayer:

Lord, grant me the serenity to accept the things I cannot change, the courage to change the things I can, and the wisdom to know the difference. Better still, Lord grant me the serenity to accept the people I cannot change, the courage to change the one I can, and the wisdom to know that it's me. (Unknown)

Good news is... you can change, you can become more achievement-oriented, but you'll have to stop blame-gaming in order to pull that off, whether you legitimately made a mistake or not. Recognize that cause and effect thinking means we hold ourselves accountable only for the things we can control, giving ourselves permission to fail while extending forgiveness to ourselves and others as we move through the learning process. There is no possibility for achievement otherwise.

I'm as convinced today as Dr. Lafferty was back in 1987. If we were simply to go about consciously reducing the amount of self-chastisement that goes on when we make a mistake (and we all do) and teach ourselves that it is not tied to our self-worth, we would increase our individual performance more than using any other gimmickry or gadgetry on the market. Dr. Lafferty believed in this so firmly that he was willing to put his money where his mouth was. I recall hearing him say to the group of media executives listening to his speech something to the effect of:

> *Let me do nothing else for your organizations than work with your sales staff on reducing their tendency toward self-defeating thoughts. I'll charge you nothing for it. You just give me 10% of the gains.* (Lafferty)

No one was known to have ever taken him up on his offer. If we don't begin to understand what gets us turned up versus what shuts us down, then we're going to continue cranking out similar problems by allowing our mistakes to hold us, and others, back.

Idea # 3 - Belief that Individual Efforts Count

All that needs to be said here can be summed up in the following:

> *It is not the critic who counts; not the man who points out how the strong man stumbles, or where the doer of deeds could have done them better. The credit belongs to the man who is actually in the arena, whose face is marred by dust and sweat and blood; who strives valiantly; who errs, who comes short again and again, because there is no effort without error and shortcoming; but who does actually strive to do the deeds; who knows great enthusiasms, the great devotions; who spends himself in a worthy cause; who at the best knows in the end the triumph of high achievement, and who at the worst, if he fails, at least fails while daring greatly, so*

that his place shall never be with those cold and timid souls who neither know victory nor defeat. (Roosevelt)

Not surprisingly, the belief that individual efforts count correlates very highly with success in schools. Dr. Lafferty used the following hypothetical example from the 7th grade as illustration:

Imagine a Math Teacher gives a test with 20 questions on it and one student asks: 'Why do we have to do 20 problems?' Typical response is straight power mode: 'Because I told you to!' But imagine for a moment that the teacher was more enlightened, and responded: 'Well, this is after all a math class and the test has been designed with 20 questions so you can prove to me that you know how to do it.' Our high-achieving student then offers this retort: 'I noticed the questions increase in difficulty from 1-20, so how about I answer questions 18, 19, and 20, which will prove to you that I know how to do it, and we can get off this Mickey Mouse and move on.' High achiever? You bet! High achievers believe their efforts count for something and know both 'how' to find out and 'why' it matters. In fact, there is an old saying that suggests those who know how and ask how will always have a job, but those who know why and ask why will always be their boss. (Lafferty)

Dr. Lafferty would also submit that this same student, 9 years later, has just finished his Bachelor's degree and is competing with 2 other folks for his first professional job as a physicist. We've all heard the common misconception about good grades, right?

It holds that we should only hire the smartest people when, in fact, studies show that a 3.5 GPA correlates as strongly with Schizophrenia as it does with Business Success. The real question is "Why did you get a 3.5 GPA?" Possible answers:

> Candidate A: I did it because I needed to maintain that GPA to meet the requirements of my scholarship and get into grad school.
> Candidate B: I did it because if I didn't my old man would kill me.
> Candidate C: To be honest, a 3.5 GPA wasn't the goal. I fell in love with Physics and the rest came fairly easily.

Which one is our student? Candidate C appears to be someone with intrinsic motivation for learning based on the sheer joy of the experience, not because a good grade was a requirement or to meet with someone else's approval. I would submit to you that this is a person who has a passion for excellence, believes in cause and effect and knows that his/her individual efforts count.

The issue is not always being right or perfect. It never has been; it never can be, if you really think about it. It is placing a value on effort. In spite of repeated failures, bounce back! Go **get** your goals, don't just set them. End of counsel on whether or not individual efforts count. Believe it and get on with it!

Idea # 4 - Moderate Risk Taking

Moderate, well-calculated risk taking characterizes high achievers. Former Secretary of State and Chairman (Ret), Joint Chiefs of Staff, Colin Powell, suggests two parts to moderate risk taking in Lesson 15 of his Leadership Primer:

Part I: Use the formula P=40 to 70, in which P stands for the probability of success and the numbers indicate the percentage of information acquired. Part II: Once the information is in the 40 to 70 range, go with your gut.

Powell's advice is don't take action if you have only enough information to give you less than a 40 percent chance of being right, but don't wait until you have enough facts to be 100 percent sure, because by then it is almost always too late. His instinct is right: Today, excessive delays in the name of information-gathering leads to analysis paralysis. Procrastination in the name of reducing risk actually increases risk. (Harari)

I couldn't agree more. Be decisive! Get on with it! Or as General Douglas MacArthur once said: "The second best decision quickly made is better than the best decision never made."

Idea #5 - Desire and Design for Feedback

The pursuit of excellence in achievement leads quickly to the desire for feedback. This happens as you begin to think differently about yourself and your ability to improve the situation you are in. This feedback, however, doesn't happen naturally. It must be programmed in by design, and there are myriad instruments/ assessments available (mentioned previously) to help determine how your thinking, behavior and performance as a leader is impacting others. Remember to maintain an openness to learning and pay attention to the results... they are eye/mind-opening.

In the final analysis, private victory heralds public victory (Covey), humility comes before honor (Solomon), or as one man quipped: "Independence precedes interdependence." You must first have in order to then give. In terms of Leadership Enrichment, excellence in achievement (personal/internal) will ultimately produce achievement in excellence (organizational/external).

No one understands this better than leaders. Leaders first attend to becoming better at who they are and what they do and can then focus on what they can do for and with others. And only then do they look to give more of themselves away. This process of "giving themselves away" yields new opportunities to lead in ways never before available, and that's where we're headed with this fourth Performance Waypoint: LEAD.

Dr. D's Reflections

My personal heuristic is 80%. But decision-making is rarely that clean—sometimes you only have 40% of the information and still need to act. Timing is a luxury we don't always have. When you do have it, use it wisely. And I know 80% is ambitious and the percentages themselves in this illustration are somewhat nebulous. That's not the point. Remember: you're not in it alone. Seeking others' perspectives can reveal angles you haven't considered. At the very least, it brings you closer to a more informed, accurate decision.

Before jumping in, here is a quick summary of all that has been discussed regarding the Leadership Enrichment LIFE-cycle, and some simple keys to remember along your journey:

L = Lifelong Learning (Enrichment Stage 1)

Emotional Connector - **Awareness**: Knowing strengths and weaknesses.

Performance Waypoint - **Learn**: Understanding how thinking/behavior impact us, others and our organizations.

I = Internal Locus of Control (Enrichment Stage 2)

Emotional Connector - **Acceptance**: Being okay with ourselves and our organizations as we/they are now.

Performance Waypoint - **Change**: Deciding to improve ourselves and our organizations.

F = Fulfillment (Enrichment Stage 3)

Emotional Connector - **Action**: Committing to a plan around worthwhile change.

Performance Waypoint - **Grow**: Monitoring progress over time.

E = Excellence (Enrichment Stage 4)

Emotional Connector - **Achievement**: Increasing personal and organizational effectiveness.

Thus, it is time for our final waypoint in the Leadership Enrichment LIFE-cycle; Building a Servant *Leadership Platform* for Personal and Organizational Mastery:

Performance Waypoint - **Lead**: Giving our best away for the glory of God, for the benefit of others and for our own good.

Performance Waypoint – LEAD

Leadership was redefined in Part 1, where we took a whole new look at what it actually means as opposed to that which we've grown accustomed. Since then, it's been a long and difficult journey. Advancing through the last three Leadership Enrichment Stages, you've proven a willingness to learn, change and grow. Now it's a matter of readiness to lead. It's about *Real Leadership*!

In this regard, there are many leadership theories, models and styles to choose from when building your platform. Leadership *theories* help us to understand *why* leaders behave the way they do and are helpful when trying to establish your Footing because they are steeped in assumptions about people and relationships that have been found to be more or less useful. As the Footing, they will transfer the load placed on the Foundation to solid and stable ground. In contrast, leadership *models* help us understand *what* leaders do, and they are helpful when building the Foundation of your platform as they "operationalize" the theories about leadership that you've adopted. As the Foundation, they represent the part of your platform that will actually distribute the load of those who choose to follow. Finally, leadership *styles* try to explain *how* leaders approach various situations and they are the part of our platforms that actually touch/impact others directly. Included in the list of style types are transactional, autocratic, bureaucratic, charismatic and democratic. These are important for the Framing of your platform. And you'll recall, the Framing is the part of your platform that is closest to your followers and responsible for carrying their weight. There's plenty of information available already on the leadership theories, models and styles, so I won't spend time on them here other than to say they are not all equal and to suggest, as a result, it is important to adopt the ones you believe are the most useful for you and for your organization.

I'd like to spend the remainder of this book presenting a particular type of *leader-in-person:* **the Servant Leader**. In fact, this type of leader often gets thrown in with the others as "just another leadership style", but this is a mistake. When it comes to *Real Leadership*, the primary passage of reference is not so much on the *why, what,* or *how* of leadership. These are important, certainly. We know that. But there is something else or, more appropriately stated, someone else to consider—someone easily overlooked in the impersonal process of coldly adopting theories, models and styles. That someone is you! We've talked so much about "others" being the object of our leadership, and we will continue to do so. But if *Real Leadership* is anything, it is first personal—it is a matter of ***who*** leaders are. That means **You** are the subject of *Real Leadership*. It really is a matter of ***who you are*** or, as you know from the very first Enrichment Stage, ***who you've allowed yourself to become*** and, more importantly, ***who you will commit to becoming*** as a *leader-in-person.*

Dr. D's Reflections

Remember, this is a choice. Just as you chose to read this book, you must also decide whether leadership holds value for you— as an individual, a member of an organization, or a contributor to society. If you choose the path of leadership, don't approach it lightly. Commit to becoming the best leader you can be. And if you do it right, you'll find that your most honest and critical evaluator... is you.

I mentioned earlier that my *Leadership Platform* was blueprinted, built and strength-tested on the Servant Model. I use the term "model" here differently than we just described above. I use it to bring the idea of role-models front and center in our thinking about *Real Leadership*. Why the Servant Model of leadership? Well, the simplest reason is; to become a better version of you and give yourself away you are going to have to do it *for and with* OTHERS. Remember the etymology of leadership presented in the Preface? Only the Servant Model places this kind of emphasis on self (i.e., Servant) in the context of others (i.e., Leader).

Doing the **right** things, extremely well *for* others is the core of service, and it requires the heart of a **servant**. Being **effective** at doing the right things *with* others, however, as they opt-in voluntarily and begin to follow your lead, automatically introduces economies of scale, skill and scope which were previously not there, and this new achievement unleashes the potential for greater, more positive and long-term impact. This is the core of leadership, and it requires the heart of a **leader**. Together, the servant *(for others)* and leader *(with others)* powerfully combine to fully enable others to become Servants and then give away the best versions of themselves as Leaders for and with others.

As just pointed out, this requires that our leadership is both effective and right. It also requires that we reach our full **"born-in" leadership potential** through a lifetime of **"made-in" leadership performance**. It is for this single reason that I renamed the LIFE-cycle from its original description: Performance Improvement; to its final description: Leadership Enrichment. *We are all created with equal born-in leadership potential, but it must be enriched through a lifetime of pursuing excellence for made-in leadership performance.* Let's explore each of these ideas in greater depth.

Effective or Ineffective Leadership– What does it mean to be an effective leader? In practical terms, it means that you have satisfied 3 basic criteria and, as a result, have been appointed to lead: 1) you have become someone who is capable of leading, 2) you have made a commitment of your will to the true good of others and 3) you have a vision of potential that is perceived as worthwhile. Those who follow will embrace your vision and produce the type of results you are trying to achieve.

It may help to remember this axiom: "Leader" is a title given to us by those who choose each day to follow our lead. If followership is compulsory (i.e., out of fear, by law, etc.) based on positional authority, we're only leading because of our title or rank or privilege. By default, if no one is following willingly, there is no leader.

When it comes to Servanthood, however, in a very practical, earthy sense, service to others is a matter of placing their interests and needs above our own. When the second greatest commandment is "Love your neighbor as yourself", there is a primary passage of reference placed on service and we'll talk about the mainspring

Dr. D's Reflections

As a Servant Leader, there will be times when the right course of action isn't immediately clear. In those moments, discerning the right things to do requires more than just logic—it calls for wisdom, humility, and a strong moral compass. I once had a mentor who lived by a simple principle: Do no harm. I interpreted that to mean our decisions should leave things better than we found them. But sometimes, this demands that we do nothing until we have greater clarity on the impact of our decisions and actions. A moral compass, rooted in ethics, can guide us through this uncertainty. I like to think of life as somewhat binary—filled with choices, either right and wrong or effective and ineffective. The difference lies not just in the outcome we're willing to live with, but can others live with it... not just in what we do, but in our motive for doing it in the first place, and the means we choose in pursuing it.

of that service in the next section. A determined focus on, and unwavering commitment to, OTHERS is what ensures that our leadership remains effective. I simply can't imagine a situation or scenario in life (at work or play; personal, social, or professional) where we would continue to voluntarily follow someone (a leader) who we did not believe had our best interest in mind (a servant). We may give them obedience out of fear to create the illusion that we are following because that's what it takes to get along and survive, but this is not real followership and, by default, not *Real Leadership*.

Right or Wrong Leadership– It does not automatically follow that effective leaders are placed in the direction of good or right. Effective leadership does not mean right leadership. One must intentionally choose right leadership over wrong leadership; otherwise leadership can be applied very effectively toward accomplishing the wrong things, in the wrong way. Juxtapose the effective and wrong leadership of Jim Jones (leader of the Peoples Temple), Adolf Hitler (leader of the 3rd Reich) and Bill Ayers (leader of the Weather Underground) with the effective and right leadership of Mother Theresa (leader of the Missionaries of Charity), Winston Churchill (leader of Great Britain) and Martin Luther King, Jr. (leader of Civil-Rights Movement). All were successful at convincing others that they were capable of leading, that they had others' best interests in mind, and that they had a vision worth following. The real difference was in their motives, the means they employed and, without question, the ends they were targeting.

I believe Jesus Christ is the greatest example of a right and effective leader—ever. He said that the greatest commandment is, "Love the Lord your God with all your heart, soul, mind, and strength," and that the second is like it: "Love your neighbor as yourself." This is the essence of right and effective leadership. To invoke the moral law and choose right leadership, we must love the moral law giver with all that we are. It will not happen with authenticity or regularity otherwise. To remain effective as a leader, we must remain steadfast in our love and affection for others as a selfless, intentional act.

Right and Effective Leadership– I want to explore the idea of both right and effective leadership in the context of our love for others and our love for God in this section. But before doing that, I believe it is important to underscore why it is imperative to bring the spiritual (i.e., being) into the LEL-c and our understanding of *Real Leadership*, which already includes the intellectual (i.e., thinking) and the emotional (i.e., feeling).

In an online post titled Beyond Emotional Intelligence: Achieving Spiritual Intelligence, Dr. Andrew Thorn recalls the following:

> *Charles P. Steinmetz, (1865 – 1923) a German-American mathematician and electrical engineer, whose work as a scientist significantly influenced the expansion of the electrical power industry in the United States, was once asked, by the founder of Babson College in Massachusetts, what line of research he thought would see the greatest development during the course of the next 100 years.*

> *Here is what Mr. Steinmetz is reported to have said:*

I think the greatest discovery will be made along spiritual lines. Here is a force which history clearly teaches has been the greatest power in the development of men. Yet we have merely been playing with it and have never seriously studied it as we have the physical forces. Someday, people will learn that material things do not bring happiness and are of little use in making men and women creative and powerful. Then the scientists of the world will turn their laboratories over to the study of God and prayer and the spiritual forces, which as of yet have hardly been scratched. When this day comes, the world will see more advancement in one generation than it has seen in the past four. (Thorn)

This is an extremely bold and compelling statement, and one I absolutely agree with. In order for us to break away from merely "playing with" leadership and move into the better alternative of *Real Leadership through the LEL-c*, I believe our enrichment efforts must give serious consideration to the spiritual. And the benefits shouldn't be ignored. Along with offering an enlightened focus on who we really are, Dr. Thorn goes on to suggest that Spiritual Intelligence helps us understand our purpose and to see things as they really are. One of the major themes of this book has been around maintaining an accurate understanding of ourselves, others and the world. This is of vital importance to *real leaders* because it is the only way we can truly learn, change, grow and lead.

Dr. Thorn's post is replete with ideas on the importance of the spiritual in our efforts to move beyond achievement. If you are familiar with his other writings, you'll quickly note that he and

I differ on the ultimate goal to be attained (i.e., perfection vs. excellence). That said, I would encourage you to read the entire post, where you'll find the following salient points [Note: relation to *Real Leadership* follows each point]:

> *A person who possesses high levels of spiritual intelligence easily identifies with his/her Higher Self or Spirit rather than with the ego. They have less need to seek after their own interests. This fosters the capacity to serve and develop others.* (Thorn)

This point relates to the Servant Model of *Real Leadership*.

> *It is worth noting that the words 'health,' 'wholeness,' 'holiness' and 'healing' all come from the same root. All of these come about because of who we are and not because of what we do.* (Thorn)

This relates to the central ideas that leadership is personal, *real leaders* are leaders-in-person and *Real Leadership* is steeped in who leaders are not just what they do or how they perform.

> *To be spiritually intelligent is to be fully engaged in becoming the best you - because it facilitates your ability to know exactly who the best you is.* (Thorn)

This relates to the *Real Leadership* mandate of continual renewal and improvement through the LEL-c. It also relates to something presented as part of the conclusion to this book... something based in the legacy of Tim Hansel, a servant leader who truly understood what it took to become your best.

All of this brings us back to our particular focus on the spiritual: a) love for God (the moral law giver) to keep our leadership right and b) love for others to secure our effectiveness as leaders. I believe these two spiritual imperatives are the essence of *Real Leadership*. Oswald Chambers is credited with putting it in the plainest, most earthy of terms in *Biblical Psychology* [emphasis added]:

> *...if you are going to live for the service of your fellow-men, you are going to be pierced through with many sorrows, unless you love God. You are going to meet with more base ingratitude from your fellowmen than you would from a dog, and you will meet with unkindness and 'twofacedness,' and if your motive is love for your fellowmen, you will be exhausted in the battle of life; but if your motive springs from a central love to God, there is no ingratitude, no sin, no devil, no angel can hinder you from serving your fellowmen, no matter how they treat you, because the mainspring of the service is love to God. Then I can love my neighbor as myself, not from pity, but from the real and the true centering of myself in God. (Chambers)*

Sounds an awful lot like what we reviewed in the etymology of leadership; particularly the part about "...moving upward and/or outward with passion, patience and suffering." I'll readily accept that most leaders have passion and a few have patience. The real rub is suffering.

But if suffering as a part of *Real Leadership* sounds difficult, C. S. Lewis underscores the inherent dangers and consequences of the alternative—never loving enough to risk suffering—in *The Four Loves*:

> *To love at all is to be vulnerable. Love anything, and your heart will certainly be wrung and possibly be broken. If you want to make sure of keeping it intact, you must give your heart to no one, not even to an animal. Wrap it carefully round with hobbies and little luxuries; avoid all entanglements; lock it up safe in the casket or coffin of your selfishness. But in that casket— safe, dark, motionless, airless—it will change. It will not be broken; it will become unbreakable, impenetrable, irredeemable. The alternative to tragedy, or at least to the risk of tragedy, is damnation. The only place outside Heaven where you can be perfectly safe from all the dangers and perturbations of love is Hell.* (Lewis, The Four Loves)

Only those who love God have the endurance to continue leading in spite of how they will be treated. Love for God comes first; then love for fellow man. This is not insignificant and explains why we spent considerable time in the FULFILLMENT Enrichment Stage ensuring that our motives, means and ends were checked against a moral framework for how things are [Morality], and also the way they ought to be [Ethics]. In fact, without our allegiance to this framework and a commitment of the will to do what is right, we will never be able to have an authentic love for ourselves, let alone a love for, and focus on, others. In other words, we will never be able to sustain right leadership and, ultimately, our effectiveness as a leader will be compromised or perverted.

This is not to say that those who don't love God preeminently are unable to exercise right or effective leadership. They certainly are, and I've met and worked with a few over the years. It's just that, when their leadership is right and effective, they simply have no basis for defending or explaining it other than personal preference or moral imperatives espoused by the society or culture within which they happen to live/work. Ethics rooted in precepts based upon principles founded in the nature and character of God is not a connection they are able to make, even though it is still there and working according to created order. Moreover, they aren't given the option of crediting the Lord for mighty works so the credit is mostly retained, even though He is still there and governing sovereignly over the affairs of men. Finally, as Mr. Chambers suggests, these individuals are more prone to sorrow and exhaustion from the ingratitude of others because the mainspring of their service is something other than a love for God.

By the same token, I'm also not suggesting that those who

Dr. D's Reflections

Being a right and effective leader isn't always easy, but neither is always popular. As the saying goes, "You can please some of the people some of the time, but you can't please all of the people all of the time." Leadership isn't a popularity contest. Even Jesus was followed by many—until he wasn't. True leadership often requires sacrifice, but never compromise of what truly matters. Your leadership should be grounded in your platform, guided by your ethical and moral compass. Use it—don't lose it. Ask yourself: Would you follow someone who compromises their values, or someone willing to sacrifice for the sake of others? Let this answer shape the leader you are becoming.

love the Lord preeminently are always adequate or able to sustain right and effective leadership. I can tell you from experience that my tendency as a leader—to be tempted away from my commitment of the will to the glory of God and the true good of others—is the same as everyone else's... particularly when I'm mistreated. In fact, I need reminders of my commitments often, which you'll read about shortly in the next personal vignette. I fall short at times. Everyone does. But that's not what counts. What counts is remembering the goals (or targets) of this Leadership Enrichment Stage:

- EXCELLENCE; not Perfection [getting better at who we are and what we do or, as the late Tim Hansel often said: "We're called to be OUR best, not THE best"].

- EFFORT; not Results [anything worth doing is worth not doing well at first].

- DISCOVERY; not Veracity [asking the right questions more than having the right answers or always being right].

The extent to which these goals are embraced by leaders will determine whether they engage in the '-cycle' aspect of LIFE for continual leadership enrichment. Any time the primary passage of reference shifts from excellence to perfection; from effort to results; from discovery to veracity; it is the beginning of demise. Watching for these tendencies in our *Leadership Platforms* is not hard. Personally, they appear when we begin to believe too highly in our own "stuff", stop learning and cordon ourselves off from others; and they carry with them the *Symptoms of Managerial Narcissism.* Organizationally, they appear as short-term thinking, micro-management by objectives and performance reviews; and they carry with them the *Symptoms of Institutionalism.* I encourage the reader to get their hands on John W. Gardner's 1965 Harper's Magazine article entitled: *How to Prevent Organizational Dry Rot* for a deeper exploration, but I've included a summary of these symptoms here, originally presented by Chuck Swindoll.

> ***Opportunity:*** *As you read the list, make a note of how many apply to your current situation. This will provide invaluable insights for where you may want to focus efforts as you lead.*

- THE LEADER BEGINS TO BE MORE IMPORTANT THAN PEOPLE. Gardner's first rule says unequivocally that people are the *"...ultimate source of renewal."*

- INDIVIDUALS START TO FUNCTION LIKE
  COGS IN A MACHINE, NOT AS INDIVIDUALS.
  Gardner's second rule point out the obvious:
  "*Individuals who have been made to feel like cogs in
  a machine will behave like cogs in a machine. They
  will not produce ideas for change. On the contrary,
  they will resist such ideas when produced by others.*"

WITH THAT...

- THERE IS A THREATENING ATMOSPHERE;
  YOU ARE NOT FREE TO ASK UNCOMFORT-
  ABLE QUESTIONS. Gardner's third rule states that
  it's a "*...basic principle of human organization that
  the individuals who hold the reins of power in any
  enterprise cannot trust themselves to be adequately
  self-critical....And the only protection is to create an
  atmosphere in which anyone can speak up.*"

- THE STRUCTURE BECOMES RIGID AND
  INFLEXIBLE. Gardner's fourth rule is a requirement for the organization's internal structure to
  remain fluid. To reinforce that idea, he adds: "*Most
  organizations have a structure that was designed to
  solve problems that no longer exist.*" Perhaps this
  is why so many unenlightened managers actually
  create problems that only they can solve. It's a
  matter of remaining relevant...of survival.

- THERE IS A COMMUNICATION BREAK-
  DOWN. Gardner's fifth rule states that the organization must have "*...an adequate system of internal
  communication....easy communication*" in order to

facilitate the near infinite variety of combinations and recombinations of diverse elements and ideas.

- A REPRESSIVE SPIRIT PERVADES; THERE IS MORE AND MORE RED TAPE TO WADE THROUGH; THE POLICY MANUAL GETS THICKER. Gardner's sixth rule is that organizations "...*must have some means of combating the process by which men become prisoners of their own procedures.*" I call this the persecution of people by proxy, the persecution of profit by policy, and the persecution of productivity by process.

- PEOPLE DEVELOP THEIR OWN SPECIAL INTERESTS AND SUDDENLY GO INTO COMPETITION AGAINST EACH OTHER AND UNITY GETS POLARIZED. Gardner's seventh rule is that organizations must find "...*some means of combating the vested interests that grow up in every human institution.*" And may I offer that catchy slogans and leadership platitudes won't cut it. What works is a concept we know today as Open Book Management, originally taught by Jack Stack in *The Great Game of Business*! If you are going to sell the idea that everyone's overriding vested interest is in the continual renewal of the organization itself, and that changes are required to secure that ongoing vitality, then sharing basic financial information, teaching them to read/interpret the statements and enabling them to opt-in and build-in the changes is a great way to do that. And at Springfield Remanufacturing Corporation

(SRC), Jack proved it was not only possible but highly effective, even when the changes threatened privileges, authority, and status.

- THERE IS A LOSS OF INITIATIVE, INNOVATION AND ENGAGEMENT; MORE TIME IS SPENT LOOKING BACKWARD THAN FORWARD. Gardner's eighth rule is that organizations capable of continual renewal must be "*… interested in what it is going to become and not what it has been.*" And this is not the responsibility of the R&D Department. Even they can't move the organization forward if everyone driving is looking in the rearview mirror.

AND FINALLY...

- THE TEAM GETS SO LARGE AND THE HIERARCHY SO THICK THAT MORE AND MORE PEOPLE OUTSIDE OF LEADERSHIP POSITIONS FEEL LIKE THEY NO LONGER MATTER. Gardner's ninth rule, as he states, "*… is obvious but difficult. An organization runs on motivation, on conviction, on morale. Men have to believe that it really makes a difference whether they do well or badly. They have to care. The have to believe that their efforts as individuals will mean something for the whole organization.*"

Born or Made Leaders– Historically, much debate is waged over whether leaders are born or made. You'll recall that I believe it's a "both/and" proposition. Leadership is first ***born in* human**

beings as potential, and then **made in** *human becomings through performance* as we continue to learn, change and grow.

Today, I believe many reject the idea that people are born with leadership potential because we tend to view leadership as an external or "corporate" thing, attached only to our careers, developed and applied only through training courses in the organizational context. But the truth is, as my good friend Anastasia Hansel refers to them, "non-neutral learning events/ environments", like the ones we experience at work, are available to us and occur in our personal and social lives.

Unfortunately, in many cases, these non-neutral learning events/ environments are overlooked and we miss our opportunity to personalize the leadership lessons they afford. And you know from the introduction that I believe this single missing element in thinking about leadership accounts for much of what we routinely observe in our organizations as lackluster performance. If leadership lessons aren't recognized, how can they be personalized? If they aren't personalized, how can

Dr. D's Reflections

One particularly valuable non-neutral learning experience comes from "management wolves in 'leadersheep' clothing." These are the Leaders-In-Position mentioned earlier. How they got there is often a mystery—though it likely has something to do with who they know. You'll recognize them easily: they take credit for others' ideas and achievements, but never own their failures. For every failure, there's either excuse or blame, and there's plenty of both to go around. They're not easy to work with, but they do present a non-neutral learning opportunity. They will force you into the uncomfortable position of having to learn how protect yourself, and others, from their lackluster leadership. But they can also serve as clear examples of what not to emulate, and what not to build into your own Leadership Platform."

they be personified? When born-in leadership potential is never developed through made-in leadership performance, it stands to reason it will be wasted.

The characteristics that define Leadership Enrichment tend to be the same in all cases. Leaders, guided by theory, commit to recognizing and using non-neutral environments to learn, change, grow and lead through awareness, acceptance, action and achievement. It doesn't matter at the end of the day whether the family these individuals grew up in promoted learning or whether the companies they worked for were "learning organizations." What really matters is that, at some point, **leadership became personal** and they were able to recognize their born-in leadership potential and develop through made-in leadership performance.

Put another way, if I had relied only on born-in leadership potential and what I learned from my family about leadership, I would have stopped learning after my formative years and my potential would have gone largely unrealized. Likewise, if I had relied on the companies I've worked for over the past 30 years to provide the right environment/opportunity for me to learn, change, grow and lead, all leadership development would have come to a virtual standstill in 1994 when I left active service in the United States Marine Corps. As soon as I took responsibility for my own leadership development and started to apply what I had learned/was learning, I began to "see" non-neutral environments everywhere. I also began to uncover more leadership potential for the organizations I served and, as a result, established highly constructive sub-cultures that successfully ran counter to the overall defensive organizational culture.

Opportunity: *Here's yours. This serves as the last of these intense callouts in the book. From here on, you will take responsibility for your own leadership development as a result of what you read and learn. Start identifying areas in the text where words like 'challenge' or 'problem' or 'opportunity' should give you pause for reflection and documentation. Then use it to* **Take Your Lead.**

One final idea about this "born-in" leadership potential, because I think more needs to be said here to increase clarity. I just want to share something I learned from Dr. Jeff Myers at the Myers Institute for Leadership and Communication. Our answer to the question: "are leaders born, made or both?" may come down to our level of thinking about life's purpose and meaning.

A few years ago, I was asked by Dr. Myers to review a few chapters from his upcoming video teaching series: *Secrets of Everyday Leaders.* I recall his conviction at that time was it wasn't

Dr. D's Reflections

I completely agree with Dr. Myers and my brother—leadership isn't just a decision; it's deliberate action. As Yoda told Luke Skywalker: "Do or do not. There is no try." If you're committed to being a *real leader*, don't try—do. And don't wait for others to validate your choice. As Napoleon Hill said, "The man who has decided to lead does not wait for consensus."

so much that we needed leaders; it was that the whole world was thirsty for people who would "...stand up, exert influence and create change." This implies that leadership is extremely rare. But Jeff didn't stop there. He went on to make the audacious claim that our willingness to accept the call of leadership—or in this case, to *Take Your Lead*—actually defines meaning in life.

I agree, and firmly believe, that every person has a purpose (born-in leadership potential as human beings). The extent to which we exercise that potential (made-in leadership performance as human becomings) is based on how we view our life's meaning and determines our overall impact. This depends, of course, on our worldview/beliefs on origins (where did I come from?), purpose (why am I here?) and destinations (where will I go when I die?). Complex subject matter but starting points like this make all the difference in whether we ever learn, change, grow or lead. They will also determine the legacy we actually leave behind.

Servanthood– What about servants? Are they born or made? Seems odd to ask, but looking back on how I built my *Leadership Platform* over the years on the principles and precepts of Servanthood, I suppose this question was inevitable. Regardless, I thought it had enough merit to deserve an answer. In my search,

I was inevitably drawn to the oldest and most reliable of all the books of antiquity: the Holy Scriptures. Drawing primarily from the perfect example of servant leadership we have in Jesus of Nazareth—it dawned on me that perhaps the answer was the same as it was for leadership. Servanthood, like leadership, is first born-in human potential and then made-in human performance. Jesus said of Himself that He *came into* the world to serve and to give (i.e., born-in). It is also recorded in Hebrews that, though He was a Son, He *learned* obedience through the things that he suffered (i.e., made-in). Likewise, we are created in His image with born-in servant potential and encouraged by the Apostle Paul to be "imitators of Christ" (Ephesians 5:1)… made-in servants who get conformed to His likeness (Romans 8:29). Yes! We all have the same born-in servant potential. The same question we asked about our Leadership remains: "To what extent are we willing to develop this potential through made-in servant performance?" To what extent are you?

Dr. D's Reflections

I've always believed there's no greater purpose than serving others. Whether in the military, politics, civil service, or volunteering, the fulfillment far outweighs any paycheck. We all serve someone or something. For the *real leader* to love what they do is simply a practical and logical outworking of their love for God and love for others. In this sense, Servanthood come naturally.

Servant Leadership– Can servants be *real leaders*? Or is it "can leaders be servants?" Knowing that the etymology of leadership included the idea of moving upward and outward with passion, patience and suffering to create value for/with others, a third question emerged. Is there really a difference between servants and leaders or are they, in the truest sense, one and the same? Who else is able to move this way, accept this kind of consequence, or have this type of impact except a *servant*...except a *follower*...except a *leader*? When you really look at this, it is amazing how interrelated, interoperable and interdependent these adjectives really are.

To understand servant leadership is relatively simple. It is based on what some have called the "follower principle": **Good Followers Make the Best Leaders**. So goes one title of Michael McKinney's LeadingBLOG posts at leadershipnow.com. Michael goes on to write:

> *There is no better way to learn leadership than by being under someone else—leading from the second chair. As ironic as that may sound, it's true. Learning to lead under someone else provides you with the opportunity (the necessity) to learn to lead without coercion. You learn to let your leadership speak for itself—authentically.* (McKinney)

Taking this a step farther—because I'm not certain it was Michael's original intent—I believe there is an inextricable link/connection between Leader-Follower-Servant. Leaders serve! Servants follow! Followers lead! I also believe this works if stated a little differently: Leaders follow! Followers serve! Servants lead!

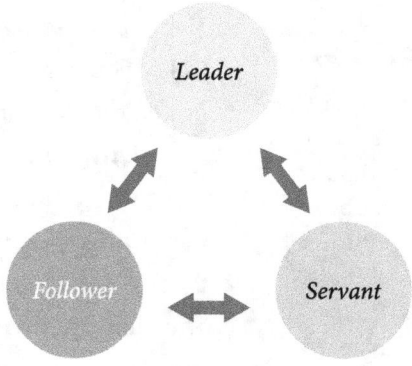

The Leader-Servant-Follower Connection.

No matter what, in the final analysis, the terms 'Leader', 'Follower' and 'Servant' are synonyms. And this statement is based in the following truths:

- To lead, one must understand the work [and the people] that he and his [team] are responsible for—re: W. Edwards Deming, Out of the Crisis.

- To understand the work/people that he and his team are responsible for, one must serve— re: Jesus Christ, Mark 10:43-44.

- To serve, one must follow—re: Jesus Christ, John 12:26.

In short: *to lead one must serve; to serve one must follow; and followers make the best leaders.* Whenever these truths are compromised you will find the beginning of a demise, and I'll spend some time on the consequences in the upcoming Leadership Vignette on Excellence.

Dr. D's Reflections

I've often heard that the smartest person in the room isn't the one who called the meeting... that's why they called it. They also aren't the one who throws out the most ideas or talks just to be hear themselves. It's really the one who speaks only when it adds value—someone who listens first, then contributes with intention. This is a learned skill, especially in a world where many feel the need to prove their worth by speaking up, regardless of impact. It all comes back to making the right choice— because in communication, timing is everything.

Before reading the vignette, I'd like you to recall when I mentioned that Servant Leadership was *relatively simple*. I'd also like you to note that I didn't say it was *relatively easy*. Considering the full weight of consequences afforded by the etymology of leadership (i.e., passion, patience and suffering), it is anything but easy. When combined in the heart of a servant leader, however, thriving rather than surviving becomes the primary passage of reference as our positive impact and influence grows through others. This is, among many other reasons, why I developed the Leadership Enrichment LIFE-cycle and why my platform is based on the Servant Model. I have found no better way to leave a real legacy...to live on through those I've impacted to the point of permanent, positive change.

Leadership (Excellence) Vignette

It was later in my career. After 15 years of professional advancement, I finally began toying around with the idea of personal achievement as it relates to leadership. The year was 1999. As a result, I started to connect some dots and recognized there was some contribution to be made by role models (a Performance

Waypoint: *Learn* skill necessary for personal accountability), some value in writing things down (a Performance Waypoint: *Change* skill useful in goal attainment) and some benefit in rituals (a Performance Waypoint: *Grow* skill essential to reaching higher levels of performance). Borrowing role models from Chuck Swindoll, goal-getting from Brian Tracy and rituals from Jim Leohr, I put into practice something to help me remember my leadership commitments to God and to others. It was nothing sophisticated or elaborate. I simply took the name of a role model, wrote it down on a piece of paper and stuck it on my wall as part of a daily ritual to read and remember. The role model's name was Uzziah, King of Judah from 791 to 739 BC, and the sign reads:

GEHAZI (Servant)
UZZIAH (Leader)

Gehazi was the servant of Elisha and his life reminds me of the perils that can befall someone committed to Servanthood. As interesting as his life story is, I'll leave that for another time and refer you to 2 Kings 5: 19-27 for the details. King Uzziah is the person of real interest here because of what was recorded about his reign as Leader of Judah.

In his exceptional Bible Study, *Can One Person Make a Difference?*, Chuck Swindoll was the first to elevate King Uzziah in my mind as a role model when it came to this idea of right and effective leadership. If you are unfamiliar with his life, work or achievements, he isn't what most would consider the definition of a role model (i.e., someone who possesses the qualities that we would like to have), at least not toward the end of his life. But keep in mind that role models are also those who have affected us in ways that make us want to be better people. It is this lesser known impact of role models where Uzziah fits. When I first heard his story, I instantly wanted to be a better person...a different kind of leader.

You can read the entire story in 2 Chronicles 26, but here are the highlights [emphasis added]:

- Uzziah was sixteen years old when he became King and reigned in Jerusalem for fifty-two years. (v. 3)

- He did what was right in the eyes of the Lord and, as he sought the Lord, God gave him success. (v. 4-5)

- His fame spread far and wide, for he was greatly helped *until* he became powerful. (v. 15)

- After Uzziah became powerful, his pride led to his downfall. He was unfaithful to the Lord his God. (v. 16a)

- While he was raging at the priests in their presence before the incense altar in the LoMr. D's temple, leprosy broke out on his forehead. (v. 19b)

- King Uzziah had leprosy until the day he died. He lived in a separate house—leprous and banned from the temple of the Lord. Jotham his son had charge of the palace and governed the people of the land. (v. 21)

- Uzziah rested with his ancestors and was buried near them in a cemetery that belonged to the kings, for people said, "He had leprosy."

Notice that his success as leader swings on the hinges of faithfulness to the moral law giver and his entire fate on the word 'until', as recorded in the last half of v. 15. The lesson from Uzziah was powerfully simple: Leadership, like any great might, does not make right. God makes (and keeps) our leadership right, whether or not we give Him the glory. And love for one another makes (and keeps) it effective. This is why my personal Servant *Leadership Platform* includes the following CAUTION:

> *Servant Leadership is extremely powerful...a great strength. But any strength, when abused, quickly trans-forms into a weakness [much the same as C.S. Lewis points out in Mere Christianity; badness is nothing more than spoiled goodness]. Since exemplary followers will do almost anything asked, even if the request places them at risk, continually subordinate your freedom as leader under the control of righteousness (i.e., love of God) and responsibility (i.e., love of others).* (Dillard)

We must continually check our motives, means and ends as servant leaders against our commitment to loving God and loving one another, otherwise we stop serving and stop leading whether we, or anyone else (i.e., our followers), notices. Recall how this also relates back to the achievement of Spiritual Intelligence, identifying with your higher Self or Spirit, taking you beyond merely fulfilling your ego to leading and serving for the benefit of others. Simple signs with GEHAZI-UZZIAH serve as reminders of our commitments. In fact, I now rotate a number of these "signs" on the wall of my office and at home as reminders of my vital commitment to right and effective leadership. Every day, world-changing servant leaders understand and are committed to this basic practice. There is no substitute for love when it comes to maintaining a right and effective leadership, and it is essential if we are to thrive.

Platform Work ... Leveraging Your Platform

Ronald Reagan is noted as saying: "Some people live an entire lifetime and wonder if they have made a difference in the World. Marines don't have that problem." This can also be said of other organizations. Pursuing excellence—striving to achieve more and lead better on the basis of what you've learned and how you've changed and grown—automatically places you or your organization in a position to leverage your platform and produce remarkable results for you, others and your organization. But there is one final component of your platform that will determine how much weight it can truly carry... how impactful your personal leadership legacy will be... how effective your organization will be in the long haul: SACRIFICE.

Personal and Organizational Platforms

Here's where your leadership begins to shine. But let the leader beware: **Anyone can shine in the brightness... it is in the darkness where you have been called to *Take Your Lead*.** Your willingness to make sacrifices for and with others will keep your leadership light on, so you can lead through the darkness—the real tough times inherent in any worthwhile journey—toward a new daybreak.

What does that really mean? From the pen of Louis Finkelstein comes this morsel of truth: "Wisdom begins with sacrifice of immediate pleasures for long-range purposes." On the personal side, Brian Tracy picks up the flavor of this nugget when he talks about the power of delayed gratification to personal leadership. On the organizational side, Dr. Deming also talks of adopting constancy of purpose and avoiding short-term thinking as essential ingredients of organizational leadership. These concepts of leadership have been around for years, yet we still have trouble swallowing or digesting this counsel as part of our leadership diet. Why is that?

Dr. D's Reflections

Remember the same sun the rises in the morning sets in the evening. You will have numerous sunrises and sunsets on your Leadership journey toward personal and organization excellence. The oil that keeps your leadership light bright for others can only be renewed by your continual and iterative movement through the LEL-c. Don't stop and stay in the EXCELLENCE stage for too long.

Ronald Wright gets credit for this in *A Short History of Progress*, but his progress trap idea may provide a central reason for why many never make the leap:

> *In a progress trap, those in positions of authority are unwilling to make changes necessary for future survival. To do so they would need to sacrifice their current status and political power at the top of a hierarchy.*
> (Wikipedia)

Perhaps this explains why many leaders (and their organizations) reach a performance plateau. Mired in past success (accumulated while climbing the corporate ladder) and trapped

Dr. D's Reflections

There isn't room to give "hier-archy" the treatment it deserves in this book; only to say this. While these types of structures originated in the old paradigm, they aren't intrinsically bad but they definitely impact culture and contribute to lowering the level of organizational effectiveness if not managed properly. In this new leadership paradigm, if you're open to exploring a better way of working, consider what my brother strongly recommends: Holacracy. It's a transformative approach to organizational structure that replaces traditional management hierarchies with distributed authority and purpose-driven roles.

by a desire to maintain position in the **hierarchy**, those at the top become unwilling to sacrifice status and power. As a result, empowerment to renew and improve dries up, yesterday's solutions become today's prob-lems, low hanging fruit grows back and all upward and outward movement grinds to a halt.

What is needed most gets practiced least: SACRIFICE. Sacrifice provides the opportu-nity to move from transactional to transformational leadership. It is embedded with the idea of suffering in the etymology of leadership, and it is an essential nutrient in the servant leader's diet. Only a leader with a sincere wish to serve others, before himself/herself, is able to make the sacrifice and transform...first personally and then organizationally.

Consider the example of General Booth, founder of the Salva-tion Army. It is reported that, just prior to his death, he articulated an incredible vision for the future focus of the organization. As the story goes, he was too sick to attend their annual convention in person, so his opening address was sent by telegram. If my memory serves, thousands of delegates gathered to hear the message General Booth intended to deliver. With great anticipa-tion, a hush moved over the crowd as the envelope was opened by the moderator. There was an immediate sigh, followed by a long pause, after which the moderator began reading. The entirety of the keynote address was one word. That word was "Others!" On August 21, 1912, William Booth died at the age of 83. There were 150,000 mourners at his funeral. If you are familiar with his life, you know of the sacrifices he made personally, and the vision of sacrifice he challenged his army to achieve as they endeavored to save the world. The Reverend General was a servant and a leader, as the organization he founded bears witness to this very day.

I believe that it is safe to say then that there is no practical difference between leaders and servants; at least not when it comes to the kind and degree of sacrifice required to secure right and effective leadership and produce positive long-term results. Those who want their leadership to thrive and transform their organizations will sacrifice and serve. Those who truly serve will be capable of leading, be appointed by others to lead, and be recognized as having a positive impact on those around them.

Summary – Enrichment Stage #4: EXCELLENCE

Awareness leads to learning and, through acceptance, releases your potential (energy) for worthwhile change! That potential is fulfilled

Dr. D's Reflections

Leadership, service and sacrifice go hand in hand. To truly serve others, you must be willing to give up something of yourself—most often, your **time**, but also your **talent** and **treasure**. As we wrote about our Dad in the Dedication of this book, it's the time you choose to invest in others instead of yourself that defines the length of your significance... it's the talent that you invest in others that will determine the breadth of your impact... it's the treasure that you invest in others that determines the depth of your service as a sacrificial leader.

by taking action on worthwhile changes in the right way and for the right reasons (for others), which produces real growth. *Pursuing personal excellence in achievement ultimately produces organizational achievement in excellence, which releases a newfound potential for leading in ways never before available to you. Teaching service as a gift will leverage your platform as others become more aware of their own potential, and through awareness learn, and by learning accept, and by acceptance, change... And so on.*

Thesis: Excellence in achievement produces achievement in excellence. Over time, the result is Unconscious Competence; a reflexive way of leading that is right and effective. Essential emotional connector is ACHIEVEMENT! Essential performance waypoint is LEADERSHIP!

Antithesis: Short-circuit our personal and organizational potential for improving performance and the positive difference we can make in the world by never daring to truly achieve and never leveraging what we have learned or how we have changed/grown on ever increasing scales.

-CYCLE ... CONTINUAL RENEWAL AND IMPROVEMENT!

By now we've established that personal leadership is perishable. Those who follow our lead must choose to do so daily and, if we're not attending to the quality of our own Leadership Platforms, they'll eventually stop following; and we stop leading. We also know that every organization that doesn't continually renew and improve its leadership begins a steady decline and ultimately reaches the natural and expected end of its lifecycle. In either case, our leadership yields to entropy, reaching a state of equilibrium and eventually breaking down entirely because there is no additional enrichment... because we did not take the new information available to us and use it to convert our born-in leadership potential to made-in leadership performance.

I again turn to John W. Gardner for perspective on renewal in his 1965 Harper's Magazine article entitled: *How to Prevent Organizational Dry Rot*. I find this as relevant in 2025 as it was in the middle of last century:

Dr. D's Reflections

A heartfelt nod to my three brothers who earned the title of United States Marine—**includ-ing author Richard S. Dillard. Your commitment, courage, and service continue to inspire. One way is in your resolute accep-tance of the reality that things change, but if I've heard it once I've heard it a thousand times from Marines...

"You adapt. You overcome. You improvise." – Clint Eastwood as Gunny Highway, Heartbreak Ridge.

May I encourage you, the reader, to embrace every new insight available to you—and use it to transform your innate leadership potential into intentional leadership performance.

> *Like people...organizations have a life cycle. They have a green and supple youth, a time of flourishing strength, and a gnarled old age. We have all seen organizations that are still going through the diseases of childhood, and others so far gone in the rigidities of age that they*

*ought to be pensioned off and sent to Florida to live
out their days. But organizations differ from people…
in that their cycle isn't even approximately predictable.
An organization may go from youth to old age in two or
three decades, or it may last for centuries. More important, it may go through a period of stagnation and then
revive. In short, decline is not inevitable, Organizations
need not stagnate. They often do, to be sure, but that is
because the arts of organizational renewal are not yet
widely understood. Organizations can renew themselves
continuously. That fact has far-reaching implications for
our future.* (Gardner)

Yes! Organizations, like the organisms (people) that work in them, can renew themselves. It's one of the basic tenets of this book. I use the word *continual*, however, because I don't believe the cycle of renewal is *continuous* (i.e., unceasing or going on without interruption). I believe leadership renewal, both per-sonally and organizationally, is something that can be frequently repeated between occasional interruptions called rest. The data in reality supports this claim in terms of burning hot and burning out… a very real danger in running the cycle continuously. Richard Swenson, M.D., wrote extensively about this in *Margin: Restoring Emotional, Physical, Financial, and Time Reserves to Overloaded Lives* (Swenson). In it, he defines margin as the space between your load and your limits—the buffer that allows for rest, reflection and resilience. He argues, I'd say very convincingly, that chronic overload in modern life—emotionally, physically, financially and in time—leads to burnout, stress and relational breakdown. These outcomes are the antithesis of *Real Leadership* in every practical and meaningful way, so I love the 75 (not a short list) practical prescriptions to restore margin and live a more balanced, intentional life. There isn't enough space to include them all here, but I've listed the key underlying themes below:

- Margin exists for relationship—with God, others and self.
- Progress is not always positive if it erodes margin.
- Slowing down is a spiritual and emotional necessity.
- Simplicity and availability are virtues worth culti-vating.

In the final analysis, what's important is how organizations gain the capacity for continual renewal and improvement. It's the same way people do, and it happens for organizations to the same extent that it happens for their personnel.

Remember Deming's statement on transformation and where it begins? It begins with the individual... the Leader. I mentioned early on that I had a "legacy complex" and was extremely concerned about whether or not I would leave others and the organizations I serve better off than they were before their encounter with me. What better way to do this than by first renewing and improving my own *Personal Leadership Platform* and then using it to renew and improve the *Leadership Platforms* of others in the organizations where I'm privileged to work... ultimately changing the organizational culture in worthwhile and sustainable ways? My encounter with these organizations may be temporal, but the impact I have doesn't have to be. And this is, in large part, what John W. Gardner is providing an opportunity for us to consider in his great article on renewal referenced above.

If an organization is to renew its leadership, its leaders must personally renew. Leaders have the unique opportunity to bring

Dr. D's Reflections

Organizational renewal is too often short-cycled by the imaginary leaders we introduced earlier... by those who lack *Real Leadership*. And we also know the power that "leadership positions" bring can be intoxicating—especially for those who become addicted to the status (and let's not forget the earnings). One of the most common and damaging ways this shows up is through poor communication—or worse, complete silence. Imaginary leaders often withhold information, believing that secrecy preserves their value and secures their position. In reality, this passive-aggressive behavior promotes *passive-defensive* responses, decision bottlenecks and trust erosion. Another telltale sign is when they belittle others or their ideas—especially in public. This isn't strength; it's insecurity disguised as authority. True leaders empower others. Those who tear people down only reveal their own weakness to those who are truly paying attention, and believe me, they are paying attention.

people together for the purpose of promoting renewal in the organizations they serve, and they do this through their impact on others and ultimately on the culture. But the key here is that this impact transcends personal leadership lifecycle boundaries. When a leader passes off the scene, which is inevitable given the predictable nature of our personal lifecycle, nothing of his/her leadership passes off the scene. There is an enduring aspect of leadership between the person and the organization that shouldn't be overlooked, and we have examples of this in both positive and negative context.

The negative impact that wrong and ineffective leaders have on an organization is verifiable and devastating. In his great work on Deming's System of Profound Knowledge, Dr. Gary Fellers proposes the "dead-boss theory" as an explanation for *Why Things Go Wrong*. Feller writes:

*A theory of mine explains why fear accumulates over time: the skeletons often stay in the closet, and build up, after the source disappears. This is the **dead-boss theory**. Employees never forget. It usually takes more continued energy to remove the skeletons than it did to put them there. The bones become dislodged and are difficult to clean up.* (Fellers)

Notwithstanding the cost and time associated with clean-up, I'd suggest the net-effect of this negative personal impact by wrong and ineffective leaders on the organization is about the same as we see from poor customer satisfaction: lost revenue and lower retention. I don't say this hypothetically, but practically. If a customer is defined as anyone who benefits from a product or service, then members of the organization are the customers of leadership. They benefit directly from the leadership services offered by the organization. When members are satisfied with leadership, retention is higher and either revenue and/or profits soar. In contrast, low member satisfaction with leadership leads to higher turnover, often to competitors, and decreased revenue or profits. It is just that simple. And, in case you're still on the fence over the legitimacy of these claims, perform a search on Google for "impact of leadership on organizational performance" and you'll find over 4 million results.

The LEL-c provides you with the means to enable continual renewal and improvement for personal and organizational leadership, if you are willing to make the required effort. There is a connection between our last Leadership Enrichment Stage (EXCELLENCE) and the first Enrichment Stage (LIFELONG LEARNING), but there is a caveat; the connection is not hard-wired. In fact,

Dr. D's Reflections

Many external forces influence organizations: government, politics, religion, social media and global events—yes, all the topics they say to avoid at family gatherings. But ignoring these influences or failing to understand their impact can stifle leadership and derail the journey. Talking about them—respectfully and thoughtfully—broadens your perspective. You may not agree with every viewpoint, but you'll gain a deeper understanding. And that understanding is what allows leaders to adapt, connect, continue the journey and lead more effectively.

none of the performance waypoints are hardwired with the next emotional connector. Just like a pilot can land at his first waypoint and choose, for whatever reason, not to continue the journey, so also we can choose to stop anywhere along the LEL-c. Unfortunately, it happens far more often than most know or are willing to admit.

Where I find hard stops occurring most often for new leaders is in the last two Enrichment Stages. Because they still remember high-school or college, they are accustomed to learning and haven't quite developed an arrogance that produces ignorance defended by hubris (e.g., they are more willing to accept new information about themselves and commit to worthwhile change). The problem is, more often than not they lack the skill/tool-set required for acting on what they've planned. Unless previously conquered during high-school or college, the "student syndrome" (a.k.a., procrastination) creeps back in and holds them up from completing Enrichment Stage #3: FULFILLMENT. As a result, growth is halted and they are never able to reach Enrichment Stage #4: EXCELLENCE.

Alternately, where I find hard-stops in the LEL-c occurring most often for more seasoned leaders, especially those with senior positions, is in the first 2 Enrichment Stages. It seems that, over time and through successive promotions, they've started to believe too much in their own stuff and have stopped learning. I referred to this in the last paragraph as an **arrogance that produces ignorance**. It doesn't happen immediately. It sets in over time, and it is extremely dangerous for anyone who has experienced the type of success that results in senior leadership roles. And it has consequences. On the personal level, just because you've been promoted to a position of leadership doesn't mean you will be appointed to lead by those who happen to be in your down-line organizationally. If they don't choose to follow your lead, at best you can expect malicious obedience until the most capable members leave your organization—usually for a competitor—to find a better leader.

On the organizational level, Human Synergistics International calls this phenomenon "defensive misattribution of success", and Dr. Robert A. Cooke, co-developer of the OCI®, explains it as follows:

> *There are quite a few successful organizations out there with defensive cultures, but they are successful despite rather than because of their cultures. The growth and profits realized by organizations result from a myriad of factors beyond culture—including ownership of patents and copyrights, geographical monopolies, historical dominance of markets, and being in the right place at the right time.*
>
> *Such advantages provide the organization with slack resources that, in turn, can allow management to get away with unenlightened leadership practices, sub-optimal technologies, counter-productive human resource*

systems, and/or rigid structures based on control and command. If management allows this to happen, these factors lead to and reinforce a defensive culture.

When managers of such organizations are presented with their [Organizational Culture Inventory®] OCI® results, they sometimes argue that defensive cultures must be good given that their firms are successful. I refer to this as the 'misattribution of success to culture,' given that people tend to attribute success to themselves or things they have created (like culture). However, their organizations are 'successful,' at least along certain criteria, despite rather than because of their cultures. (Nesbitt)

Either way, it is absolutely vital that we understand what holds us back and take pains with it on the personal and organizational level if we are to adopt the LEL-c, which is intended, by design, to be a LIFE-cycle for renewal.

If we are able to successfully cycle through our first iteration of the LEL-c, we must still be willing to learn. We can't view our achievement in excellence as having arrived at a final destination. It takes a lifelong commitment, which is why the first Enrichment Stage is LIFELONG LEARNING.

The cycle repeats as long as we continue learning, and this increases our potential to lead in new ways as we advance through the second and third Enrichment Stages. Ultimately, pursuing excellence for and with others by leveraging our *Leadership Platforms* in the last Enrichment Stage will afford fresh perspectives and new information about our leadership; the catalyst for learning that is absolutely essential to personal and organizational renewal.

You're now moving to the *Conclusion* of this book, but it's really just a prelude to the beginning. It's been quite the journey already and my hope is that you've taken advantage of the numerous opportunities presented throughout this book. Don't stop here. This powerful and inspiring approach to renewing and improving your *Personal Leadership Platform* first sets a strong foundation for influencing others authentically and sustainably. Then, by modeling the change you want to see, you create credibility and trust—two essential ingredients for cultural transformation. But I understand how overwhelming this can seem, no matter where you are in the journey. As one of my old, long-time mentors, Galen McPherson, Intellectual Capitalist, would say: This can become a lot more complicated than it looks… and it already looks very complicated."

So, here's how you might structure your way forward in 3 simple (not easy) steps:

1. **Renew Your Personal Leadership Platform**

   ▸ *Clarify your "Why":* Revisit your purpose and values.

   ▸ Assess your current leadership habits: What's working? What needs refining?

   ▸ *Build margin:* Apply principles like those from Swenson to avoid burnout.

   ▸ *Commit to continuous learning:* Stay curious and adaptable.

2. **Influence Others' Leadership Platforms**

- *Mentor and coach:* Share your journey and tools with others.

- *Create safe spaces:* Encourage reflection and growth in your teams.

- *Model vulnerability and integrity:* Show that leadership is a journey, not a destination.

3. **Transform Organizational Culture**

- *Align systems with values:* Ensure policies and practices reflect the desired culture.

- *Celebrate small wins:* Reinforce positive change.

- *Foster shared ownership:* Culture change is a team effort.

Remember, it's a journey—and your greatest opportunities still lie ahead.

CONCLUSION

[Written by Mr. D with reflections by Dr. D.]

This section is as much a closing for this book as it is a tribute to you; those who will take the information presented in its pages and use it to **Take Your Lead** *and improve the organizations you serve. Between Dr. D's insights and Tim Hansel's legacy of modeling Leadership as a Service (LaaS) to others, we hope you take it in the spirit with which this entire book was intended:*

- *Motivational: Encouraging you to act in the pursuit of new goals.*
- *Encouraging: Providing you with support and confidence.*
- *Uplifting: Raising your countenance and expression.*
- *Empowering: Elevating your authority or power to do something great.*
- *Visionary: Establishing clearer ideas about who you want to be in the future.*
- *Ambitious: Strengthening your desire for success or achievement.*
- *Hopeful: Inspiring your optimism about the future.*
- *Influential: Exercising power to affect others' actions, decisions, or thinking.*

If you want to transform your organization or team, focus first on transforming yourself into a *real leader*. If you want to improve your *rightness* as a leader, design and build the Footing and Foundation of your personal *Leadership Platform* with virtues/ core values and guiding principles that place a primary passage of reference on others and always consider motive, means and ends in each decision or action. To improve the *effectiveness* of your leadership, design and build the Framing of your personal *Leadership Platform* with strategies that are more prescriptive than restrictive across the key areas or domains that promote positive individual, group and organizational outcomes. If you want to maintain and leverage your personal *Leadership Platform* (a human becoming the best version of you), strive to adopt the Leadership Enrichment LIFE-cycle on a continual basis... literally, over a lifetime.

Committing to the LIFE-cycle for a lifetime of service to others is what it means to be truly remarkable and exceptional as both servant and leader. In my humble estimation, if anyone ever met the definition of a servant with a well-defined *Leadership Platform* who could easily be described as remarkable and exceptional by their followers, it would have been Tim Hansel.

It is in Tim's honor—out of my great love and affection for this man and a heart filled with gratitude—that I include the following outline of these 10 keys, in his "flesh and bones" terms. Honestly, I couldn't have said it better, and it is truly only a small fraction of the legacy that Tim Hansel created as a servant leader while still this side of eternity.

Tim taught these 10 keys to personal peak performance in his magnificent video aptly titled *Holy Sweat* (Hansel), first produced back in 1986. They are as essential today as ever: start, vision, goals, courage, teamwork, excellence, ability to fail, perseverance, joy and giving it all away. More practically, Tim lived these 10 keys. They proved invaluable to me as I developed as a leader, and I believe it can make a positive difference in your adoption of the LEL-c and in the creation of a *Leadership Platform* for yourself and your organization.

KEY 1 - YOU'VE GOT TO START:

The great tragedy in life is that most people spend their lives indefinitely preparing to live. — Paul Tournier, Swiss Psychologist

I can't tell you how many times I've gotten stuck on start. And I see it happen far too often with good managers who are struggling to be good leaders in our modern organizations. They have the best intentions but never really get out of the blocks. Tim actually uses the illustration of a locomotive to underscore the point. A locomotive, of course, is the railway vehicle that provides the motive power for a train, and it has been reported that one inch blocks of wood can keep the train from getting underway. It will not move forward with those one inch blocks of wood when placed in front of and behind the drive wheels. In contrast, remove the one inch blocks and get the locomotive underway, and it can break through 5 feet of concrete laced with rebar. Enough said!

KEY 2 – YOU'VE GOT TO HAVE VISION:

The essential sadness of the human family is that very few of us ever approach the realization of our full potential. I accept the estimate of the theoreticians that the average person accomplishes only 10% of his promises, sees only 10% of the beauty of the World around him, hears only 10% of the music and poetry of the universe, smells only a 10th of the World's fragrance and tastes only a 10th of the deliciousness of being alive. He's only 10% open to his emotions, to tenderness, to wonder. His mind embraces only a small part of the thoughts, reflections and understandings of which he is capable. His heart is only 10% alive with love. He will die without ever having really lived or really loved. — John Powell

Here are some things to consider when creating a personal Vision of Potential:

- Who are your heroes?

- Who do you admire most?

- Who would you most like to meet, learn from and emulate?

- What do you love to do?

- What are you nuts about?

- What are your special gifts/abilities?

- What are you good at?

- Where will you be in 5 years?

KEY 3 – YOU'VE GOT TO GET GOALS:

Goal *getting* beats goal *setting* every time. Make sure you follow these patterns when getting your goals:

- Have them, and make sure they are Clear – Specific – Concise (characterizes top 15% of society)

- Write them down in 1st Person, with Potent Emotion, in Present Tense (characterizes top 2% of society)

- Plan your work; Work your Plan (we covered this as part of the ACTION emotional connector to the GROW performance waypoint in the Fulfillment stage of leadership enrichment)

- Key is to become OUR BEST... not THE BEST

CAUTION: Focus on starting one goal/objective/task at a time. Prioritize to avoid over-tasking or multi-tasking. To further this concept, I've drawn the following from Bill Tenny-Brittian's BLOG post from June 6, 2012:

> *Have you ever wondered how a locomotive can over-come the inertia of so much weight? We're talking about 12,000 tons. Even though the locomotive may weigh 270,000-pounds and makes 3,200 horsepower (some generate 7,000 horsepower) generating over 64,000 pounds of thrust it could never pull 12,000 tons from a dead stop. The fact is the locomotive doesn't pull them all*

at once. It only pulls one car at a time. The engineer does this by backing up the locomotive so that all of the slack is removed from the couplers as the cars are bunched together. While in motion, the brakes are set enough to prevent coasting, and the train comes to a stop. The engine then starts forward having only to pull one car at a time to get it rolling, which it can easily do for about an inch, then the second car is pulled, and so on until the slack comes out of all the couplers. By the time the caboose is pulled, the engine is sometimes traveling as much as 10 to 15 miles an hour. (Tenny-Brittian)

By the same token, avoid falling into the traps of the Student Syndrome, which we discussed earlier; or Parkinson's Law, where work expands to fill the time allotted for it. Don't be afraid to correct for either of these natural tendencies related to goals. Finally, if you really want to get good at this idea of goal getting rather than goal setting, take a little encouragement from Brian Tracy in *Eat That Frog! 21 Great Ways to Stop Procrastinating and Get More Done in Less Time*. It is a great resource for those in need of goal getting.

KEY 4 – YOU'VE GOT TO HAVE HEART:

Courage – comes from the French word Cœur, which means HEART. It means extended effort, bravery or valor. Or, if you prefer the American Translation: GUTS! It is life's greatest intangible... its middle name. There IS NO Substitute for COURAGE, especially the courage of self-affirmation.

If there is a seventh wonder of this world, it would be self-affirmation. It means I have a positive self-concept. Again borrowing from Brian Tracy, our self-concept is representative of our self-portrait, our self-ideal and our self-esteem, and there are seven ways of developing a positive dominant image for all three: 1) recognize you are the best and only version of you; 2) don't compare; 3) accept that you are NOT your actions; 4) employ solid decision-making; 5) acknowledge mistakes are NORMAL; 6) enjoy the present; and 7) give yourself plenty of praise and encouragement. (Tracy)

Sound advice! But have you ever actually applied it? It is tough. And I suppose that's why courage is required. Honestly, I've never met someone who complained of suffering from too much encouragement.

KEY 5 – YOU'VE GOT TO LEARN HOW TO COOPERATE:

Cooperation has become the optimum survival strategy.
It no longer has to be you or me. 'Selfishness,' he declared,
is unnecessary and hence-forth unrationalizable....
— R. Buckminster Fuller

Buckminster "Bucky" Fuller was the person most responsible for making **synergy** a common term. Much of his work was about exploring and creating synergy. He found synergy to be a basic principle of all interactive systems. He developed a subject called *Synergetics*, a "Geometry of Thinking." Simply put, synergy occurs when two or more people come together to accomplish something they can't do separately. It has also been defined as "when the whole exceeds the sum of its parts."

The BOTTOM LINE is: We need each other! As mentioned earlier, every healthy cell in our body lives to enable all the other cells—that's what makes us work. When cells live only for themselves, we call this cancer. Consider also that there are more than 600 voluntary muscles in the body. If all your muscles could cooperate to pull in one direction, you could create a force of 25 tons. Imagine what you could accomplish with a pair or small group if everyone voluntarily cooperated to move in one direction.

KEY 6 – YOU'VE GOT TO PURSUE EXCELLENCE; NOT PERFECTION:

Striving for perfection is the greatest stopper there is. You'll be afraid you can't achieve it . . . . It's your excuse to yourself for not doing anything. Instead strive for excellence, doing your best. — Sir Laurence Olivier

The pursuit of excellence is gratifying and healthy. The pursuit of perfection is frustrating, neurotic and a terrible waste of time. — Edwin Bliss

Drs. J. Clayton and Lorraine Lafferty captured this idea in the title of their book: *Perfectionism: A sure cure for happiness*. And since we have covered this a lot already, I'll stop at sharing only one more story from Dr. Lafferty's great presentation: *The Roots of Excellence.* At one point, he reminded the media executives in attendance of Kitty and Peter Carruthers skating performance in the 1984 Winter Olympics (where they won the Silver Medal). After they skated off the ice following one performance, a news reporter noticed that they weren't looking at the judges' scores. When asked about it, they replied: "We came here to skate well, and when you skate well, you win." (Lafferty)

KEY 7 – YOU'VE GOT TO HAVE THE ABILITY TO FAIL:

Success is never final; failure is never fatal...it is courage that counts. — Winston Churchill

Failure is NOT the enemy of Success. Thomas Waters, former President of IBM, had a long-term formula for success: "Double Your Failure Rate." Edison referred to 8,000+ failures at inventing the light bulb as "Education." Attitude is everything!

KEY 8 – YOU'VE GOT TO PERSEVERE:

Press on. Nothing in the world can take the place of persistence. Talent will not: nothing is more common than unsuccessful men or woman with talent: Genius will not; unrewarded genius is almost a proverb. Education

alone will not; the world is full of educated derelicts.
Persistence and determination alone are omnipotent.
— Calvin Coolidge

What is perseverance? The ability to Bounce Back. Courage Stretched Out. Patience plus Endurance. Illustration: Glenn Cunningham (World's Fastest Human Being) is a perfect example. As Kyle R from Sycamore Junior High so eloquently states in his paper for *The My Hero Project*: "He was just eight years old when it was his turn to light the school house heater. Then boom!... Glenn Cunningham's physicians told him that he would never walk again. He had severe leg burns from the explosion....Cunningham not only walked again but was one of the top-notch milers in the 1930s. For three years, from 1932 to 1934, he won the Big Six indoor titles and was at the Olympics again in 1936. Then in 1938 Cunningham became the world's fastest runner as he set a new record at Dartmouth College."

KEY 9 – YOU'VE GOT TO CHOOSE JOY:

There is no box, made by God nor us, but that the sides can be flattened out, and the top blown off, to make a dance floor on which to celebrate life. — Kenneth Caraway

In spite of all you may have heard, joy is a choice. It is also a gift. It is based on who we are, not what we have or what happens to us. Happiness, in contrast, comes from the same root word as 'happening', which would suggest that in order for us to be happy, something has to happen. Happiness is based on circumstances. Joy is deeper... it defies circumstance, occurs in spite of difficult situations and coexists with ambiguity and pain. Louis Smead, now a deceased professor at Fuller Seminary once wrote, "You and I were created for joy, and if we miss it we miss the reason for our existence. If our joy is honest joy however, it must somehow be congruous with human tragedy. This is a test of joy's integrity; is it compatible with pain? Only the heart that hurts has a right to joy." The reality is, when we try to cut ourselves off from pain—not possible, by the way—we cut ourselves off from joy.

KEY 10 – YOU'VE GOT TO GIVE IT ALL AWAY:

In this context, 'it' means YOU! It means giving yourself away for the benefit of others, and there is no position on earth where this quality needs to exist more than that of a Leader. Remember the essential ingredient in a leader's platform? **Sacrifice!** It is a combination of the Latin *sacra*, meaning "sacred rites" plus the root of *facere*, which means "to do, perform." According to the Online Etymology Dictionary, it was first recorded in the 1590's and conveys the sense of "something given up for the sake of another." To servants, this comes naturally.

With this type of sacrifice, is it all that hard to imagine why high-achievers in excellence (i.e., peak performers), like Tim Hansel, become great leaders? It is the actual point at which we truly begin to draw a following through the basic "law of attraction." I'd dare say, it is also a prerequisite to investing in our enrichment as leaders in the first place. The only way we'll ever be able to truly leverage our *Leadership Platforms* is to ensure that they carry more weight for those who choose to follow. The LEL-c was developed with this purpose in mind.

If you never stop learning, changing, growing or leading through awareness, acceptance, action and achievement, you'll always be ready to...

AFTERWORD

T HE JOURNEY TO writing this book was both highly professional and deeply personal for the Authors. I know this both personally and anecdotally.

Personally, because we've shared experiences as brothers — Richard, Brian, and I — and have witnessed together how leaders can falter under the weight of flawed and distorted paradigms. We've also seen how they flourish when they embrace adaptability, authenticity and self-awareness. Anecdotally, because I've heard the stories — many of them of the horror variety — over the past 41 years.

I also know this empirically. My own professional experience over the past 35 years validates the patterns, pitfalls and possibilities of leadership and organizational culture explored in the pages of this book.

But this book isn't just a chronicle of what's broken. It's a blueprint for what's possible.

In Part 1, you were introduced to the concept of the **Leadership Platform** — a metaphor and a model that reflects the structure, the strength and the intentionality required to lead with lasting impact. You learned that platforms aren't inherited. They're built — by hand, by heart and by hard work. They are unique to each leader, shaped by purpose, tested through adversity and proven through application.

Part 2 brought this to life through the **Leadership Enrichment LIFE-cycle (LEL-c)** — a pathway grounded in real-world insight and emotional depth. From **awareness to acceptance, action to achievement,** you explored the work of becoming a more grounded, more effective and more fulfilled leader. This wasn't about theory — it was about transformation.

And that, ultimately, is what this book is — a guidebook for personal and organizational transformation. By now, through the multiple **Opportunities** offered throughout, you have a head start. Don't Stop!

The world doesn't need more managers who can manage. It needs more managers who can lead — people with the courage to reflect, the humility to grow and the resilience to build something that lasts. That's why your Leadership Platform isn't a final destination. It's a practice. A mindset. A commitment.

What lies ahead for you in leadership will not be easy. The future is uncertain, the pressures are immense and the pace of change is relentless. But what remains true — and what this book hopes to remind you — is that **your platform matters.** You don't need to be perfect, but you do need to be present… leading with clarity, consistency and conviction.

So I leave you with this:

- Take what resonated with you and put it into practice — even if imperfectly.

- Revisit your platform regularly. Strengthen it. Reinforce it. Share it.

- Remember that growth happens in the work — not just the reading.

To my brothers, Richard and Brian — thank you for leading this effort and for continuing to challenge the leadership status quo with integrity, insight and intrepidity.

To the reader — this is not the end. It is an open invitation to **Take Your Lead** with an RSVP attached.

Along with a world in need, we await your Acceptance.

> — Christopher J. Dillard,
> Chief Value Officer at Tyleum Group LLC
> Sr. Finance & Accounting Leader

BACK MATTER
FOR THE PREFACE

REFERENCES

12manage.com (2012). 12manage Smart Card [Company webpage entry]. Retrieved from https://www.12manage.com/sc.asp?RS=dl00

Bateman, T. S., & Snell, S. A. (2011). *Management: Leading & Collaborating in a Competitive World* (9th ed.). New York, NY: McGraw-Hill/Irwin.

Cooke, R. A. (2012). Leadership/Impact® (L/I) [Company webpage entry]. Retrieved from https://www.humansynergistics.com/change-solutions/change-solutions-for-leaders-and-managers/assessments-for-leaders-and-managers/leadership-impact/

Cooke, R. A., & Rousseau, D. M. (1989). Organizational Culture: Not Just Another Name for Climate. Adapted from *Behavioral norms and expectations: A quantitative approach to the assessment of organizational culture*. Group & Organization Studies, 13, 245-273.

Deming, W. E. (1986). *Out of the Crisis*. Cambridge, MA: Massachusetts Institute of Technology, Center for Advanced Educational Services.

Deming, W. E. (1994). *The New Economics*. Cambridge, MA: Massachusetts Institute of Technology, Center for Advanced

Educational Services. Retrieved from https://deming.org/explore/sopk/

Dillard, R. S. (2009). *Miracle Cure: The Amazing New Elixir of Corporate Culture*. Retrieved from https://www.slideshare.net/slideshow/miracle-cure-the-amazing-new-elixir-of-corporate-culture/9941081

Gitelson, G., Bing, J.W., & Laroche, L. (2001). *The Impact of Culture on Mergers & Acquisitions*. Retrieved from https://buscreative.blogspot.com/2014/12/the-impact-of-culture-on-mergers.html

Human Synergistics® International (2025). *How Culture Works*. Retrieved from https://www.humansynergistics.com/about-us/how-culture-works/

Human Synergistics® International (2012). *The Impact of Leaders on Culture* [Company webpage entry]. Retrieved from https://www.human-synergistics.com.au/wp-content/HSFiles/Publications/Why-Culture-and-Leadership-Matter.pdf

Human Synergistics, Inc. (1988). Behavioral norms and expectations: A quantitative approach to the assessment of organizational culture. *Group & Organization Studies*, 13, 245-273.

Human Synergistics, Inc. (Producer). (1987). *The Roots of Excellence: Achievement in Sales Thinking* [VHS]. Available from Human Synergistics, Inc., Plymouth, MI.

McCarthy, S. (2005). *The Leadership Culture Performance Connection*. Unpublished manuscript, Human Synergistics® International.

Redgrave (2025). *The state of US workplace culture in 2025.* Retrieved from https://redgravesearch.com/insights/publications/the-state-of-us-workplace-culture-in-2025/

Right Management (2010). Leadership Insights. *Organizational Effectiveness: Discovering How to Make It Happen.* Originally sourced from http://www.right.com/thought-leadership /research/organizational-effectiveness-discovering-how-to-make-it-happen.pdf

Sanders, E. J., & Cooke, R. A. (2005). *Financial Returns from Organizational Culture Improvement: Translating "Soft" Changes into "Hard" Dollars.* Article for Presentation at the ASTD Expo in Orlando, FL, June 6, 2005.

Schwartz, T. (2010). *Six Secrets to Creating a Culture of Innovation.* Originally sourced from http://blogs.hbr.org/schwartz/2010/08/six-secrets-to-creating-a-cult.html

Stewart, A. (2021). *How Leaders Impact Culture.* Retrieved from https://www.humansynergistics.com/en-ca/blog/2021/10/04/how-leaders-impact-culture/

Szumal, J. L. (1998). *Organizational Culture Inventory® Interpretation and Development Guide.* Plymouth, MI: Human Synergistics, Inc.

ENDNOTES

1 Christina Garsten and Tor Hernes concluded in *Ethical Dilemmas in Management* (New York: Taylor Francis, 2008) that the stability of Enron's house of cards had been eroded by the very culture that had allowed it to be built. The very results Enron had sought to prevent—falling stock prices,

lack of consumer and financial market confidence—came about as a direct result of decisions that had been driven by Enron's culture.

2 According to the Columbia Accident Investigation Board (CAIB) report, Volume 1, August 26, 2003: "The accident was not a random event but rather a result of the spaceflight program's culture, which had as much to do with the accident as the foam did. The organizational causes of this accident are rooted in the space shuttle program's history and culture, including the original compromises that were required to gain approval for the shuttle, subsequent years of resource constraints, fluctuating priorities, schedule pressures, mischaracterization of the shuttle as operational rather than developmental, and lack of agreed national vision for human space flight."

3 The conclusion of one study project funded by AHRQ on "The Culture of Safety" at 15 California Hospitals (2001) was: "…while short term efforts to work on specific interventions (such as computerized physician order entry implementation) are laudable, they may be insufficient if the managerial structures and cultures of institutions do not sufficiently favor patient safety. Long term progress may need to include interventions specifically aimed at improving safety culture and breaking down barriers between managers and front line workers" (Singer, S.J. et. al, *The Culture of Safety: Results of an Organization Wide Survey in 15 Hospitals*, Quality & Safety in Health Care 2003;12:112-118).

4 A 2002 report on the reliability and validity of Leadership/Impact (L/I)™ included an evaluation of self-reports from 4,950 leaders along with descriptions by others from 32,470

people. The report concluded, in general, that leaders who use Prescriptive strategies have a constructive impact that is positively associated with effectiveness and success while leaders who use Restrictive strategies promote defensive styles that are negatively associated with long-term effectiveness and success: "...regardless of organization type or geographic location, L/I data from around the world show that the leaders who create truly effective organizations are those who have a Constructive rather than...Defensive impact" (Szumal, J. L., *An International Study of the Reliability and Validity of Leadership/Impact (L/I)*™, Human Synergistics/Center for Applied Research, 2002).

5 Sanders & Cooke (2005) "...discuss five different studies that validate and support the importance of the work...to improve organizational culture. The studies referenced use quantitative data to measure both organizational culture via the Organizational Culture Inventory® (OCI®) (Cooke and Lafferty, 1987) and financial performance (based on corporate financial reports), and draw strong correlations between the two. The OCI® is a well-respected survey that has been completed by over 2 million individuals over the past twenty years and is statistically reliable and valid (Cooke and Szumal, 1993)."

6 The organizations with the strongest "adaptive" cultures saw their revenue grow four times faster, experienced job creation seven times faster, enjoyed stock prices that increased twelve times faster and had 750 percent higher profit performance (Kotter, J. P. & Heskett, J. L., *Corporate Culture and Performance*. New York, NY: Free Press, 1992).

7 Barrett, R. (1998). Liberating the Corporate Soul, New York, NY: Butterworth-Heinemann.

8 One Denison study found that the average return on equity for organizations with the lowest culture scores was six percent, while the average return on equity for organizations with the highest culture scores was 21 percent (Denison, D., *Linking Culture to the Bottom Line*, Denison Research 2007, Zurich, Switzerland: Denison Consulting, 2006).

9 Wolf, J., *Healthcare Heal Thyself: Seven Simple Truths that Drive Performance,* High Performance Research Project, Hospital Corporation of America, 2006.

BIBLIOGRAPHY

Air Force Insitute for Advanced Distributed Learning. *Noncommissioned Officer Academy*. Gunter Annex: Air University (AETC), 2010. Print.

Carlson, Dawn. *Balyor Business Research*. n.d. Web. 12 November 2010. <http://www.baylor.edu/business/research/index.php?id=48209>.

Chambers, Oswald. *Biblical Psychology*. 1914. Document. 4 December 2012. <http://openlibrary.org/books/OL24996451M/Biblical_psychology>.

Cooke, Robert A and Janet L Szumal. "Using the Organizational Culture Inventory to understand the operating cultures of organizations." *Handbook of Organizational Culture and Climate*. Ed. N M Ashkanasy, C P M Wilderom and M F Peterson. Thousand Oaks: Sage, 2000. Print.

Cooke, Robert A. *Leadership/Impact Feedback Report*. Plymouth: Human Synergistics International, 2011. Print.

Deming, W. Edwards. *The Deming System of Profound Knowledge*. 2012. Web. 23 December 2010. <http://deming.org/index.cfm?content=66]>.

Dillard, Richard. *The Leadership Platform of Richard S. Dillard, PMP, SSBB*. Dillard Partners LLC, 2012. Document.

Dwoskin, Hale. *The Sedona Method*. Sedona: Sedona Press, 2007. Print.

Fellers, Gary. *Why Things Go Wrong*. Gretna: Pelican Publishing Company, Inc., 1994. Print.

Gardner, John W. *EXCELLENCE: can we be equal and excellent too?* New York: W. W. Norton & Company, Inc., 1987. Paperback.

—. "How to Prevent Organizational Dry Rot." *Harper's Magazine* October 1965: 20-26. Document.

Gill, Roger. *Theory and Practice of Leadership.* 2006. Web. 29 November 2012. <http://www.amazon.com/ Theory-Practice-Leadership-Roger-Gill/dp/1849200246/ ref=sr_1_1?ie=UTF8&qid=1354201460&sr=8-1&keywords =Roger+Gill#reader_1849200246>.

Harari, Oren. *Quotations from Chairman Powell: A Leadership Primer.* n.d. 29 November 2012. <http://govleaders.org/ powell2.htm>.

Hendricks, Kathlyn and Gay Hendricks. *The Openness - to - Learning Scale.* n.d. Document. 30 November 2012. <http:// www.hendricks.com/links/Openness-To-Learning-Scale. pdf>.

Holy Sweat. Perf. Tim Hansel. Word Publishing. 1987. VHS.

Huls, J. *FROM THEOLOGY TO MYSTAGOGY.* 2006. Document. 4 December 2012. <http://www.ajol.info/index.php/ actat/article/viewFile/52316/40941>.

Lewis, Clive Staples. *The Four Loves.* New York: Harcourt, 1960. Print.

—. "The Weight of Glory." n.d. *Verber Consulting.* Ed. Mark Verber. Web. 20 April 2013. <http://www.verber.com/mark/ xian/weight-of-glory.pdf>.

McKinney, Michael. *LeadingBLOG.* n.d. Web. 29 November 2012. <http://www.leadershipnow.com/leading-blog/2008/03/followers_make_the_best_leader.html>.

MCRD SD Boot Camp 1980s. United States Marine Corps. Traditions Military Videos. n.d. DVD.

Nesbitt, Mary. *A Conversation about Changing Newspaper Culture.* 30 November 2001. Document. 3 December 2012. <http://www.readership.org/culture_management/culture/ data/interview_culture.pdf>.

Noebel, David. *Understanding the Times.* Eugene: Harvest House Publishing, 1991. Print.

Roosevelt, Theodore. *The Man in the Arena.* n.d. Speech. 29 November 2012. <http://www.theodore-roosevelt.com/ trsorbonnespeech.html>.

Szumal, Janet L. "Leadership/Impact Facilitator's Manual." Arlington Heights: Human Synergistics/Center for Applied Research, 2001. Print.

Tenny-Brittian, Bill. *The Summer Express ... What I've Learned from Locomotion.* 6 June 2012. Web. 29 November 2012.

The Roots of Excellence. Perf. J. Clayton Lafferty. Human Synergistics, Inc. 1987. VHS.

Thorn, Andrew. *thoughtLEADERS, LLC: Leadership Training for the Real World.* 13 February 2013. Web. 25 February 2013. <http://www.thoughtleadersllc.com/2013/02/ beyond-emotional-intelligence-achieving-spiritual-in- telligence/?utm_source=feedburner&utm_medium=e- mail&utm_campaign=Feed%3A+ThoughtleadersLlc- Blog+%28thoughtLEADERS+Blog%29>.

Tracy, Brian. "Psychology of Achievement." Nightingale Conant, 1987. Cassette.

Wikipedia, Contributors. *Progress Trap.* Vers. 517431392. n.d. 29 November 2012. <http://en.wikipedia.org/w/index. php?title=Progress_trap&oldid=517431392 >.

CREDITS AND POST SCRIPT

The authors wish to thank the staff at Human Synergistics International for their effort in reviewing the content of the original books—CultureIMPACT™ and Real Leadership! Are You Ready?—herein combined and updated.

All Human Synergistics International material referenced throughout is based on research and development by Robert A. Cooke, Ph.D. and J. Clayton Lafferty, Ph.D., and is protected by copyright. All rights reserved. For more information, please contact them directly (info@humansynergistics.com) or one of their certified consultants directly. — Copyright 1973-2025 by Human Synergistics International.

Human Synergistics International created a general theoretical model for "How Culture Works"—interactive model still available on their website (https://www.humansynergistics.com/about-us/how-culture-works/—beginning with the way assumptions and values are related to behavioral norms and expectations, as well as other organizational variables.

Organizational Culture Inventory® and OCI® are registered trademarks of Human Synergistics International. Used with permission.

Constructive, Passive/Defensive and Aggressive/Defensive are OCI® terminology: From *Organizational Culture Inventory®* by R. A. Cooke, Human Synergistics International. Copyright 2013 by Human Synergistics. Adapted by permission.

Navigation Aid

THE ROADMAP ON the following pages will help enable your journey, as well as track your progress through the Leadership Enrichment LIFE-cycle. As a "trip-ticket"—some of you are old enough to remember when AAA Insurance used to provide them for traveling in the Continental USA—they include common navigation terms like "mile marker" and "landmark" that serve as natural check points along the way. The check points will not only help you understand where you are at in the journey, but they also contain specific questions to help you assess whether you are ready to continue moving forward or need to spend more time at the mile marker or landmark. Moreover, they can serve as much needed rest-stops that will revitalize your Leadership Enrichment efforts.

Your journey continues, so...

MILE MARKER #1: MENTOR/COACH

Do you have one?

If no, find a mentor interested in investing themselves in you or hire a coach.

If yes, proceed to the next Mile Marker.

MILE MARKER #2: LEADERSHIP & CULTURE ASSESSMENT

Have you completed one?

If no, select/complete a personal leadership or organizational culture/effectiveness inventory.

If yes, proceed to the Landmarks.

LANDMARK #1: OPENNESS TO LEARNING

DO YOU KNOW HOW OPEN YOU ARE TO LEARNING IN THIS MOMENT?

· If not, evaluate your current level of Openness to Learning, whether about your personal leadership or your organization's culture.

· If so, determine what you must do to shift up the scale (rather than drift farther down) and proceed to the next Landmark.

LANDMARK #2: POTENTIAL TO LEARN

HOW DO YOU USUALLY LEARN (BY EXPERIENCE OR THEORY)?

· Try formulating a theory to inform the right questions when confronted with a non-neutral learning opportunity.

· Then use your experience, an experiment and the wisdom of others (i.e., mentors/coaches) to find the right answers.

HOW DO YOU USUALLY RESPOND TO PROBLEMS PRESENTED ABOUT YOU OR YOUR ORGANIZATION?

· Begin looking at them as non-neutral learning opportunities.

· Realize your behavior and resulting impact on others is not a measure of your self-worth, but a measure of your worth to others.

HOW OFTEN DO OLD PARADIGMS PREVENT YOU FROM LEARNING NEW INFORMATION?

· Review Joel Barker's work on Paradigms and learn how to overcome their limiting effects.

MILES MARKER #3: ACKNOWLEDGEMENT

Are you ready to acknowledge what isn't working in yourlife or your organization?

If not, commit right now to reject the lies you've been telling yourself and accept that you and your organization can be better than you've allowed yourself and it to become.

MILE MARKER #4: UNLIMITING EMOTIONS

Related to your prior acknowledgement, are you presently experiencing any limiting emotions?

If so, move through the basic releasing questions in the Sedona Method and commit to releasing any emotion that will prevent you from making meaningful changes in leadership for you or your organization.

If not, take up courage to accept the feedback as useful and necessary for worthwhile change, accept yourself and your organization for who and what you are today, and advance to Landmarks.

LANDMARK #3: CHANGE SELECTION

BASED ON YOUR FULL ACCEPTANCE OF WHAT YOU LEARNED ABOUT YOUR LEADERSHIP AND ORGANIZATIONAL CULTURE, HAVE YOU SELECTED A COUPLE OF THINGS YOU'D LIKE TO CHANGE?

· If not, work with your mentor/coach or a consultant to identify the areas you should work on first.

· If so, move to the next Landmark.

LANDMARK #4: CASE FOR CHANGE

FOR WHAT YOU HAVE DECIDED TO CHANGE, HAVE YOU DEVELOPED A CLEAR AND COMPELLING CASE FOR CHANGE?

· If not, move through the Formula for Successful Change and clearly document your level of dissatisfaction with the way things are, a clear vision of future potential (how things could be), the practical first steps to get there and belief that change is possible and will leave you better off than when you are today. Then document the perceived or estimated cost of change to ensure that, in your mind, at this point in the process, there is a compelling case for change.

· If so, advance to the next Mile Marker.

LANDMARK #4

MILE MARKER #3

MILE MARKER #4

LANDMARK #3

MILE MARKER #5

MILE MARKER #5: ACTION SEQUENCE

Based on your case for change, have you developed a complete understanding of what it will take to pull it off successfully?

If not, move through the proven action-sequence to ensure your efforts will produce the type of growth you are looking for.

If so, document your Virtues as Values, Vision & Strategy, Support Structures, and essential Skills to enable and empower your effort, begin taking action, and advance to Landmarks.

LANDMARK #5

LANDMARK #5: GROWTH MINDSET

FOR WHAT YOU ARE NOW TAKING ACTION ON, DO YOU HAVE THE RIGHT MINDSET TO STICK WITH IT AND SEE IT THROUGH TO FRUITION?

· If not, commit to following Dweck's advice and reject the mindset that suggests your intelligence and talents are fixed, and adopt a growth mindset in which you see yourself as fluid and adaptable; a work in progress.

· If so, continue checking your motives and means against your values to ensure you are growing for the right reason (i.e., doing things right) and in the right ways (doing the right things), and move on to the next Landmark.

LANDMARK #6

LANDMARK #6: ASSESSMENT REFRESH

IF YOUR ACTION IS COMPLETE, HAVE YOU REPEATED OR REFRESHED EARLIER ASSESSMENTS TO ENSURE YOUR ACTION PRODUCED THE TYPE OF GROWTH YOU WERE LOOKING FOR?

· If not, repeat the assessment and refresh the results to show progress and/or uncover any additional development opportunities. The results will either support the fact that you have learned, changed and grown successfully (i.e., you really are thinking in new ways) and effectively (i.e., you are having the impact you intended to have, as documented in your platform). In other words, it will help confirm that you are leading in ways consistent with changes to your personal platform and that your organization's Operating/Current Culture is becoming more like its Preferred/Ideal Culture.

· If so, advance to the next Mile Marker.

Enrichment Stage #4: Excellence Navigation Aid

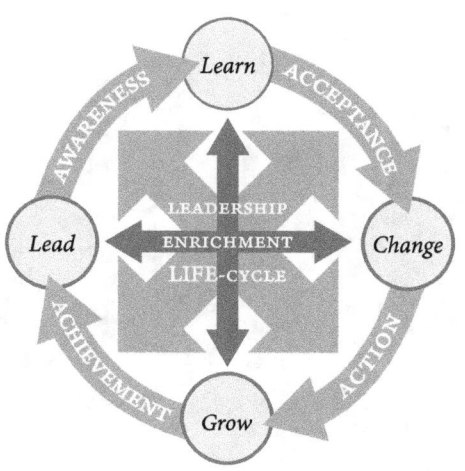

Based on the Growth produced, have you comitted to using it in ways that will help you and others achieve greater levels of performance excellence?

If not, go back and review the five ideas about Achievement that Dr. Lafferty shared in The Roots of Excellence and commit to maintaining Passion for Personal Excellence, Cause-Effect Thinking, Belief that individual Efforts Count, Moderate Risk Taking and Desire for Feedback.

If so, proceed to the next Landmark.

LANDMARK #7: LEADERSHIP MODELS

FOR WHAT YOU INTEND TO ACHIEVE FOR AND WITH OTHERS, HAVE YOU SELECTED THE TYPE OF LEADER YOU ARE BECOMING BASED ON WHAT YOU BELIEVE MOST ENABLES EXCELLENCE IN ACHIEVING IT?

· If not, evaluate the various types of leaders you encounter and how they incorporate various leadership theories, models, and styles in order to have the greates, most positive impact on others and their organizations. Then select the type of leader you most want to emulate and adopt the particular strategies that most align with your values and vision.

· If so, lead onward and upward with passion, patience and perseverance and organizationally, and commit to repeating the LIFE-cycle to continually renew and improve your leadership and the culture of your organization.

· Now proceed to the first Mile Marker and repeat the LIFE-cycle for Leadership Enrichment.

MILE
MARKER
#6

Leadership Platform

FOOTING

One Vision (driven by Mission)...
One Mission (guided by Vision)

With a platform that "rises to the bottom," I am a capable, enthusiastic and committed Lean-Agile Manager-Teacher Servant-Leader who endeavors...

TO continually move upward and outward with passion, patience, and perseverance with and for others...

SO THAT we can co-create and then perpetually grow products and services of extraordinary and lasting value.

Built on Trust

Constructive relationships built on trust and service form the basis of positive influence for Servant Leadership. With trust, teams (leaders and followers) can truly commit to accomplishing successful work together—whatever it may be. Without trust, people cannot work together authentically, and the disrupted/ strained relationships that result will have a negative, direct impact on any attempt to create value for/with others...your Vision/Mission.

As Servant Leader, remember that others must choose to follow my lead, otherwise I am not leading... regardless of my title, rank or position. Therefore, through the judicious (i.e., fair) and effective (i.e., balanced) use of both personal and positional power—primary and secondary sources, respectively—with high content of moral character, I strive to develop trust and sound reasoning among my followers, inspiring them to become service-oriented leaders who will advance and sustain the value movement.

The "leaders that follow" will automatically take pride in their work and hold themselves accountable for the things they can control. Through their service-oriented focus and commitment, these exemplary follower-leaders add more value. They know what it means to be a team player (not just a team member), to share ideas that advance the movement, to "go the distance".

This is possible because, as history reveals and science verifies, constructive **relationships** become conduit for the exchange of constructive **information** (i.e., communication for learning). In the process of approaching others and our successful work in this way we can create a new **vision** of potential for the team, the organization and the world. Barriers break down, paradigms shift and a whole new level of thinking begins to form around becoming our best. As Meg Wheatley suggests in *Leadership and the New Science*: "When [we] begin to fully explore these principles, a wealth of creative energy is unleashed and a new found capacity for learning is realized."

CAUTION: Servant Leadership is extremely powerful... a great strength. But any strength, when abused, quickly transforms into a weakness. Since exemplary followers will do almost anything asked, even if the request places them at risk, continually subordinate your freedom as leader under the control of righteousness (i.e., love of God) and responsibility (i.e., love of others). This will enable you to guard against abusing the strength of your platform, pushing things to self-defeating points, or taking advantage of those who choose to follow your lead. Remembering to "keep those who follow FIRST" will enable you to rise to the bottom…to truly support their weight as leader, accomplishing your mission as servant and finding your vision advanced beyond what you could dare imagine and your purpose fulfilled beyond what you could dare dream.

Reinforced by Personal Accountability

To develop and maintain trust, to truly be effective as a Servant Leader, personal accountability for this platform is imperative. Accountability establishes trust (ethos), which enables a powerful, lasting movement of effective leadership and excellence in performance.

Preserved by a Practical Warning

As the leadership goes, so goes the value movement (and the organization). As such, beware the traps of believing too much in your own "stuff", which leads to the destructive consequence of 1) *untamed passions in gifted men* caused by an abandonment of traditional moral standards and restraints, 2) *wanton power in weak men* caused by a growing voracity within and 3) *unteachable temperament in privileged men* caused by an arrogance that ultimately produces ignorance.

Guarded by 3 Virtues as Values

Honor: It is a way of thinking, behaving and doing... a *true north moral compass*. You either have it, or you don't. You either live by it or you just talk about it. It is the true measure of the self-worth of the individual, the team and the organization. Honor requires you to exemplify the ultimate standard in ethical and moral conduct. Honor is many things; honor requires many things. A Leader must never lie, never cheat, never steal, but that is not enough. Much more is required. Each Leader must cling to an uncompromising code of personal integrity, accountable for his actions and holding others accountable for theirs. And, above all, honor mandates that a Leader never sully the reputation of his compeers, company or Country.

Courage: Simply stated, courage is *honor in action*... an unlimited energy in motion (emotion) – and more. Courage is having the moral strength to use the compass for navigation, the will to heed the inner voice of conscience, the constitution to do what is right regardless of the conduct of others. It is mental discipline, an adherence to a higher standard. Courage means willingness to take a stand for what is right in spite of adverse consequences, a willingness to act without hesitation... to learn, change, grow and lead whenever needed. It is the willingness to let go, when necessary, and move on for more constructive outward action. It is the ability to laugh out loud, even at our own mistakes. Life is fun. This courage, throughout history, has sustained Leaders during the chaos, perils and hardships of combat, famine, depression, slavery and all manner of evil known to man. And every day, it enables each leader to look in the mirror – and smile.

Commitment: In a nutshell, commitment is *courage stretched out…over time*. It is a pledge of the personal will to the true good of others…a total dedication to the team. All for one…one for all! By whatever definition or cliché, commitment is a combination of: (1) selfless determination and (2) a relentless pursuit of excellence. Leaders never give up, never give in and never willingly accept second best. Excellence is always the goal…not perfection. And, when a leader's position changes within the organization or team, he/she remains steadfast in his/her allegiance and affection toward those with (and for) whom they have served. There is no such thing as an ex-Leader or former-Leader. Once a Leader, always a Leader. Commitment never dies.

FOUNDATION

Moving Toward 1 Goal/3 Objectives

Continually make prosperous differences in our world by helping individuals and organizations build capital, supported by these objectives:

- Create high-quality, productive and sustainable relationships with internal and external customers (continual growth through relational capital),

- Develop and deliver innovative, best-in-class products and services through a dedicated, fully-engaged and empowered workforce (continual innovation through human capital) and…

- Hardwire robust business processes supported by a highly-constructive culture for the relentless pursuit of excellence in all we do together (continual improvement through structural capital).

Empowered by 11 Guiding Principles

(Adapted from the United States Marine Corps)

- *Know yourself and seek self-improvement.* – Temet Nosce! This requires lifelong learning, changing, growing and leading through awareness, acceptance, action and achievement. Remember that "success is never final and failure is never fatal…it is courage that counts". – Winston Churchill

- *Be technically and tactically proficient.* – You either get it or you don't. Know the job…be someone who gets it.

- *Develop a sense of responsibility among your juniors, peers and seniors.* – 360⁰ Leadership. Ethos (appeal based on the character)…Pathos (appeal based on emotion/empathy)…Logos (appeal based on logic/

reason)! "An individual without information cannot take responsibility; an individual who is given information cannot help but take responsibility." — Jan Carlzon, CEO, Scandinavian Airlines Systems

- *Make sound and timely decisions.* – "The second best decision quickly made is better than the best decision never made." — General Douglas MacArthur

- *Set the example.* – Applied Leadership is spherical – 100% of the time. The only thing that changes is your relative position to the center (those standing on your platform and following your lead). Leading from the top is built into the organizational hierarchy if you are in the unique position of leading others. Here the portion is to set-up, fill-up and free-up your team to pursue goals mutually set, and then negotiate the means and remove barriers around their success in achieving them. A portion of Leadership is also from the front, and its creed is "Follow me!" Another is from the bottom, as you support the weight of your followers. Yet another is from the rear (developmental), as you push your team to and just above (never beyond) their current limits. And finally, it is from the flank, as you get out of the way and let the team accomplish their goals, effectively removing "the law of the lid" from the leadership equation. In any of its forms, Leadership by example is the antithesis of the "Do as I say, not as I do" mentality. Always let the authority of your example outweigh the authority of your rank, position or title.

- *Seek responsibility and take responsibility for your actions.* – In large part, this is achievement orientation and includes the following elements:

1. Passion for Excellence (not winning).

   - Paradox: The more pre-occupied you are with winning the more likely you are to lose.
   - Correlates with Performance at greater than .54.
   - Translates best through the not-so-new concept of participative management.
   - Highly distractible by Approval, Convention, Power, Prestige, Influence, Status and Control.

   Excellence pursued not as measure of self-worth but simply because it can be done characterizes outstanding individuals and organizations.

2. Cause and Effect Thinking.

   - Things are caused. This is the antithesis of a belief in luck, fate, chance and magic.
   - Illustration: Management by Objectives.
   - Implication: Holding people accountable for things they can't control.
   - Translation: A sophisticated game of "Gotcha".
   - Effect: Self-defeat, Demotivation, Low Morale, Poor Performance.

3. Belief in the Idea that Individual Efforts Count (Self-set Goals).

   ◆ Self-set goal characteristics are measurable as early as 4-5 years of age. Set goals for yourself.

   ◆ Lead the goal setting process, but don't impose goals. Any time you try to impose a goal you will diminish the thinking of the other person.

4. Moderate Risk Taking.

   ◆ Set modest goals, reach them and continually raise the bar. Avoid stretch goals/targets…it is a huge demotivator.

   ◆ Once realistic, modest goals/targets have been set for the organization, use the Hoshin Kanri method of "catch ball" to participatively set targets for the group and negotiate the means to accomplish them.

   ◆ Shift the focus from managing numbers (after-the-fact) to leading people by removing barriers around accomplishment of self-set goals.

5. Desire for Feedback from Others and Design for Feedback from the System.

   ◆ The further you get into this, the more you want to know how you, others and the system are doing.

   ◆ Constructive localized feedback from the system and your internal customer (the

employees) should be continuous, not once
or twice a year. Avoid at all costs the trap
of a "suggestion box", which is another way
of saying to your employees/customers:
"stick your ideas in here and someone will
eventually get around to looking at them".
Wisely select and skillfully employ 180^0, 360^0
and 540^0 (external suppliers and customers)
feedback mechanisms.

- ◆ Responsiveness is critical to closing the
  feedback loop. All feedback, like theories,
  are valid…some are simply more useful than
  others at creating and sustaining change that
  is worthwhile. Seek clarity and ensure understanding from feedback received and then act
  appropriately on what you've learned.

- ■ *Know your team and look out for their welfare.*
  – Webster defines relationships as "natural associations." There is nothing more natural to a leader
  than *knowing* the team they lead and nothing more
  powerful to a leader than supporting the weight of
  those who follow. But knowledge and power for
  what? Successful work. It is widely held that 80% of
  our successful work comes from superior human
  relations. Always consider the following:

  1. What are our FORMAL relationships and do
     they reflect the way in which work is done?

     - ◆ Formal relationships include manager-
       subordinate, team leader-team member,
       mentor-mentee, peer relationships, etc., and

they are typically what appears on organizational charts. When power is shared through formal relationships such as participative management and self-managed teams, positive creative power abounds.

2. What are our REAL relationships through which we are most effective?

   ◆ We are most effective through positive relationships, not negative ones. Positive relationships generate power. Power shows up as a significant increase in productivity and personal satisfaction.

3. Is there agreement or discord between my FORMAL and REAL relationships?

   ◆ Because organizational power is purely relational, what gives power its charge, positive or negative, is the nature of the relationship. Power in organizations is measured through the capacity generated by relationships. If power is the capacity generated by our relationships, then we need to attend to the quality of those relationships.

As the old saying goes: "No one cares how much you know until they know how much you care!" Management by Roaming, Management by Walking Around or Rounding for Employee Outcomes…by whatever name it is known, spending time at the front and in the trenches with your team is essential. Welfare certainly involves maintaining proper work-life balance and instilling real self-life skills, but it also includes making tough, unpopular decisions when required, for the good of the team.

- *Keep your team informed.* – Information drives the individual, team and organization. Consider life itself. It uses information to organize matter into form, resulting in all the physical structures that we see. The role of information is revealed in the word itself: in-formation. When a new structure materializes, we know that the system has in-formed itself differently. In a constantly changing and dynamic universe, information is a fundamental yet invisible player, one we can't see until it takes physical form. Something we cannot see, touch, or get our hands on is out there, influencing life. So in order for information to become a helpmate in creating greater order in our organizations, we have to work with information the same way that life does. We have to create much freer access to it and become much more astute at noticing new information as it emerges. Continually ask and answer the following questions:

1. What information do I need?

  - Everybody needs information to do their work. We are so in need of this resource that if we can't get the real thing, we make it up. When rumors proliferate and gossip gets out of hand, it is always a sign that people lack the genuine article—honest, meaningful information.

2. What information do I have the may be beneficial to others?

◆ If a system has the capacity to process information, to notice and respond, then that system possesses the quality of intelligence. Intelligence is a property that emerges when a certain level of organization is reached which enables the system to process information. The greater the ability to process information, the greater the level of intelligence.

3. What restricts information flow?

◆ Given that we all need to be continually nourished by information, it is no wonder that employees cite "poor communication" as one of their greatest problems. People know it is critical to their ability to do a good work. They know when they are starving.

■ *Ensure Vision, Mission, Core Values, Long-term Goals, Short-Term Actions and Assigned Tasks are understood, and that those assigned are empowered to accomplish them.* – If employees don't understand what is expected, it is very hard—if not impossible—to meet those expectations. If you want someone to do a good job, give them a good job to do. This requires understanding of Purpose, Picture, Plan and Part. Consider first that VISION is organizational clarity about purpose and direction. Vision has long been thought of as the creation of a destination...a place. What if vision were a field instead? What if field theory was applied to organizational vision? If nothing else, at least thinking about the possibility of organizational fields is an interesting exercise in metaphoric thinking.

1. Is there a shared understanding of who we (you and your team) are?

   - In a field view of organizations, attend first to clarity. Say what you mean and seek for a much deeper level of integrity in your words and acts than ever before. And then make certain that everyone has access to this field, that the information is available everywhere. This will enable you to have a shared understanding of who you are.

2. Are you working from the same sense of shared purpose?

   - If vision were a field, vision statements would move off the walls and into the corridors, seeking out every employee and every recess in the organization. In the past, you may have thought of yourself as a skilled designer of organizations, assembling the pieces, drawing the boxes, exerting energy to painstakingly create all the necessary links, motivation and structures. Now imagine yourself as a beacon tower of information, standing tall in the integrity of what you say, pulsing out congruent messages everywhere. This will move everyone else to begin stating, clarifying, reflecting, modeling and filling all of the space with the messages that are collectively cared about. As you do that, a powerful field develops—and with it, the wondrous capacity to organize into coherent, capable form.

3. How would you know…what evidence or history do you share that reinforces your sense of identity?

• The difference would be recognizable. For example, in creating a vision, you would be creating a power, not a place…an influence, not a destination. This field metaphor would then help everyone identify whether or not there was congruency in the air; visionary messages match by visionary behaviors. You also would know whether that vision permeated through the entire organization as a vital influence on the behavior of all employees, because that behavior would be consistent with the message. And finally, everyone would begin to feel genuinely threatened by incongruous acts because they would understand their disintegrating effects on what they dream to accomplish. This is all the evidence we would ever need.

Empower means to "put power into" or "give power to". Ensure that your delegation of assignments includes the necessary "power" (authority, resources, knowledge, skill, distribution of influence, etc.) to complete them…otherwise the assignments become nothing more than "dirty delegation" that results in frustration or anxiety, which ultimately leads to grief at best and apathy at worst.

- *Train your team as a team.* – Instill a spirit of cooperation, not competition. Give them a chance to practice regularly making effective, synergistic team decisions based on interpersonal skills that strive for consensus and higher levels of acceptance and rational skills that strive for quality and higher levels of thought leadership. Then, always cognizant of individual contributions, reward team performance.

- *Employ your team in accordance with its capabilities.* – In a crisis situation, your team will not rise to the occasion, but default to the level of their training (or, more appropriately, their thinking). Train your team to accomplish what is expected of them and only employ them for this purpose. Remember that in all of life, crisis is inevitable, training is optional...survival is at stake.

Enabled by 3 Strategic Priorities

[1st Priority Adapted from the Organizational Culture Inventory® (OCI®) and Organizational Effectiveness Inventory® (OEI), the Group Styles Inventory™ (GSI) and Leadership/Impact® (L/I), Copyrighted © and Trademarked by Human Synergistics. All rights reserved.]

1. Organizational, Group and Individual/Leadership Development

   ▸ As the **organizational design and development expert**, assess organizational culture and effectiveness using advanced diagnostic and development tools in order to understand assumptions, values, vision, mission and operating philosophy and align with structures (i.e., role definition, distribution of influence, decision-making models), systems (i.e., training, appraisal, reinforcement, goal setting), technology (i.e., job design, variety, feedback, inter-dependence) and skills/qualities (leadership, communication, bases of power) that: (1) increase the efficacy of business performance improvement methods, models and theories-in-use, (2) affect the full utilization of human, structural and relational capital and (3) improve individual, group (department/team) and organizational outcomes.

   ♦ Organizational *culture* is viewed here as the commonly shared assumptions (about people, behaviors and the business), beliefs and values of organizational members that lead to expectations for, and general patterns of, work-related behaviors in what is called a "Ideal Culture". The stronger the underlying base of values and beliefs and underpinnings of behavioral assumptions, the more pervasive and consistent the behavioral norms and associated patterns.

◆ The *assumptions* referenced here are initially established by organizational founders and subsequently refined and tempered by key leaders and organizational circumstances. These assumptions—concerning the organizations purpose, mission and the roles of people—are deeply seated. They are largely subconscious convictions (Schein, 1985) or "theories in use" (Argyris, 1976) about relationships and the world and how it works.

◆ *Values* are at a somewhat more conscious level and define normative principles or the behaviors expected of organizational members. Values and assumptions may be linked in a way that helps establish a coherent foundation from which expected behaviors emerge. If the sets of assumptions and values are coherent, they provide a broad base for viewing, feeling and approaching the world—an ideology for subsequent generations of organizational leaders. If they are shared widely and strongly, they provide a basis for a consistent pattern of expected behaviors.

◆ Emerging *mission* and *operating philosophy* (i.e., goals, strategies and policies), and the emergence of specific behaviors from the philosophical underpinnings, are all part of the organization's maturation and development process. Over time, ways of people relating to each other that feel right and seem to work (i.e., organizational *structures*, human resource management *systems*,

technology/job functions and individual *skills/
qualities*) are collated into a comprehensive
framework of the organization's current "way
of doing things", which can be described as
the "Current Culture". This, in turn, produces
measurable individual, group and organizational outcomes that determine effectiveness,
financial performance and overall success for
the company.

▸ As **team builder**, improve the effectiveness of
team decision-making through the assessment
and development of rational skills (i.e., analyzing the situation, setting objectives, simplifying
the problem, considering alternatives and
discussing consequences) and interpersonal
skills (i.e., listening, supporting, differing, par-
ticipating and striving for consensus) designed
to broaden the quality of thinking available
to teams and increase the level of solution
acceptance. Synergy, simply defined as two or
more people coming together to accomplish
something they could not do separately, can be
realized by high-performance teams. Synergy is
the goal of rational skill processes and, as a measurable result, can be detected using diagnostic
instruments designed to assess whether a team
exceeded the level of knowledge available to
them (i.e., high quality of thinking) in divining
the solution to a "simulated" problem. Consensus, simply defined by the idea: "it may not
be exactly what I want, but I can live with the

results and will support the decision", is the goal of interpersonal skills and can be measured by the level of solution acceptance on the team. An effective decision (ED) then can be said to equal the quality of thinking (QoT) times the level of acceptance (LoA) or ED = QT x LA.

▸ As a **Servant Leader**, raise the level of leadership within the organization by first modeling the attributes and traits of effective leaders, and then by designing and implementing assessment and development programs to produce "real-world" results through worthwhile leadership change. Leaders have a real and significant impact on individuals and, by extension, teams and the whole organization. That impact can be either positive (achieved through Prescriptive strategies that facilitate activities and promote behaviors) or negative (achieved through Restrictive strategies that constrain activities and prohibit behaviors). The impact itself can be Constructive (i.e., a task and people orientation that stimulates higher order needs for satisfaction) or Defensive (i.e., a people/task orientation that stimulates lower order needs for safety and security). As a result, the actual effectiveness of leaders can be measured at the organizational level in terms of how visionary/future-focused, empowering/motivating, and long-term oriented they are when it comes to performance. At the personal level, effectiveness can be viewed as the extent a leader is viewed as relaxed and "at ease", promotable and growth oriented (i.e., interested in self-development). Effectiveness can also be viewed as having a proper balance in value (i.e., neither overvalued or undervalued by the organization), authority (i.e., somewhere between having too much and too little) and success (i.e., advancing organizational as much as personal). A leader can increase short and long-term "bottom-line" performance through more prescriptive strategies that create and reinforce an organizational culture around constructive norms and expectations. According to Human Synergistics International, "Constructive behaviors not only lead to better performance than do Defensive behaviors, they also result in higher levels of personal satisfaction and lower levels of stress....Given that the performance of leaders ultimately depends upon the quality of the performance of the people around them, Prescriptive leaders are generally more effective that those who are Restrictive." – *Leadership/Impact® Facilitators Guide.* The real BOTTOM LINE: Leadership is cause, everything else is effect.

2. Strategic Planning, Policy Deployment and Change Management

    ▸ As **strategist**, work with Executive-level Steering Committees to create a viable growth strategy based on vision/mission (what), values/guiding principles (how) and current state analysis (SWOT), resulting in clearly defined, long-term strategic priorities.

- As **policy deployment specialist**, dim the long-term vision to actionable, short-term objectives and put them into circulation, including Key Performance Indicators (KPIs) to monitor progress through regular reviews of dashboard metrics.

- As **project manager**, ensure successful planning, timing and execution of short-term objectives and focused business initiatives, managing tasks to plan, costs at or below budget and quality beyond expectations.

- As **facilitator and logistics coordinator**, work with internal stakeholders to ensure that critical meetings get scheduled, that the appropriate people attend them, and that they achieve their intended purposes.

- As **on-site business mentor and coach**, explain, demonstrate, practice and give feedback in order to introduce new activities into the organization.

- As **data analyst**, assist operating unit leaders and monitoring teams with building and interpreting charts, graphs and reports.

- As **change agent**, remain positive, encourage patience, communicate clearly and frequently, and recognize all progress.

3. Operations Excellence – Quality, Lean Six Sigma and Problem Solving

   - As **quality consultant**, provide internal and/or external customers and suppliers with insight gained from experience and understanding, and support them as they implement systems designed to improve quality, productivity and competitive position, including proper application of methods, models and theories-in-use.

- As **problem solver and trainer**, implement and facilitate team problem solving using appropriate methodology and tools (i.e., Six Sigma DMAIC, PDCA, Kepner-Tregoe, Shainin TranXactional, TRIZ, P/D-FMEA, et al).

- As **lean/six sigma expert**, install and exploit continuous improvement as well as waste/non-value add/variation reduction methods, including the skillful application of 6S, Standardized Work, Process/Value Stream Mapping with Kaizen, Mistake-Proofing, SPC and MSA for greater efficiency, higher customers satisfaction and less net organizational pain.

- As **lifelong learner**, maintain textual knowledge of the following methods, models and theories-in-use:

  - Theory of Constraints (TOC) and Focused Factory for operations performance,

  - Business Process Reengineering and Capability Maturity Model Integration (CMMI) for enterprise-wide process performance,

  - ITIL for information technology performance and

  - Critical Chain and Critical Path methods for project performance.

FRAMING

Defined by 4 Managerial Properties

[Adapted from W. Edwards Deming's System of Profound Knowledge]

- *Systems Thinking.* Knowledge about the interaction, interdependence, interrelatedness and
  interoperability of forces. The discipline of looking
  at wholes. To understand anything necessarily
  involves understanding its relationships to larger
  wholes – the larger the whole and the more
  extensive the relationships that are understood, the
  truer the understanding.

- *Knowledge of Variation.* All systems exhibit natural,
  inherent variation from both common and special
  causes; hence, the information needed to create
  optimum systems is unknown and unknowable
  without the scientific method and statistics. Iterative application of the scientific method (plan, do,
  study, act learning cycle) reveals what's unknown
  but knowable about the system faster. Determining
  if the system is stable and on target—whether its
  distribution of output is predictable—requires
  the use of statistics. By observing the operation
  (behavior) of the system over time using statistical
  process control, built-in flaws can be detected,
  isolated and removed in order to reduce complexity, variation and/or entropy. When this happens,
  the system has an aim and a definable capability of
  hitting its target.

- *Theory of Knowledge.* Experience without theory teaches nothing. Be guided by theory rather than experience when seeking to understand the system so as to avoid paradigm paralysis. Theory asks the right questions, experience can only provide the answers. Knowledge requires that you can make a prediction. To do this you must develop a theory that can be tested and compared to what you predict will happen. It's not the only way to learn about the world but it is a higher form of learning then common sense.

- *Psychology.* Understanding of people; how they relate to each other, how they think/learn, how they approach their daily work and accomplish tasks. Includes knowledge of motivation (i.e., intrinsic vs. extrinsic), the management of change (i.e., levels of dissatisfaction with the way things currently are, a clear vision for how things could be, practical first steps for getting there and a belief that change is possible) and achievement orientation (i.e., high standards of excellence, cause and effect thinking (self-set goals), belief that individual efforts count, moderate risk taking and feedback from the system).

Driven by 14 Operational Imperatives

[Adapted from W. Edwards Deming's 14 Points]

1. *Create a constancy of purpose around continuous improvement of all efforts in all company operations.* Work on constantly reducing scrap, waste, rework and accidents to improve the competitive position of the company, to stay in business and to provide prosperity for employees and jobs for the community. Top Management is responsible to all employees in this effort.

2. *Adopt the new management philosophy.* There are new competitive pressures to continually renew and improve. Recognize that all forms of waste… that property damage and injuries from accidents are the same as producing scrap and result from variation in the system. We can no longer live with commonly accepted levels of employee injuries, delays, mistakes and defective or improper equipment. Management must awaken to the challenge, learn their responsibilities and take on leadership for change that is worthwhile.

3. *Cease dependence on mass inspection (or any after-the-fact activity) to achieve quality, productivity or safety.* Require instead statistical evidence that quality is built in and eliminate the need for firefighting routines that do not change and improve the system.

4. *Work with all Suppliers on improving the quality and timing of their products/services, while reducing*

overall cost. Move toward single-sourcing as a long-term strategy.

5. *Improve constantly and forever the system of production and service to improve quality and productivity and decrease internal costs.* Find problems. It is Management's job to work continually on the system (i.e., Manpower, Materials, Methods, Machines, Measurement and Mother-Nature). Target your performance. To do this Management must participatively work on improving the system, using the thinking of Statistical Process Control, with the help of all employees. Learn how to determine "common" or "special" causes of defects, delays, rework, accidents and other forms of waste (i.e., "Muda") and work on continually reducing them. Use teams for decision-making (consensus) and problem-solving of systemic quality, productivity and safety problems.

6. *Institute training.* A firm foundation of Profound Knowledge (Systems Thinking, Knowledge of Variation, Theory of Knowledge and Psychology) is needed for every manager/leader. Moreover, the foundation of the Customer Principle and Standardized work is needed for every worker. Employees will need the opportunity to do a good job and the information (feedback) from the system to know when they've done it in order for better decisions to be made and for work to become smarter, rather than harder, for everybody.

7. *Provide leadership instead of managership.* The responsibility of supervision must be changed from managing the numbers to being leaders, facilitator's, coaches and counselors of work systems, including people and the goal-setting process. A leader's job is to remove the barriers around the successful work of employees...barriers that prevent them from doing their jobs safely and with the highest quality output.

8. *Drive out fear so everyone can work effectively and safely for the company.* Eliminate the use of reprimands and incentives (bribes) as some management tools to control the action of employees. Reprimands destroy the intrinsic motivation everyone has, and incentives destroy any intrinsic value in the work itself.

9. *Break down barriers between departments.* All departments must learn to cooperate with each other so they can work together on solving common and special causes of variation. Applying the customer principle and using operational definitions for anything that requires a specification that two or more people must see, understand and agree on (i.e., what is "safe", what is "quality", what is a "defect") will eliminate barriers between departments, suppliers and customers. Eliminate all activities that prevent people from contributing to improving the organization by working on the system (i.e., Demotivators).

10. *Allow business/process units and employees to set their own goals.* Eliminate management-set objectives which are put forth in numerical quotas, incentive programs, posters and gimmicks/slogans; none of these improve quality, safety or the production system.

11. *Eliminate numerical quotas.* For the workforce and management team, unnecessary numerical quotas create internal competition, breakdown cooperation and prevent everyone from working effectively and safely at all times of production and service. They also create the need for making choices of Quality vs. Productivity vs. Safety. All are important and none will be optimized if the other is ignored.

12. *Remove barriers around pride of workmanship.* Build a leadership practice that responds immediately to reports from teams on barriers which prevent continual never-ending improvement of quality, productivity or safety. Use the problem solving methods of the Plan, Do, Study and Act Learning Cycle to implement change. Work on chronic problems such as; superficial training, persistent and consistent sources of waste, unclear operational definitions of "quality", et al. Return pride and joy to work by eliminating annual or merit ratings and management by objectives that nourish short-term performance, annihilate long-term planning, build fear, demolish teamwork and nourish rivalry and politics. All of these so-called performance management systems

deliver precisely the opposite of what they portend and leave people bitter, crushed, bruised, battered, desolate, despondent, dejected, feeling inferior (some even depressed), unfit for work for weeks after receipt of rating and unable to comprehend why they are inferior. These unfair appraisals of work performance ascribe to the people in a group those differences that are, in most cases, caused totally by the system that they work in...a system that leadership determines and controls.

13. *Encourage and exemplify lifelong learning and self-improvement for everyone.* Offer opportunities like job shadowing, coaching and mentoring to enhance knowledge, skills and abilities of workers at all levels. Acquire and apply self-improvement tools (i.e., diagnostics, simulations) and methods (i.e., goal setting, development planning, etc.), in addition to standard college tuition reimbursement programs, for those who would like to increase their life skills or performer skills in lieu of a degree.

14. *Create a structure in Top Management and through-out your organization that will push every day on the above 13 points.* End of counsel...enough said.

Characterized by 14 Traits/Qualities

[Adapted from the United States Marine Corps]

1. *Bearing* - Creating a favorable impression in carriage, appearance and personal conduct at all times.

2. *Courage* - The mental quality that recognizes fear of danger or criticism but enables a man to proceed in the face of it with calmness and firmness.

3. *Decisiveness* - Ability to make decisions promptly and to announce them in a clear, forceful manner.

4. *Dependability* - The certainty of proper performance of duty.

5. *Endurance* - The mental and physical stamina measured by the ability to withstand pain, fatigue, stress and hardship.

6. *Enthusiasm* - The display of sincere interest and exuberance in the performance of duty.

7. *Initiative* - Acting in the absence of orders; ensuring the action is lawful/ethical and consistent with the letter and spirit of the other 13 traits.

8. *Integrity* - Uprightness of character and soundness of moral principles; includes the qualities of truthfulness and honesty. For others to follow your lead, they must see you as first being trustworthy. From the followers' perspective, trust leads to respect and respect to admiration and admiration to commitment. From the leader's perspective, admiration leads to respect and respect to trust and trust to empowerment.

9. *Judgment* - The ability to weigh facts and possible solutions on which to base sound decisions. Includes the rational skills of Analyzing the Situation, Setting Objectives, Simplifying the

Problem, Considering Alternatives and Discussing Consequences.

10. *Justice* - To judge according to merits of the case in question. The ability to administer a system of accountability impartially and consistently.

11. *Knowledge* - Understanding of science and art, task accomplishment and people orientation. The range of information and capacity for learning, including professional knowledge and an understanding of yourself, your team and your environment/ surroundings.

12. *Loyalty* - The quality of faithfulness to God, Country, the company, the team, to one's seniors, peers and juniors.

13. *Tact* - The ability to deal with others without creating offense. This includes the interpersonal skills of Listening, Supporting, Constructive Differing and Striving for Consensus where agreements should be reached.

14. *Unselfishness* - Avoidance of providing for one's own comfort and personal advancement at the expense of others.

Supported by 4 Pillars of Success (Transformation Leadership)

This model is based on the notion that effective and worthwhile change is a combination of culture, direction, implementation and leadership. Ensure that each one is addressed and none are optimized at the expense of the others. It highlights the leadership-culture-performance connection, which is appropriate given that everything rises and falls on leadership.

- *Assumptions and Values Alignment– CULTURE*
  (assessing the most important and valid assumptions and values regarding employee motivation and effective management, and the level of commitment that senior leadership has to each). This is important to understand early on because the assumptions and values held by the organization's senior leaders will affect the problems identified and the solutions proposed (i.e., direction), as well as the actions taken (implementation) and the approach to management (leadership)... a direct result of leadership's impact on current culture and culture's impact on the performance of employees and the efficacy of methods, models and theories-in-use. Fact is, all of the 400+ business management and improvement methods, models and theories combined, no matter how robust, can't compensate for a defensive organizational culture. Farther back and higher up, organizational culture ultimately determines the efficacy of people/teams (human capital), process/technology (structural capital) and product/throughput (relational capital) that we need to manage and grow business. And with this firmly established, organizational leadership takes on a whole new meaning and teams quickly emerge as the means by which a more constructive organizational

culture can be established. When this happens, a wealth of creative energy is unleashed and a newfound capacity for learning, changing, growing and leading is realized.

- *Change Identification/Prioritization and Objectives/ Measures – VISION-MISSION-STRATEGIC PRIORITIES (DIRECTION).* Changes are often recommended or implemented before real problems and issues have been identified/verified. Subsequently, goals/objectives, action plans, management approaches and feedback/communication tend to be based on symptoms rather than true problems. Take pains to identify real issues based on values (ensures that change is worthwhile), vision (reduces confusion), the voice of internal and external customers (enables consensus-based, interpersonal decision-making that increases solution build-in and acceptance through participation) and the voice of systems (enables data-based, rational decision-making by engaging process and technology as a part of the answer). Follow the progressive elaboration of Vision -> Strategy -> Structure -> Function -> Form to align action steps (below) with assumptions and values (above) when answering the questions of 'what needs to change?' and 'what do we change to?'. Once strategy aligns with vision, consider how structures (role definition, distribution of influence, decision-making models, etc.), systems (training, evaluation, reinforcement, goal-setting, etc.), technology (job-design, variety, feedback, interdependence, etc.) and skills/qualities (leadership, communication, bases of power, etc.)

may need to be redesigned in order to support the strategic priorities/objectives and sustain the changes.

- *Action Planning and Implementation – CHANGE MANAGEMENT.* Necessary to achieve the objectives, actions are informed by the decisions above and include elements of change management like stakeholder identification, current vs. future state planning (i.e., fit-gap analysis between policy, processes, practices/behaviors, etc.) and field analysis of driving and restraining forces. This mitigates risk and produces the following essentials to successful change:

1. Learning solutions to shore up new skills through training/development,

2. Process improvements to ensure resources are effectively and efficiently engaged through elimination of waste/non-value-added work activities and

3. Performance management solutions to manage and monitor changes through teams, project plans and dashboard systems/reporting tools.

Implementation also includes the often-over-looked aspect of recognition/celebration and lessons learned/read-across for each milestone accomplishment along the way.

- *Approach to Management and Feedback/Communication - LEADERSHIP.* As W. Edwards Deming once quipped: "To manage, one must lead". How senior leaders view/deal with people, problems and issues has a strong influence on their ability to take action, achieve goals/objectives and ensure sustainable results. Refer back to Operational Qualities and Imperatives for details, but more constructive approaches include removing barriers around successful work/providing support; reducing conflict/increasing common understanding; creating opportunities for growth; promoting self-evaluation, learning and goal-setting; and advancing systems thinking, discovery by inquiry and designed experiments (PDCA learning cycle). Moreover, a desire to get feedback from the system and share it through frequent progress assessments/reports using methods like open book management actually improves performance while creating opportunities to collaborate, and constant two-way communication encourages participation, buy-in and ownership. Remember, we are all inelegant learners so we must continually ensure there is forgiveness in the learning process.